REFRAMING CAMPUS CONFLICT

NO CONFLICT MANAGEMENT

DIALOGUE/DEBATE/DISCUSSION

CONFLICT COACHING

FACILITATED DIALOGUE

MEDIATION

RESTORATIVE PRACTICES

SHUTTLE DIPLOMACY

ADJUDICATION (INFORMAL)

ADJUDICATION (FORMAL HEARING)

# REFRAMING CAMPUS CONFLICT

## Student Conduct Practice Through a Social Justice Lens

*Edited by*
*Jennifer Meyer Schrage*
and *Nancy Geist Giacomini*

Foreword by Edward N. Stoner

Stylus

STERLING, VIRGINIA

Published by Stylus Publishing, LLC
22883 Quicksilver Drive
Sterling, Virginia 20166–2102

**Library of Congress Cataloging-in-Publication-Data**
Reframing campus conflict : student conduct practice through a social justice lens / edited by Jennifer Meyer Schrage and Nancy Geist Giacomini ; foreword by Edward Stoner.—1st ed.
    p.   cm.
    Includes index.
    ISBN 978–1-57922–408–0 (cloth : alk. paper)
    ISBN 978–1-57922–409–7 (pbk. : alk. paper)
    1. Campus violence—United States—Prevention.
2. College campuses—Social aspects—United States.
3. Conflict managment—United States.   4. Social justice—United States.   I. Schrage, Jennifer Meyer, 1973–   II. Giacomini, Nancy Geist, 1961–
LB2345.R44 2009
378.1′95—dc22                    2009026556

13-digit ISBN: 978–1-57922–408–0 (cloth)
13-digit ISBN: 978–1-57922–409–7 (paper)

Printed in the United States of America

All first editions printed on acid free paper
that meets the American National Standards Institute
Z39–48 Standard.

Bulk Purchases

Quantity discounts are available for use in workshops and for staff development.
Call 1–800–232–0223

First Edition, 2009

10  9  8  7  6  5  4  3  2  1

*For my son—may you learn and live peaceful
and just resolution of conflict.*
J.M.S.


*In memory of my parents, who were schooled on the adage that "nobody
ever said life was fair" and still devoted their lives to raising three
daughters to believe that it could be.*
N.G.G.

# CONTENTS

# PART TWO
## PATHWAYS WITHIN THE SPECTRUM MODEL

# PART THREE
## SUSTAINABLE INNOVATION

     **Assessing Conflict Resolution Programs**
        *Richard T. Olshak*

15.  TEACHING SOCIAL JUSTICE ON CAMPUS FOR SELF-
     AWARENESS, COMMUNITY SUSTAINABILITY, AND
     SYSTEMS CHANGE                                     *219*
        *Judy Rashid*

16.  AN IMPLEMENTATION MODEL                            *227*
     **Campus Conduct and Conflict Management at the University
     of Michigan**
        *U-M Division of Student Affairs Office of Student Conflict
        Resolution and Housing Student Conflict Resolution Staff*

17.  SHARING STORIES                                    *241*
     **Program Innovations of Our Colleagues**
        *Nancy Geist Giacomini*


     ABOUT THE EDITORS                                  *259*

     ABOUT THE CONTRIBUTORS                             *261*

     INDEX                                              *267*

# ACKNOWLEDGMENTS

This book is a product of conversations and collaborations with many colleagues in the fields of conduct and conflict resolution and social justice education. We honor the contributions of those professionals who first introduced the idea of adding mediation and related dispute resolution practices to conduct programs decades ago. We acknowledge the Association for Student Conduct Administration (ASCA) for its commitment to offering professional development and encouraging grassroots change from within ASCA's membership. We also acknowledge the leadership and faculty involved with the 2008 Donald D. Gehring Academy for Student Conduct Administration's Conflict Resolution Specialist Program. The synergy and collegial dialogue that developed during our time and work together in creating that groundbreaking program provided inspiration for this volume.

The Spectrum of Resolution Options visual model referred to throughout this book is a shared creation by Jennifer Meyer Schrage and Monita C. Thompson. Originally introduced at the 2008 Gehring Academy, Schrage and Thompson developed the Spectrum Model concept to bring together the ideals of social justice, diversity, and inclusive conflict resolution inspired by their work at the University of Michigan (U-M). A special thank-you goes to the U-M Division of Student Affairs Office of Student Conflict Resolution (OSCR) staff and divisional colleagues. The Spectrum Model is in many ways a reflection of the OSCR program's evolution. The imprint and influence of the staff, graduate students, and undergraduate students involved with the office since 2006 is acknowledged and appreciated. We also thank Associate Vice President Simone Himbeault Taylor and colleagues in the U-M Program on Intergroup Relations. Your "positive pressure" and reminders of the *so what* for OSCR's work with students prompted a paradigm shift, subsequent innovation, and the commitment to add this perspective to the national dialogue through this book.

We owe a great deal to those who provided review and assistance, sometimes under very short deadlines. Thank you to Ed Stoner, Bill Fischer, Robert Hosea, Veronica Hipolito, and Malinda Matney. We express deep appreciation to Jordan England for her thorough review and commitment to excellence in academic research and related support. Also, many thanks to those who provided related assistance, including Sophia Chang, Robert Coffey, Agustina De Majo, Jenna Keefe, Carrie Landrum, Amethyst Saldia, and Vu Tran. Thanks also to our indexing team, K. Page Boyer, Sarah Fike, Carmen McCallum, Ronald Perkins Jr., and Stephen Sanney.

We pay tribute to our contributing authors. Thank you for your commitment to ensuring a timely, relevant, and meaningful volume informed through many lenses. Finally, we thank our partners and families for their support, as we invested significant time, energy, and attention to this endeavor.

# ENDORSEMENT

The Association for Student Conduct Administration (ASCA) was founded in 1988. At that time its primary objective was to serve as a higher education association for student conduct professionals to come together and develop best practices, educate ASCA members, provide educational resources in the specific area of student conduct administration, and provide training to conduct student hearings in an objective, unbiased, and professional manner. During ASCA's infancy, conduct officers often adjudicated student conduct cases through a formal dualistic process. In the 1990 article "Harnessing the Spirit of Insubordination: A Model Student Disciplinary Code"[1] Ed Stoner and his colleague Kathryn Cerminara emphasized the need for a formalized process ensuring due process, along with other rights, by the university to the charged student. The model code has been recognized over time as the foundation fair adjudication models are built upon.

However, as the profession advanced and society became more complex, students and universities across the country required incident response models that addressed their unique situation and individual complexities. Mediation and conflict resolution were introduced as alternatives to the traditional adjudicatory model. Over the past several years ASCA has embraced best practices for training conduct professionals, which include alternative dispute methods. In 2008 the ASCA deliberately expanded its mission statement and developed a vision statement and set of core values to specifically reflect its commitment to diversity. In doing so, the ASCA also endorsed alternate forms of conflict resolution models as viable conduct administration options.

Today, ASCA endorses the use of diverse forms of conflict resolution. This includes conflict resolution pathways based upon social justice theories, restorative justice, conflict coaching, and facilitated dialogue. By providing a variety of conflict resolution methods practitioners are able to shape and mold their processes to fit their unique campus culture and give additional stakeholders, that is, the victims, an opportunity to have a voice not only in

---

1. In *Journal of College & University Law*, 17(2), 89–121.

the outcome but in the actual resolution process. These models allow for diverse approaches at multiple levels, and ASCA believes that having a variety of dispute resolution mechanisms tailored to a unique student situation is ideal.

This approach serves to enhance the student's ability to fully comprehend the seriousness of the conduct, appreciate the people, community, or institutions affected by his or her conduct, restore the people, communities, and institutions affected, and hopefully eliminate a repeat of inappropriate behavior. When students comprehend the impact of their behavior on others, it truly allows them to participate not only in an educational process but a transformative one as well. The students walk away from the experience with a greater appreciation for the community they belong to and a deeper respect for others.

This book is endorsed by ASCA as a collaborative, collegial new lens for considering how social justice practices and student conduct administration can come together to inform best practices in conduct and conflict management on college and university campuses.

Tamara L. King, JD
2009 ASCA president

# FOREWORD

T his book is a welcome addition to the resources available to every student affairs professional. It provides concrete suggestions designed to improve the way you deal with student conduct, thus enhancing your efforts to create a good living/learning environment for everyone on campus.

The chapters in this book start to fill an opening left by the model student code.[1] They explore many methods of dealing with a student who has apparently violated campus standards *before* you use your version of a more formal hearing process.

In our model student code, we acknowledged that after becoming aware of a potentially troubling student conduct situation a student affairs professional first would take a preliminary look at the alleged misconduct. Then, using the resources available at the institution, the professional would try to dispose of the matter "administratively by the mutual consent of the parties involved on a basis acceptable to the Student Conduct Administrator."[2]

What we did not do in the model code, however, was to try to discuss the various approaches that might be used prior to the formal code process to reinforce the type of living/learning environment desired for a campus. Those approaches are the focus of this book.

There are many ways to deal with questionable conduct before you invoke your student conduct code hearing process, ranging from the tried-and-true meeting with the dean to the many alternatives suggested by contributors to this volume. Of course, the more resources in personnel, expertise, and funding that are available to you, the more flexibility you will have in selecting the best options for the social system of your campus.

That is the beauty of this book. It is written by student affairs professionals with, collectively, centuries of student affairs experience. They have worked in large and small institutions, public and private, all across the country and have experimented with (and used successfully) a wide range of approaches.

---

1. E. N. Stoner & J. W. Lowery, "Navigating Past the 'Spirit of Insubordination': A Twenty-First Century Model Student Conduct Code with a Model Hearing Script," *Journal of College and University Law, 31*, no. 1 (2004).

2. Stoner & Lowery, p. 39.

This book contains not only suggestions but also models. You probably will not find one that fits your campus exactly. But what you will find is a treasure of careful thought given to many different approaches. If you are lucky, you will find a nugget here and a kernel there that together will be just the new approach that perfectly fits your campus history and expectations.

As always, your judgment as an experienced professional in higher education—who knows your institution's students, values, and history—will be the best guide in selecting portions of this book to add to your own policies.

In addition, using your professional judgment in this manner is also the best protection for all your efforts in a legal sense, because courts do respect and honor the judgment of college administrators—when that judgment is to pick approaches that thoughtfully address the students and institution they serve.[3]

There are no easy answers to students' spirit of insubordination. But, just as Thomas Jefferson relied upon his colleagues James Madison and James Monroe to try to figure out how to deal with unruly University of Virginia students nearly two centuries ago, you may rely upon the wisdom of these authors in trying to create the most desirable living/learning environment for your campus.

Good luck!

Edward N. Stoner
Coauthor of the Model Student Conduct Code

---

3. E. N. Stoner & J. M. Showalter, "Judicial Deference to Educational Judgment: Justice O'Connor's Opinion in *Grutter* Reapplies Longstanding Principles, As Shown by Ruling Involving College Students in Eighteen Months Before *Grutter*," *Journal of College and University Law, 30,* 583 (2004). See Stoner & Lowery, p. 6, n. 16.

# INTRODUCTION

*Jennifer Meyer Schrage and Nancy Geist Giacomini*

With this volume, we invite our readers to embrace a broad and diverse menu of conflict resolution options in higher education. The proposed approach offers not only an inclusive visual image of the informal to formal pathways available to manage student conduct and conflict but also provides the answer to why these fuller menu options are necessary in today's campus climate. The why rests on the core values that we share, including commitment to student development, freedom of expression, the value of diversity and accessibility, individual rights, and shared responsibilities in a community of learners. The why breathes life into underused resolution practices and reminds us that systems and models are simply vehicles for us to act on our values.

Student development theories have paved the way for new and best practice models for administrators to meet the needs of students in appropriate developmental ways, and legal precedents have influenced procedural considerations in campus conduct codes. Social justice theory provides the lens through which we expand our view and encourages us to consider systemic change in student conduct administration. This lens, when added to our historic reference points, provides a clearer vision of how expanded resolution practices can empower today's students to resolve their own conflicts; help account for power, privilege and oppression; and effect systemic change.

To present a variety of perspectives, voices, and practices, this text is divided into three parts. Part 1, "Responding to Conflict on Campus: Foundations for Student Affairs Educators," consists of four chapters. This section provides a framework for transforming student conduct administration using conflict resolution methods and social and restorative justice practices. Chapter 1 describes the current campus climate and the challenges associated with creating a community in which learning and personal development can take place using the current adjudication-only model. Chapter 2 describes how the theoretical and legal foundations for student conduct work support the increased use of conflict resolution methods and social and restorative justice practices in this field. Chapter 3 discusses social justice and its connection to student conduct and conflict resolution. Chapter 4 lays out Schrage and Thompson's Spectrum of Resolution Options as a visual model expanding Stoner and Lowery's (2004) Model Student Conduct Code to meet the needs of today's diverse campuses while honoring the student development theory, legal rights, and social justice commitments that are core to our work as student affairs educators.

Part 2, "Pathways Within the Spectrum Model," devotes eight chapters to explaining each of the conflict resolution pathways introduced under the spectrum's menu of options. The order of these chapters is intentional and follows the model. We begin with pathways that are less formal, involve minimal structure, and little to no third-party facilitation or administrator intervention. Chapter 5 describes and explains the value of dialogue, chapter 6 explains conflict coaching, chapter 7 describes facilitated dialogue, and chapter 8 provides an overview of mediation. Chapters 9, 10, and 11 introduce the middle pathways of the spectrum, providing an overview of restorative justice practices and philosophy and shuttle diplomacy. The section closes with chapter 12, which considers conflict resolution practices and social justice theory to inform the most formal student conduct code pathways.

Part 3, "Sustainable Innovation," provides practical application tools and the big picture for the ideas presented in this text. Chapters 13 and 14 offer important program development considerations with discussions of change management and assessment. Chapter 15 serves as a reminder of the value of teaching social justice on campus, in the classroom, and as part of student affairs practice. Chapter 16 describes a theory-to-practice example of a spectrum approach for educators to consider as they craft their own campus version of the model. In chapter 17, we conclude with an overview of programs from across the country using inclusive and creative conflict resolution methods in student conduct work.

In this book we bring a variety of voices together, elevate each pathway of resolution to equal scrutiny and consideration, and conceptualize individual practices into a model for a full and balanced review by our reader. We invite robust dialogue with colleagues whose paths have led them to study, research, teach, practice, design, and evaluate systems of student conduct and conflict resolution over the years in the name of access and justice for the individual student as well as restorative, safe practices for the campus community.

Everybody brings something to the table. Every individual matters. It is with this respect for diversity, inclusion, and innovation that we begin this conversation with you.

## Reference

Stoner, E. N., & Lowery, J. W. (2004). Navigating past the "Spirit of Insubordination": A twenty-first century model student conduct code with a model hearing script. *Journal of College and University Law, 31,* 1–77.

# PART ONE

# RESPONDING TO CONFLICT ON CAMPUS: FOUNDATIONS FOR STUDENT AFFAIRS EDUCATORS

# BUILDING COMMUNITY
# IN THE CURRENT
# CAMPUS CLIMATE

*Nancy Geist Giacomini and Jennifer Meyer Schrage*

Accept all students as individuals, each with
rights and responsibilities, each with goals and
needs; and seek to create and maintain a campus climate in which learning and personal
growth and development take place.

*Association for Student
Conduct Administration (ASCA, 2009)*

I n this chapter we explore the current campus climate to consider the
extent to which it promotes or inhibits student learning and personal
growth and development. Capturing the nature of today's campus climate is important. It lays the foundation for this book; namely, that the
diversity of our students and the issues they face demand creative and educational solutions in addition to the conscientious application of procedural
safeguards traditionally provided by campus disciplinary processes.

From this foundation, contributing authors will further expand the
premise that current campus adjudication models are not keeping pace with
(a) stated individual and organizational core values, (b) tracked and reported
diversity trends in our student bodies, and (c) our own developmental con-
victions to balance student learning with justice, not just in our practice,
training, and language, but within our systems.

It is an optimistic sign that the Model Student Disciplinary Code
(Stoner & Cerminara, 1990) has been revised with significant changes
including the endorsement of more developmental and less-legalistic language (Stoner & Lowery, 2004). The revisions mark a positive movement
away from what many campus administrators have shaped into quasi-
courtroom proceedings in the name of due process (something the model

code's authors never intended), and toward embracing the more educational, collaborative, and inclusive approach typically found in the language and processes of conflict resolution, restorative justice, and social justice work.

This call for change in student conduct administration gained significant momentum in recent years, as made evident in the official name change and expanded mission for the higher education association devoted to student affairs educators doing this work. Moving from the Association for Student Judicial Affairs (ASJA) to the Association for Student Conduct Administration (ASCA), this organization modified its mission to include conflict resolution and affirmed its commitment to diversity in revised vision and core values statements.

Recognizing a revolution in the field, the *Chronicle of Higher Education* devoted a three-part series in early 2009 to covering the profession's move away from its formalistic and punitive past. *Chronicle* reporter Sara Lipka captured the essence of this shift through interviews with leaders in the field and practitioners implementing new and innovative restorative approaches (Lipka, 2009). The series was complemented by a column in which Peter F. Lake, director of the Center for Excellence in Higher Education Law and Policy at Stetson University College of Law, made the case against a legalistic approach to student discipline (Lake, 2009). We embrace this momentum forward and assert that best practices now require that we actively explore, endorse, and normalize conflict resolution and social and restorative justice practices as equally viable conduct management approaches in a spectrum of conflict and conduct resolution pathways explored in detail throughout this book.

In the pages that follow, we turn first to some widely held demographic statistics and climate issues to shore up our common ground. We then consider these indicators against the present service model in student conduct administration that favors formal adjudication over less-formal conflict resolution pathways. We highlight who is being served and who is not being served by this approach. The chapter concludes with an invitation to educators to engage in dialogue around the philosophies, values, and language that make our work together and with students so compelling.

## Today's Campus

Exploring the nature of campus climate in today's colleges and universities requires an understanding of demographic trends within the populations we are committed to serving. This is particularly true because all readily available indicators point to significant current and future changes in the diversity of our campus communities. We need to understand whom colleges and universities attract and why; which students stay and which ones leave, and how best to meet students' needs as they make their way through the college experience.

One comprehensive source of demographics relied on by U.S. colleges and universities is the Western Interstate Commission for Higher Education (WICHE). Its seventh edition, the March 2008 publication, "Knocking at the College Door," includes projections of public school graduates by race/ethnicity (WICHE, 2008). Figures 1.1 and 1.2 summarize national highlights from this publication that can inform our understanding of the modern campus environment. One notable trend is the significant increase in Hispanic graduates and the decline in White non-Hispanic graduates.

## FIGURE 1.1
### High School Graduates: 2004–2005

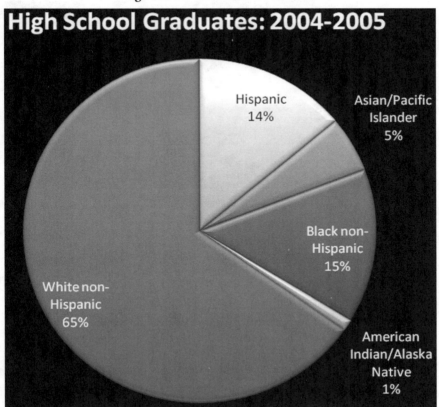

**FIGURE 1.2**
**High School Graduates: 2014–2015**

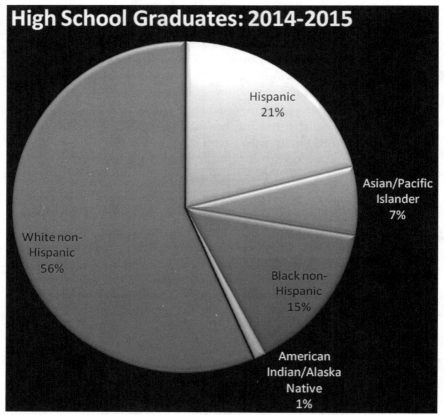

What we know about the disciplinary experience for the growing population of students of color in the K–12 school system is relevant to this
research concerning high school graduates. In 2006 the University of California, Los Angeles Institute for Democracy, Education and Access (IDEA)
issued a report titled "Suspension and Expulsion At-A-Glance." The report
was aimed at highlighting potential bias and discrimination in campus conduct policy. It revealed that, systemically, students of color are most often
referred and suspended for vaguely classified nonviolent conduct such as
"disrespect of authority" or "disobedience." The report also concluded that
African American students are overly represented in disciplinary referrals. In

fact, while African American students represent just 17% of public school enrollment, they account for a full 33% of disciplinary suspensions.

Tomorrow's incoming classes will join campus communities already experiencing and responding to over a decade of significant changes in the sexual, racial, and ethnic makeup of the student population. Figures 1.3 and 1.4 represent data from the U.S. Department of Education, National Center for Education Statistics (NCES, 2008, 2006) and provide a big picture perspective of some of these changes in demographics.

Fully understanding campus demographics also requires consideration of our population of international students. The number of undergraduate international students enrolling in higher education institutions in the United States increased by 7% in 2007–08 (Institute of International Education [IIE], 2008a). This record-high increase raised the number of international students in the United States to 623,805 (IIE, 2008b).Table 1.1 offers an additional perspective on the variety of cultures that convene on our campuses.

Diversity in ability, sexual orientation, and socioeconomic status has also influenced the makeup of our campus populations:

- According to NCES (2006), "eleven percent of undergraduates reported having a disability in 2003–04. Among students reporting a

**FIGURE 1.3**
**Number of Graduate Students by Gender**

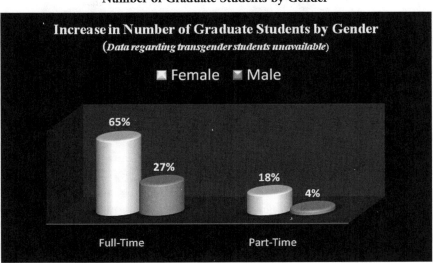

Increase in Number of Graduate Students by Gender
(*Data regarding transgender students unavailable*)

■ Female  ■ Male

65%

27%

18%

4%

Full-Time          Part-Time

## FIGURE 1.4
**Underrepresented Populations in Higher Education**

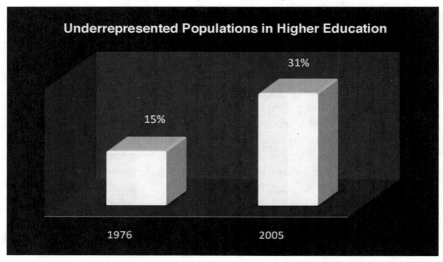

## TABLE 1.1
**Leading Places of Origin of International Students 2007–2008 Academic Year**

| Place of Origin | No. of Students in the United States |
|---|---|
| India | 94,563 |
| China | 81,127 |
| South Korea | 69,124 |
| Japan | 33,974 |
| Canada | 29,051 |
| Taiwan | 29,001 |
| Mexico | 14,837 |

*Note.* From "Leading Places of Origin," Figure 2B: Top 20 Leading Places of Origin of International Students, 2006/07 & 2007/08, http://opendoors.iienetwork.org/?p = 131534

disability, one-fourth reported an orthopedic condition, 22 percent reported a mental illness or depression, and 17 percent reported a health impairment" (p. 133).

- According to the 2005 U.S. Census American Community Survey, the number of same-sex couples in the United States grew from nearly

600,000 couples in 2000 to almost 777,000 in 2005. This is a more than a 30% increase from 2000 to 2005 and is five times the 6% rate of growth in the U.S. population (Gates, 2006). Reliable data concerning estimates of the number of students on campus who identify themselves as lesbian, gay, bisexual, or transgender (LGBT) are unavailable, as most education institutions do not track this information. However, the experience of this campus community is striking. In a recent study, more than one-third (36%) of LGBT undergraduate students reported having experienced harassment within the past year (Rankin, 2003).

- NCES (2000) reports that in 1995–96, 26% of all undergraduates were low income. At the time of this writing, the U.S. and global economic climate is in significant and historic degradation, suggesting that the number of low-income students struggling to earn a higher education may well increase significantly.

Contributors to this volume walk a fine line when sharing statistics. We wish to be thorough, balanced, and concise all at once to provide an objective and fair picture of our student populations by the numbers. This is important because our case for broadening student conduct models begins with a shared regard for the relative importance of these changing numbers to our campus climates. More important than debating the merits or agreeing on the significance of a single campus statistic is creating a general understanding and ongoing atmosphere of inquiry regarding our changing campus demographics. In this way, we can be thoughtful and proactive in our responses to the unique characteristics and social pressures of our changing student population.

In sharing this information, we strive not to be conclusive but simply to pique your curiosity and encourage you to seek out more information of relevance to your own institution, state, and region. Ongoing collaboration with your Institutional Research Office or Office of the Registrar at your institution is a great first step toward understanding trends and statistics related to present and anticipated campus demographics and trends.

## The Student Experience of Diversity, Conflict, and Campus Climate

Behind these demographics and statistics exist real individuals and communities. These diverse populations that make up our campus communities interact with, respect, and include one another in various ways. Student affairs educators have come to conceptualize the feeling or tone of a campus with regard to how students interact with one another within the community as *campus climate*. It is an aptly coined term. The challenge in defining the climate of a campus, however, is that it is not adequately communicated as a simple statistic, report, or retelling of an event or story. Neither is climate a fixed target. Instead, it is a fluid marker in time. Some markers are pervasive, seeping into the fabric of a community, while others are short lived and sustainable only until a more sensational incident appears.

Reports and statistics are important in gauging the current climate or reviewing the climate in retrospect, but these markers are not necessarily good predictors of the future. Additionally, once there is a breech of trust for an individual or community harmed by a pervasive and hostile climate, it is hard if not impossible to repair it.

Finally, climate is perceptual not just intellectual. Stand a dozen people outside in an atmosphere ripe with snow. All can report that it is snowing. That's intellect. Perception is that unique individual reaction that causes some to shiver, zip up their wraps, and raise their hoods while others forgo their mittens, fling open their coats, and spread their arms into the wings of snow angels. The experience of campus climate is as individual as snowflakes.

We make the distinction between the perceptual and intellectual in order to be genuine in reflecting the importance of campus climate to systems work in student affairs. It is easy to make the case that diversity-related conflict or bias-related acts of ignorance or hate have a substantial impact on campus climates. Today, incidents are broadcast through the written word as readily as in startling photographs and videos on student-favored Internet sites. News coverage is ample, nationally and in campus and local papers and other media outlets. Independent reports, as well as information gathered by the U.S. Department of Education and the Office for Civil Rights, frame our collective experience and perception of campus climate. We might argue among ourselves over the degree of impact these records reflect, but the fact is that on any given day we can find incidents that chill our campus climates.

Tosheka Robinson refers to Utopia University in chapter 5, and there seems to be ample visual evidence that it exists. Pictures of ideal campus landscapes, timeless ivy-covered buildings, gripping sporting events, eager student faces, and diverse collegial friendships abound. It is the stuff of campus brochures, recruitment fairs, student orientations, and, indeed, some of our own most cherished memories of campus life as students.

However, these compelling public relations images stand in stark contrast to the pictures that surface now and again in the media and on the Internet. Sometimes these pictures expose the anonymous noose left hanging in a residence hall, campus courtyard, or academic building. Others document the swastikas that surface as overnight graffiti. Perhaps for some, the picture of a survivor of campus sexual violence or the organization party gone wild or the beaten LGBT student leader resonate. Like stories, these pictures of campus life also speak to each of us in unique and personal ways.

Our campuses are full of such contradictions that have an impact on how we tailor not only our personal approaches but also our systems for managing the conduct and conflict that arises from these contrasts. We must care what the experience is like to be a young Black man on campus who at once celebrates the election of our first African American president only to be confronted with racist graffiti in his own residence hall. How do we fully embrace what that feels like and then demonstrate care in our personal dealing with students? How do we imbed that understanding and care in our service models?

We must care that female students struggle to reconcile the images of safety and community in a brochure with the need to never go to a party alone because of real fears of sexual violence based on alarming national statistics revealing that a college that has 10,000 female students could experience more than 350 rapes in a year. Further, we must ask ourselves why only 5% of completed and attempted campus rapes are reported to authorities (Fisher, Cullen, & Turner, 2000).

These and similar experiences across the country no doubt affect student trust, and that trust carries over into the overall sense of the climate in which students live and learn. It influences how students receive other students and experience safety in the classroom. These experiences directly influence learning and a student's trust of and interactions with the systems established within a given climate, systems such as student conduct administration.

## Conflict Cultures on Campus

To investigate the full impact of demographics and cultural expressions on campus climate, it bears mention that our increasingly diverse student populations also bring with them a variety of conscious and unconscious responses when faced with conflict. We name this *conflict culture*. Conflict culture speaks to the unique lens or story an individual brings to the table in a dispute and the ways in which this surfaces or influences his or her engagement in a conflict. The convergence of varying conflict cultures on our campuses also provides insight on climate.

For privileged populations coming from social groups historically provided access to higher education (i.e., White, upper middle class, male), the dominant conflict culture of the United States will likely resonate. This dominant conflict culture places significant value on third-party decision makers, competition, individual responsibility for choices, autonomy, and self-reliance (Pillay, 2006). These are what anthropologist Edward T. Hall (1976) called *low-context communication styles*. That is, direct and verbal communication is emphasized, words maintain literal meaning and messages are explicit. The dominant conception of identity in these populations is *individualistic*, as labeled by Charles Hampden-Turner and Fons Trompenaars (2000).

These cultural orientations, however, are not universal. Many international students and students coming from historically marginalized and/or underrepresented communities may embrace very different conflict cultures. Many of these cultures function with high-context communication styles. Disputants in such cultures will emphasize nonverbal and indirect communication, look for the implicit messages, and consider the context and implied meaning associated with a situation. Further, for some of these populations *communitarianism* is the prevailing conception for self and identity. This means cooperation, deference toward elders, interdependence, and group harmony are considered cultural norms in such communities (Pillay, 2006).

Further, knowing what we know about the multiple social identities and cultures that intersect within an individual, it is likely that many of our students' ideas about conflict and conduct are informed by a range of cultures and personal experiences rather than from a single cultural identity or experience. This is further complicated by the likelihood that personal circumstances, peer group, and identity development during the college years often cause a student to adjust his or her approach to conflict over time.

Attempting to make broad assumptions about any one individual student's conflict culture based on social identity is ineffective. Nonetheless, the diversity of our campuses and the many conflict cultures expressed within provide another angle of insight on the campus experience and climate for all our students. It casts light on the possible disconnect of current student conduct service models with the needs of our students.

We can be sure that every student carries challenges based on their various social identities, together with their personal conflict cultures and levels of self-awareness and personal development. These stories directly affect how a student will experience, respect, comply with, and engage or not engage in an adjudication process. Even traditional adjudication models imbedded with developmental language and educational sanctions are largely premised upon and guided by the authoritarian, punitive model reflective of the legal system. Such models send a message that the discipline policy is in place to rein in or turn out a student who fails to respect an ultimately subordinate role at the institution.

## Is Adjudication Enough?

Nearly every contributor to this book has a long and rewarding history leading campus adjudication programs across the country. In form and function, adjudication is arguably the favored model in our schools and in our country to date for managing policy violations. Nonetheless, shortcomings exist in a one-system model for managing student conduct and conflict.

First, adjudication-only models fail to address conflicts that often underlie behavior brought to the attention of student conduct administrators. In this failure, students do not have a structured and informed chance to challenge their role and actions in a conflict, consider alternative conflict resolution options in the future to resolve or de-escalate their own conflicts, or see a process modeled for them that would in turn help develop this skill set. The Council for the Advancement of Standards in Higher Education (CAS, 2008) deems these conflict resolution skills to be necessary, citing "manages interpersonal conflicts effectively" (p. 3) as a desired learning outcome for the college years.

Second, adjudication seldom acts to intentionally restore a community harmed by a student's actions. Sanctions may caution, hold accountable, and even remove a student from campus. Regardless, they seldom promote restorative justice for a community. In fact, more than an act of omission, individual rights of privacy for a student completing a student conduct process most often win out over the disclosure of consequences to those in the community with a stake in the outcome of the misconduct of another student.

Finally, a single-process option does not appreciate the diversity of the population it attempts to serve. A campus incident response model that offers adjudication under the conduct code as the only or predominantly favored venue for resolving a conflict ignores the variety of needs associated with the many student identities, experiences, and conflict cultures within the population. An adversarial and narrow disciplinary process that relies on competition and individualism as central values does not model inclusion or increase tolerance. Again, CAS (2008) speaks to the importance of appreciating diversity and social justice, listing "understands one's own identity and culture; seeks involvement with people different from oneself; articulates the advantages and impact of a diverse society" (p. 4) as desired learning and development outcomes. These learning outcomes resonate with our work as student affairs educators to encourage students to engage moral dilemmas in a way that involves equal consideration of the points of view of all individuals involved in a conflict (Kohlberg, 1976). Adjudication-only policies encourage polarization and a win-lose or right-wrong framework. Such an approach risks discouraging students from going below the "violation" to gain a deeper understanding of other participants and their different perspectives. In the adjudication process, participants are actually discouraged from introducing or considering the larger dynamics in society that inform an experience.

This collected work does not advocate for the abandonment of traditional models crafted carefully over the years by schools to meet the unique demands and circumstances of their communities. The diverse voices coming forward in support of a fuller menu of options to address conflict and conduct on campus were educated in traditional student development theories and administrative standards of fundamental fairness. These colleagues are respectful of case law relevant to the field and of the historic differences celebrated between campuses across the country. But we are also advocates for a new direction in student conduct administration. This new direction empowers practitioners, educators, and students alike to go beyond creating fair administrative systems based on the laws, policies, and mandates relevant to higher education to embrace the core values that support civil discourse, inclusive and restorative communities, and practices that support personal, healthy resolution of conflict.

## Testing for Inclusion and Access

We acknowledge at this juncture that as two White women we are limited in our ability to fully inform campus climate issues not by lack of effort, ability, or good intention but simply by our own unique personal lenses. In fact, a cornerstone to the collaborative, inclusive work we promote is that every one of us must become better equipped to recognize and account for our own complex personal lenses. We have sought to balance what we bring to the table with colleagues from across perspectives and practices. This collaboration has netted some common and important themes. As we leave you our readers to the considered expertise of our contributing authors, we encourage you to draw on your own personal experiences, records, hard data, and expertise by considering the following questions.

Before you move through this book, we invite you to conduct your own informal assessment of how well the student conduct program at your institution attracts and serves students fairly and maintains "a campus climate in which learning and personal growth and development can take place" (ASCA, 2009) for all members of the community.

- First, review the statistical breakdown of the student population on your campus based on social group identities. Next, review the numbers of disciplinary cases for the past semester based on the type of incident, severity of sanction, and social identities of the student charged. Then, consider those seeking services as complainants in such cases. Do the statistics match, or is a category of student overrepresented or underrepresented in your conduct process based on overall population? Who is using your services and who is not? Have you ever considered these service gaps?
- Now consider documented and "personal notes" cases of alleged sexual violence, harassment, and hate or bias incidents on campus based on gender, race, culture, sexual orientation, religion, and so on. How many completed a formal resolution process of some kind, and what happened? How many students, if they had the choice, opted out of filing formal charges for these alleged assaults?
- How many hate or bias incidents that occurred on campus this past year went unaddressed based on freedom of expression considerations?
- Consider those cases referred to adjudication or other formal conduct processes that might better have been served by a conflict resolution process that allowed for resolution through coaching, dialogue, negotiation, mediation, or a restorative justice conference. Or, if you are fortunate and have a viable conflict resolution practice like mediation in place, consider the social identity of those students who have engaged in that process. What do these cases tell you about your accessibility to all students?
- Consider the visual diversity represented by the first three people a student with a conflict or conduct issue will meet as he or she enters the student conduct office. Give some thought to the impact of first impressions, particularly for a student who may feel defensive, apprehensive, underrepresented, or harmed by the community in some way.
- Consider the training offered to staff and students charged with managing the student conduct system at your institution. How much is specifically aimed at building skill sets not related just to "diversity awareness" but to creating multipartial (instead of impartial), culturally competent facilitators? How much training or dialogue directly

addresses notable campus, regional, and national demographic and campus climate trends?

## Conclusion

Many of the concepts and pathways introduced in the chapters that follow are not new. Conflict resolution advocates and practitioners have been on campuses for many years, along with leaders and allies promoting diversity, multiculturalism, and social justice. The purpose of this volume is to bring these areas of thought together in a new and ongoing dialogue to inform student conduct and conflict work.

Students are different and should have access to resolution pathways that best meet their diverse social, educational, and developmental needs. The histories and personal stories they use to navigate their campus worlds are as unique and complex as their perceptions of and reactions to the changing weather. Student affairs educators are not called upon to be all things to all students. And yet, we do aspire to be fair and just in our dealings with students and through our systems.

Improving and sustaining a healthy campus climate is a shared community responsibility that must not rest solely on the backs of those targeted by incidents that leave them feeling left out in the cold. We must broaden resolution pathways with early, institutionalized, and easily accessible community systems that invite all to participate fully and allow for the telling of unfamiliar stories safely and effectively. Single pathways for resolving conduct issues, nearly all of which are imbedded with some degree of conflict, do not express the best version of ourselves as educators.

## References

Association for Student Conduct Administration. (2009). Ethical principles and standards of conduct. Retrieved January 14, 2009, from http://www.theasca.org

Council for the Advancement of Standards in Higher Education. (2008). *Statement of learning and development outcomes.* Retrieved May 1, 2009, from http://www.cas.edu/CAS%20Statements/CAS_outcomes_chart.08.pdf

Fisher, B., Cullen, F., Turner, M. (2000). U.S. Department of Justice Institute of Justice. *The sexual victimization of college women.* Retrieved January 14, 2009, from http://www.ncjrs.gov/pdffiles1/nij/182369.pdf

Gates, G. J. (2006). *Same-sex couples and the gay, lesbian, bisexual population: New estimates from the American community survey.* Retrieved January 14, 2009, from http://repositories.cdlib.org/uclalaw/williams/gates_8

Hall, E. T. (1976). *Beyond culture.* New York: Doubleday.

Hampden-Turner, C. M., & Trompenaars, F. (2000). *Building cross-cultural competence: How to create wealth from conflicting values.* New Haven, CT: Yale University Press.

Institute of International Education. (2008a). *Newly enrolled international students.* Retrieved January 23, 2009, from http://opendoors.iienetwork.org/page/131548/

Institute of International Education. (2008b). *Leading places of origin.* Retrieved January 23, 2009, from http://opendoors.iienetwork.org/?p=131534

Kohlberg, L. (1976). Moral stages and moralization: The cognitive-developmental approach. In T. Lickona (Ed.), *Moral development and behavior: Theory, research and social issues* (pp. 31–53). New York: Holt, Rinehart and Winston.

Lake, P. (2009, April 13). Student discipline: The case against legalistic approaches. *The Chronicle of Higher Education, 55*(32).

Lipka, S. (2009, March 27) Part 1: Discipline goes on trial at colleges. *The Chronicle of Higher Education, 55*(29).

Lipka, S. (2009, April 6) Part 2: Colleges sharpen tactics for resolving academic-integrity cases. *The Chronicle of Higher Education, 55*(31).

Lipka, S. (2009, April 13) Part 3: With "restorative justice," colleges strive to educate student offenders. *The Chronicle of Higher Education, 55*(32).

National Center for Education Statistics. (2000). *Low-income students: Who they are and how they pay for their education.* Retrieved January 14, 2009, from http://nces.ed.gov/pubs2000/2000169.pdf

National Center for Education Statistics. (2006). *Fast facts.* Retrieved January 14, 2009, from http://nces.ed.gov/fastfacts/display.asp?id=60

National Center for Education Statistics (2008). *Fast facts.* Retrieved January 14, 2009, from http://nces.ed.gov/FastFacts/display.asp?id=98

Pillay, V. (2006). Culture: Exploring the river. In M. Lebaron & V. Pillay (Eds.), *Conflict across cultures: A unique experience of bridging differences* (pp. 25–55). Boston: Intercultural Press.

Rankin, S. R. (2003). *Campus climate for gay, lesbian, bisexual, and transgender people: A national perspective.* New York: The National Gay and Lesbian Task Force Policy Institute.

Stoner, E. N., & Cerminara, K. L. (1990). Harnessing the spirit of insubordination: A model student disciplinary code. *Journal of College and University Law, 17*(2), 89–121.

Stoner, E. N., & Lowery, J. W. (2004). Navigating past the "Spirit of Insubordination": A twenty-first century model student conduct code with a model hearing script. *Journal of College and University Law, 31,* 1–77.

University of California, Los Angeles Institute for Democracy, Education and Access. (2006). *Suspension and expulsion at-a-glance.* Retrieved January 14, 2009, from http://idea.gseis.ucla.edu/publications/suspension/index.html

Western Interstate Commission for Higher Education. (2008). *Knocking at the college door: Projections of high school graduates by state and race/ethnicity, 1992–2022, executive summary.* Retrieved January 14, 2009, from http://wiche.edu/policy/knocking/1992–2022/knocking_exec_summary.pdf

# 2

# WHEN STUDENT LEARNING AND LAW MERGE TO CREATE EDUCATIONAL STUDENT CONFLICT RESOLUTION AND EFFECTIVE CONDUCT MANAGEMENT PROGRAMS

*Simone Himbeault Taylor and Donica Thomas Varner*

Learning is a complex, holistic, multi-centric activity that occurs throughout and across the college experience. Student development and the adaptation of learning to students' lives and needs, are fundamental parts of engaged learning and liberal education. . . . Learning, development and identity formation can no longer be considered as separate from each other; they are interactive and shape each other as they evolve.

*National Association of Student Personnel Administrators (NASPA) & American College Personnel Administrators /College Student Educators International (ACPA) 2004, p. 8.*

I n this comprehensive chapter, we explore how a commitment to legal compliance is not at odds with but rather aligns well with an educationally driven approach to the work of student conflict resolution and student conduct management. This approach advances students' holistic learning and is a recurring theme throughout this book. In the area of student conflict resolution and conduct management, higher education institutions are constantly managing their responsibilities to safeguard the community's well-being and to develop and educate the individual student. Ideally, we are able to meet the individual student's needs without compromising the health and safety of the community or the institution's overall fiduciary responsibilities. Similarly, the institution's commitment to educating the whole student requires an intentional focus on the student's academic/professional development as well as the student's psychosocial development. We are constantly and intentionally engaged in student development and learning in the ever-expanding extended classroom. The disequilibrium created from student conflicts and student conduct issues, therefore, becomes a natural experiential stage from which educators can direct a student's personal growth and influence the community's definition of a just society.

Historically, the response to student conflict and misconduct is rooted in legal theories designed to determine a student's guilt or innocence through a traditional hearing model. While current Model Student Conduct Code (Stoner & Lowery, 2004) advocates move away from legalistic language modeled after the courts (e.g., guilt vs. innocence), the code's fundamental purpose remains to provide a standard corrective or disciplinary response to guilty behavior. This rubric ensures that students are not deprived of fundamental rights without due process, students are treated similarly for similar misconduct, the institution's compelling interest in maintaining a safe and healthy community is satisfied by prompt corrective action, and scarce resources are efficiently managed through the use of a standard disciplinary process.

What is lacking in this risk-reduction model is the conscious decision to support individual growth in the areas of moral and ethical decision making, social identity development, cultural competency, and other components of psychosocial development theory. In many cases, student learning is an unintended consequence rather than an intentional outcome. In our one-dimensional effort to protect people from disparate treatment, arbitrariness, and capriciousness, there is insufficient latitude to grapple with the complexity of the individual student that an institutional commitment to student learning, diversity, and inclusiveness demands. Similarly, in our isolated effort to minimize liability and risk (e.g., legal exposure, bad publicity, stakeholder backlash), we may simply postpone or even escalate the emergence of more serious problems by placing narrow policy standards over the individual needs and experiences of people. Harwood (2008) describes this dynamic in an article promoting the use of campus threat assessment teams:

> There are times when an assessment team finds that the subject is simply enraged about being charged administratively with a minor violation of a

university rule. The situation then escalates because a campus bureaucrat holds strong and says he or she can't overlook the subject's infraction. "Sometimes," says Martin, "we have to say 'Break the rule. Make the exception . . . if that's what it takes to defuse a volatile situation.'" Of course, students also have to know that threats and violence are not the way to resolve such problems. So at the same time that the team may help to address the issue, it also has to address the student's behavior." (p. 76)

Infusing an educationally grounded approach with an institutional risk-reduction model creates the opportunity to break out of the false dichotomy of doing the right thing versus doing the thing right. Drawing on theories of moral and ethical development as well as psychosocial development, we offer in this chapter a conceptual framework for accomplishing the essential intra- and interpersonal development work implicit in student conflict and conduct management. This chapter makes the case for how an informed approach grounded in clarity about educational purpose can result in meaningful student interventions that become the rule, not the exception. These interventions encourage individual ethical development and teach/practice the fundamentals of good citizenship in a diverse society, and at the same time responsibly manage the legal and risk management concerns of the university. We argue that intentionally engaging in student development and learning through conflict resolution pathways, such as negotiation, restorative justice circles, mediation, or facilitated dialogue, actually complements the institution's legal compliance and risk management programs.

## Principles for Grounding Conflict Resolution Work in Student Learning

As educators, wise practice will be informed by our understanding of

- *what* students are learning (intra- and interpersonal competency and character)
- *where* they are learning it (every "where" physically and virtually)
- *how* they are learning (concretely, experientially, abstractly)
- and *with whom* (educators, intimate and virtual peers, themselves)

With this grounding, we may be more likely to conceive of educational interventions and environments that meet today's students where they are and stretch them toward their best "possible selves," a borrowed term suggesting that it is only when individuals have awareness of what options are available for their lives, can they aspire to these futures (Markus & Nurius, 1986). The purpose of this section is to provide the foundations for educators who manage conflict to ground their work in the principles, theory, and research of student learning.

## *What Is Student Learning?*

The constructs of student *learning* and student *development* were at one time regarded as separate. A more sophisticated understanding of learning exists today that accounts for the "complex, holistic, multi-centric activity that occurs throughout and across the college experience" (NASPA & ACPA, 2004, p. 8).

What learning are we trying to inspire in students, and to what end? Over at least the past two decades, numerous reports have emerged from national associations and governmental agencies articulating desired college outcomes. While the language associated with the aims of higher education might shift over time and across reports, the fundamental purpose that guides educators has remained steady and is captured broadly within the following, not necessarily mutually exclusive, constructs:[1]

- Knowledge acquisition
- Intrapersonal competence
- Interpersonal competence
- Cognitive and moral/ethical complexity
- Practical competence/skill development
- Global civic engagement and social responsibility
- Life-long integrative learning/self-authorship

Taken together, these outcomes might be aggregated to describe what Gardner, Csikszentmihalyi, and Damon (2001) call developing *competence and character*. That is, "Individuals exhibit a sense of autonomy and maturity, while at the same time maintaining a connection to the wider community, to vital traditions of earlier times, and to people and institutions yet to come" (p. 243). Yet, in their study of individuals identified as rating highly in competence and character, Gardner et al. revealed an even greater intercultural development outcome reaching beyond individualistic virtues—that of differentiation and integration.

> Optimal development of a person involves fulfilling two potentials that we all have: *differentiation* and *integration*. A differentiated person is competent, has character, and has achieved a fully autonomous individuality.

This is the highest goal of Western cultures. An integrated person is some-one whose goals, values, thoughts, and actions are in harmony; someone who belongs to a network of relationships; someone who accepts a place within a system of mutual responsibilities and shared meanings. In many Eastern cultures, it is integration that is held to be the highest goal of human development. A future worth striving for, in our opinion, is one where a person can develop both differentiation and integration to their fullest extent. (p. 243)

According to the authors, differentiation and integration are the foundation for engaging in *good work*. Gardner et al. describe good work as "work of expert quality that benefits the broader society" (p. ix). Within the context of learning outcomes being grounded in optimal individual development and contribution to the greater good, we argue that student conflict resolution work has the capacity, if done with intentionality, to guide competence and character, differentiation and integration. Choosing to approach student conflict work with these learning outcomes at the forefront is a commitment by student affairs professionals to serve as educators in the higher-learning enterprise.

### What Fundamental Theories Ground Student Conflict and Conduct Work?

"Thin" theor[ies] . . . leave out the unwieldy bulk of human personality and the untidy commingling of real lives filled with dread and aspirations. Philosophers of thin theories treat similar cases similarly, without much regard for moral psychology or the particularity of individual persons. Thin theories are clean and neat. . . . Thick theories require qualifications about the nature of societies and differences among the human animals who live in them. They involve a more complex moral psychology that views human beings as motivated by more—and less—than reason. (Laney, 1990, p. 49)

A theoretical orientation informs how educators influence development along an array of learning outcomes. Being theory grounded informs practice and, employed wisely, elevates perfunctory activities to educationally purposeful interactions. For example, when can community service or a reflective paper transform from a standard sanction into a vehicle for integrative learning for students to better understand themselves and their role in a just society? As educators, intentionality of action informed by knowledge must be the measure for effective work with students. This framing offers an important reference point for the theory-to-practice model and pathways presented in subsequent chapters. The theories, the model, and the pathways are neither clean nor neat and yet must be considered as we strive to increase our effectiveness with students.

Current research in the physiology of brain development suggests that the prefrontal cortex, that region that controls judgment and impulse, is one of the last areas to develop and may not reach maturity until one's mid-20s (Giedd, 2004; Reyna & Farley, 2006; Winters, 2008). This suggests a greater degree of influence for higher education in terms of affecting moral and ethical development in students. Developmental theories inform us about what students learn and how they make meaning. A substantial cognitive psychology literature base demonstrates the relationship between intellectual and moral development. Cognitive, moral, and ethical development and learning theory help explain *how* students make meaning and approach experiences. It also explains how making meaning may be influenced and mediated by their own unique selves including social identities and learning styles. While much of the research literature is based on 18- to 22-year-old college students, the use of the term *student* here is intended to include students of all social identities and of all class levels, from entering to PhD (Astin, 1993; Chickering & Reisser, 1993; Erikson, 1968; Feldman & Newcomb, 1969; King & Kitchener, 1994; Sanford, 1962; Terenzini, Pascarella, & Blimling, 1996; Upcraft, 1994).

Most cognitive development theories assert that as students gain cognitive complexity, they develop the capacity to shift from an externally driven to an internally driven sense of self and evolve in their moral reasoning and reflective judgment. They more fully integrate from an authority-defined right from wrong to a more nuanced sense of who they are, who they desire to be, and the extent to which there is congruence between their thoughts and their behaviors (Baxter Magolda, 1998; Gardner, 2006; Gardner et al., 2001; King & Kitchener, 1994; Kohlberg, 1976; Kolb, 1981; National Research Council, 2000; Pascarella & Terenzini, 2005; Perry, 1970). Understanding the relationship between moral development and conduct and conflict work creates a bridge for the work to be used as the vehicle for practicing the individual skills associated with developing what Gardner et al. coined as competence and character.

Psychosocial development literature also informs conflict resolution work as it concerns itself with the *what* of higher learning. Closely aligned with the learning outcomes discussed earlier, these developmental tasks include mastering knowledge, developing competence, managing emotions, and establishing a sense of self, purpose, and integrity (Chickering & Reisser, 1993). When students abuse substances, argue with their roommates, or inappropriately assert themselves with others, they reveal the personal work required to better understand the alignment between who they are and who they aspire to be.

Psychosocial tasks cross as students gain the knowledge, awareness, and skills to understand the complexities of their diverse social identities and their relationship to others in a society that bestows different power and privilege to these different identities. This includes but is not limited to social diversity of race, ethnicity, nationality, class, sexual orientation, gender and gender orientation, disability, religion, age, and intellectual diversity of ideas, and their intersectionality. The grasp of the complex intersectionality across multiple identities leads to intercultural understanding, and, per Gardner et al. (2001), to gaining the tools to engage meaningfully in good work. Gaining that grasp requires taking risks to understand oneself more fully and to learn from interactions with others. One can see the clear vision line between these tasks, the conflict this may create, and the role conflict resolution educators can play. In this respect, conflict resolution work is in the service of a greater goal for individuals and society (Hardiman & Jackson, 1992; Jones & McEwen, 2000; McIntosh, 1992; Pope, 2000; Robinson, 1993; Schlossberg, 1989; Tatum, 1997; Zuniga, Ratnesh, Nagda, Chesler, & Cytron-Walker, 2007).

Current conceptualizations of the student experience advance *thick theories*, bringing together the wealth of knowledge garnered across multiple theory bases. In her study on the relationship of moral development to enhancing tolerance for diversity, Taylor (1998) introduced a model that was a confluence of cognitive and psychosocial development, interactionist theory, sociological theory, and college impact. *Self-authorship*, a concept first introduced by Kegan (1982) and expanded by Baxter Magolda and King (2004), brings together epistemological, intrapersonal, and interpersonal foundations for the development of cognitive maturity, integrated identity, and mature relationships that converge to create effective citizenship (Baxter Magolda, 1998; Baxter Magolda & King; Kegan).

Taylor (2008) has introduced a comprehensive model that is a synthesis of multiple theories and models, which themselves derive from multiple perspectives that integrate key constructs from decades of research about college students, including Baxter Magolda and King's (2004) self-authorship model. From her synthesis, she draws a conceptual map to describe the student journey from Following External Formulas to Standing at the Crossroads, Becoming Self-Authored, and Building an Internal Foundation (Figure 2.1). Such an integrated approach allows researchers and practitioners alike to live into the holistic concept of learning by reinforcing the inextricable links between cognitive and psychosocial growth and the role played by environmental/social influences to foster and/or impede this growth.

A well-documented component for fostering growth is the presence of disequilibrium or "crisis" that causes students to challenge (with support) previous assumptions about themselves, their external influences, and their micro and meta relationships in society (Erikson, 1968; Light, 2001; Sanford, 1962). Adapted from Taylor (2008), Figure 2.1 aligns some of the types of questions prompted at each stage of development. Student conflict resolution educators can perhaps easily imagine how using this integrated map could inform how one would engage meaningfully with a student presenting with a disequilibrium opportunity, whether addressing drinking behavior or allegations of harassment. The student, and the conduct and conflict resolution educator, are offered a teachable moment. Consistently, that teachable moment is in service of encouraging individual competence and character and in building these qualities to enhance one's contribution to the greater good.

## Where Do Students Learn?

Students are learning to negotiate complex relationships, including the one they have with themselves. Moreover, they are learning to be good citizens

### FIGURE 2.1
**Mapping Intricacies of Young Adults' Developmental Journey**

|  |  Following external formulas |  Standing at the crossroads | 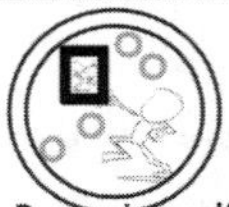 Becoming self-authored |  Building an internal foundation |
|---|---|---|---|---|
| **Cognitive** | What authorities say about what I should know | How do I know? | I know because... | I know because...but I also accept ambiguity |
| **Intrapersonal** | What authorities say about what I should be | Who am I? | I am.. | I am...even when environmental forces pressure me to change |
| **Interpersonal** | What authorities say about kinds of relationships I should have | What type of relationships do I want to have? | I want relationships that... | I want relationships that...but negotiate to meet both my needs and others' needs |

*Note.* Adapted from "Mapping Intricacies of Young Adults' Developmental Journey" (K. Taylor). *The Journal of College Student Development*; May/June 2008, *49*(3); p. 226.

and leaders in a global community. In total, students have a 24-hour-a-day job mastering content, learning sophisticated critical thinking skills, establishing a moral compass, and developing the knowledge, skills, and awareness associated with becoming a global citizen. Those 24 hours are spent in the classroom, in cocurricular activities, at work and at study, and in their living environments. These are 24 hours of potential time to "become habituated to a vision of the good society by inhabiting a good community of scholars" (Laney, 1990, p. 59); 24 hours making wise decisions and at times employing poor judgment, sometimes simultaneously.

In keeping with Taylor's (2008) model, we can imagine students negotiating an array of internal and external conflicts as they journey from socially prescribed to internally driven modes of being. Representative conflicts are illustrated in Table 2.1 and Table 2.2.

### How Can Students Be at the Center of Their Own Learning? With Whom Are They learning?

How best might students learn to negotiate these untested and uncertain territories? Advocates of active student learning propose placing students at the center of their own learning. Astin (1993) refers to this as *engagement*, the notion of the required physical and psychological energy directed at a learning task. When learning occurs at the cognitive and affective levels and as a result of *active learning* through experience, it is more likely to become truly integrated. Kolb's (1981) experiential learning model provides an iterative learning cycle for active learning. This model describes types of learning

### TABLE 2.1
#### Examples of Negotiating Internal Conflicts

| *Presenting Concern* | *Internal Conflict* |
| --- | --- |
| Choosing major and career | Will I choose what my parents have selected for me or follow my passion? |
| Determining one's value system in a competitive environment | Will I (or to what degree will I) compromise my value system to ensure I advance well? To what extent can I "do well" if/when I "do good?" |
| Reconciling multiple social identities and related privilege and subjugation | Will I acknowledge and live into my life as a White, gay male? |
| Determining one's personal identity | Who am I? Why do I believe what I believe? |

## TABLE 2.2
### Examples of Negotiating External Conflicts

| Presenting Concern | External Conflict |
|---|---|
| Roommate conflict | How can I reconcile differences with someone so different from myself? |
| Romantic and/or sexual relationship | How can I understand what are the appropriate boundaries with a potential partner? |
| Adhering to rules, regulations, and laws set by society and the institution | How can I decide when I can assert my own will and when I need to follow external principles and directives? |
| Hazing | How do I reconcile my desire to engage in traditional bonding activities with my peers with my responsibility not to harm myself or others? |

from concrete to abstract and proposes that a student may enter at any access point in the cycle, depending on his or her learning style, and engage in learning. This engagement occurs within and throughout the extended classroom. Kegan (1982) places an emphasis on the learners themselves and advances three principles critical for effective learning, which he says occurs when students

- bring their own life experiences to their learning
- are validated as knowers
- work with educators to mutually construct meaning

The idea of mutually constructing meaning supports Freire's (1997) concept of educators and students together engaging as "simultaneous teachers *and* students" (p. 53) in the enterprise of creating knowledge together. It is an empowerment model that represents a recurring motif in the literature for promoting active student learning. Another recurring motif in the college impact literature concerns itself with the influence of role models and, in particular, peers (Alwin, Cohen, & Newcomb, 1991; Astin, 1993; Pascarella & Terenzini, 1991, 2005). In their qualitative study regarding good workers, Fischman, Solomon, Greenspan, and Gardner (2004) identified six factors influencing good work, that is, work derived from competency and character. These factors align substantially with college impact research conducted over time and include

- Long-standing belief and value system (often derived from family, religion, philosophy, and organized groups and then internalized)
- Role models, mentors (learning positive lessons from those admired and also lessons from negative antimentors)
- Peers (the ethical standards of peers can reinforce or undercut tendencies)
- Pivotal experiences (experiential tipping points can influence a more or less ethical course)
- Institutional milieu (includes norms, observed behaviors, organizational histories)
- Periodic inoculations (this reinforces pivotal experiences to strengthen resolve) (adapted from Fischman et al., pp. 167–183)

According to Fischman et al. (2004), "when [these factors] all point in a positive direction, one is likely to encounter a good worker. When the signals are weak or decidedly mixed, or when they point collectively in a negative direction, one is likely to encounter a worker of indifferent or poor quality" (p. 173).

Taken together, educators are led to the conclusion that students learn best what they discover for themselves cognitively, affectively, and experientially (Blimling, Whitt, & Associates, 1999). This is a compelling case for structuring conduct and conflict work to empower community members to engage educationally and intentionally with students across the expanse of the formal and extended classroom. It is a particularly compelling case for students themselves, whether directly involved or affected by a conflict or incident of misconduct or part of the educational community at large, to play an active role in constructing their own learning and making their own meaning (Astin, 1993; Baxter Magolda, 1999; Freire, 1970/1997; Kegan, 1982; Kolb, 1981; Kuh, Schuh, & Whitt, 1991, 2005; Light, 2001; Pascarella & Terenzini, 1991, 2005).

Because we are reminded that "learning is a complex, holistic, multicentric activity" and that learning and development are not separate entities (NASPA & ACPA 2004, p. 5), the sight line between learning, conflict, and conduct work is made. Yet, to gain a fuller understanding of conflict resolution and conduct management, legal principles must also be fully integrated into the conflict equation. Together with an educational orientation, the balance of individual growth and community accountability may be aligned and actualized. We now turn to legal considerations.

# The Role of Law in Student Conflict and Conduct Management

Understanding the legal principles that the traditional judicial approach to student conflict and conduct management are based on is necessary to challenge the either/or view that legal compliance is at odds with conflict resolution methods premised in student learning theories. The legal cornerstones of student conduct management are the concepts of due process and nondiscrimination. We are legally compelled through constitutional requirements or contractual obligations to provide students with fundamental fairness before imposing sanctions affecting their continued enrollment. We are also required to respond to similar misconduct in similar ways, suggesting that fairness requires sameness. As a result, the primary focus from a legal compliance perspective in developing student conflict and conduct management policies is the establishment of clear behavioral standards and resolution procedures that can be applied uniformly to all students. Consistent with this legal framing, all students who set off the fire alarm/sprinkler system in a residence hall are generally subjected to the same disciplinary procedures and set of sanctions regardless of whether subsequent damage or community disruption resulted from the careless use of a microwave, intentional attempted arson, or the burning of paper shoes as an expression of a traditional Chinese death ritual. The impact of the student's misconduct supersedes the student's intent.

An educationally grounded approach to student conflict and conduct management suggests that student learning theories should inform the *institutional process* for managing misconduct as well as the *institutional response* to the misconduct through sanctioning. In this case, the student's intent supersedes the result of the student's misconduct. The careless student, the deliberate arsonist, and the culturally conscious student may be at different points in their cognitive, intrapersonal, and interpersonal development. Likewise, each student poses a different risk to the health and safety of the overall community.

How then do we meet the individual student at his or her unique developmental stage without engaging in disparate treatment? How do we move beyond the comfort and ease of a uniform response to student conflict and conduct issues to create a space for individualized intervention and growth for all participants in the conflict? How do we appropriately balance the individual student's needs and the institution's interests and fiduciary responsibilities to maintain a healthy and safe community?

To answer these questions, we must first challenge the premise that fairness requires sameness. Fairness is not about everyone being treated the same, but rather it is about everyone getting what they need. This is a foundational principle of social justice.

> [Thick theories] do not lend themselves to severing values from facts and making moral decisions on the basis of general empirical induction. They frequently begin . . . with a vision of what is good rather than a vision of what is right, and they speak more about virtue and character and tradition than they do about law and obedience and duty. (Laney, 1990, p. 50)

When we rely on established student learning and development theories to tailor an appropriate institutional response to student conflict and conduct issues, we are able to advance the overall academic mission. Similarly, when we invest in a spectrum of conflict resolution methods that are able to meet the variety of student conflict and conduct issues that arise, we are then able to be truly fair.

## Due Process

The concept of due process stems from federal and state constitutional law. At the core of the Fourteenth Amendment to the U.S. Constitution (Section 1) is the belief that before the government can take away or burden a citizen's fundamental life, liberty, and property interests, the citizen must be given due process (*Goss v. Lopez*, 1975). The due process clause of the Fourteenth Amendment of the Constitution encompasses the idea that an individual's liberty and property interests are protected by substantive and procedural due process rights (*Goss v. Lopez*). Over many decades of American jurisprudence, the Supreme Court has determined that *substantive due process rights* are rooted in the Constitution and represent those individual freedoms that are so necessary to the foundation of the American judicial and political systems that neither liberty nor justice would exist if these rights were abolished. Examples include the right to marry, to have children, to determine the education and raising of one's children, the right to marital privacy, the use of contraception, bodily integrity and abortion, and refusal of unwanted lifesaving medical treatment (*Palko v. State of Connecticut*, 1937; *Washington v. Glucksberg*, 1997).

The U.S. Supreme Court has yet to conclude that continued enrollment in a public college or university is a constitutionally protected interest entitled to substantive due process protections. On two notable occasions, the Supreme Court has considered whether public universities violated the Fourteenth Amendment when dismissing students for unsatisfactory academic performance (*Soong v. University of Hawaii at Hilo*, 1992). In the *Board of Curators of the University of Missouri v. Horowitz* (1978) case, the Supreme Court assumed for the sake of argument that the student was entitled to substantive due process protection and then quickly determined that because there was evidence that the university was careful and deliberate in its decision making that the university did not act arbitrarily or capriciously in reaching its conclusion, that the student failed to meet the academic standards of the program. In doing so, the court recognized that

> the educational process is not by nature adversary; instead it centers around a continuing relationship between faculty and students, "one in which the teacher must occupy many roles—educator, adviser, friend, and at times, parent-substitute." . . . This is especially true as one advances through the varying regimes of the educational system, and the instruction becomes both more individualized and more specialized. (p. 90)

In the other case, *Regents of the University of Michigan v. Ewing* (1985), the Supreme Court assumed that the student had an implied contractual right to continued enrollment but decided there was no evidence the university acted arbitrarily when the record showed that the university's process was fair, that the university acted in good faith, and the university offered good reasons for its dismissal decision. In fact, Justice Lewis F. Powell opined in a concurring opinion that a student's interest in continued enrollment at a public institution "bears little resemblance to the fundamental interests that previously have been viewed as implicitly protected by the Constitution" (pp. 229–230).

The duty to make reasoned and rational decisions regarding student conflict and conduct issues is usually viewed as a contractual duty that is created by the educational institution's conduct policies, handbooks, and codes of conduct (*Dixon v. Alabama State Board of Education*, 1961).[2] The existence of an implied contract is a matter of state law (*Bishop v. Woods*, 1976; *Regents of the University of Michigan v. Ewing*, 1985). Private institutions may also obligate themselves, through their student handbooks and policies, to be fundamentally fair in the administration of student conduct policies by avoiding arbitrary and capricious actions (Tenerowicz, 2001).

While it remains uncertain whether continued enrollment at a public institution is a property interest protected by substantive due process, it has been clearly established that public institutions must comply with the procedural due process requirements of the Fourteenth Amendment before suspending or expelling a student for nonacademic misconduct (*Dixon v.*

*Alabama State Board of Education,* 1961).[3] The Supreme Court held in *Goss v. Lopez* (1975) that "at the very minimum, therefore, students facing suspension and the consequent interference with a protected property interest must be given some kind of notice and afforded some kind of hearing" (p. 579). The required notice consists of specific information regarding the charges of misconduct and the policies that are alleged to have been violated, so the student can adequately respond to the charges (*Goss v. Lopez,* 1975). In terms of a hearing, all that is required is that the student be provided with a meaningful opportunity to be heard and tell his or her version of events (*Goss v. Lopez,* 1975).[4] In fact, the notice and hearing can occur simultaneously (*Goss v. Lopez,* 1975).[5] As such, an informal interview is sufficient in most situations (*Dixon v. Alabama State Board of Education,* 1961). In short, procedural due process simply requires fundamental fairness (*Dixon v. Alabama State Board of Education,* 1961).[6]

The Supreme Court has recognized that procedural due process is not a technical rule that should be mechanically applied in all cases (*Cafeteria & Restaurant Workers v. McElroy,* 1961). On the contrary, the court has consistently held that "due process is flexible and calls for such procedural protections as the particular situation demands" (*Morrisey v. Brewer,* 1972). In fact, in certain emergent circumstances where it is necessary for the state to act quickly, due process may be provided after a temporary suspension has been ordered (*Gilbert v. Homar,* 1997).[7] Similarly, the idea that schools must provide a formal, adversarial hearing model to satisfy the constitutional requirements of procedural due process has been completely and consistently rejected by federal courts beginning with the case of *Goss v. Lopez* (1975), in which the Supreme Court held that "formalizing the suspension process and escalating its formality and adversary nature may not only make it too costly as a regular disciplinary tool but also destroy its effectiveness as part of the teaching process" (p. 583).

Having a spectrum of conflict resolution pathways available to resolve student conflicts or to manage student behaviors in a manner that is consistent with student learning and social justice theories is aligned with the constitutional concepts of substantive and procedural due process. Pathways selected and applied in a responsible manner are inherently thoughtful, deliberate, and reasoned (as opposed to being arbitrary or capricious). Similarly, no matter which pathway is most appropriate, the student is still guaranteed notice and an opportunity to be heard. Pathways such as facilitated dialogue, mediation, and restorative justice circles actually provide a greater opportunity for the student to be heard than the more formal adjudication pathways. Moreover, these forums are intentionally tailored to provide the affected students with a safer and more egalitarian space to share their personal narrative than what can be provided in a traditional arbitration/hearing process.

Conflict resolution educators can determine the desired learning outcomes that students should master as a result of their participation in campus conflict resolution procedures and then infuse student learning theories into the establishment of conflict resolution programs/policies without compromising the institution's due process obligations. If the goal is to teach students to understand themselves as part of a community and to appreciate how their actions affect others, this can be achieved through a traditional judicial hearing by holding the student strictly accountable for violation of community rules and regulations. But this goal may also be achieved through pathways offered as a diversion from the judicial hearing process, such as restorative justice practices or mediation. If the goal is for students to become aware of their internally driven selves and evolve their moral and ethical decision making based on an appreciation of the source of their motives and intent, then a facilitated dialogue between parties coupled with a reflective writing exercise may be appropriate. The range of possibilities to support student learning is endless within the legal framework of fundamental fairness (i.e., notice and opportunity to be heard).

## *Nondiscrimination*

Civil rights laws enacted by federal, state, and local governments in addition to institutional nondiscrimination policies prohibit disparate treatment of students based on their protected status, and protect people against rules and practices that disparately have an impact on a group of students based on their membership in a protected classification.[8] Key to a disparate treatment claim is evidence of an intentional discriminatory motive that is proven by either direct or indirect evidence. Also key to a disparate impact claim is evidence that an otherwise neutral policy or practice disproportionally negatively affects certain protected groups. Therefore, it is understandable that educational institutions prefer a uniform disciplinary process to protect students from the possibility of unbridled discretion, discriminatory animus, bias, or poor judgment of educators who administer conduct and conflict resolution programs. The effectiveness of the student conflict or conduct management program can suffer if there is no consistency in the institutional response or outcome. Uniform disciplinary processes help to neutralize the impacts of structural privileges and disadvantages that exist within an institution.

In addition, uniform disciplinary processes help to ensure that over time and across decentralized institutions, students are treated similarly for similar misconduct. Complying with a standard disciplinary protocol limits the ability of others to influence the institutional response to student misconduct because of the identity of the accused student, the identity of the other involved student(s), or the negative consequences for the institution. The more options that are available in a student conflict and conduct management program and the less obvious the desired learning outcomes are, the greater the opportunity for intentional or unintentional discriminatory treatment exists.

Yet, treating everyone the same, without regard to the interplay of intent versus consequence, or individual versus community, or thin theories versus thick theories can also result in unfair and discriminatory outcomes for individual students. This is because of structural biases inherent in institutions and the primacy of the dominant narratives on each campus.

Consider the case of undergraduate student "Sarah" labeled a threat by a professor who desires her immediate removal from future classes. The professor describes Sarah's classroom behavior as intimidating, confrontational, and disruptive. According to the professor, Sarah takes over classroom discussions without allowing other students' voices to be heard and inappropriately challenges authority. This conflict has resulted in a verbal altercation between Sarah and the professor. As a result some students no longer want to attend class. The professor refuses to teach the class if Sarah remains in it.

Before initiating the disciplinary hearing process, the associate dean interviews Sarah and learns that Sarah is an adult in her mid-50s who is returning to school to finish her undergraduate degree. She is an African American woman who appears to be thoughtful and confident. Sarah acknowledges the tension between her and the professor, a White male in his 40s, and explains that she is frustrated at being ignored and marginalized by the professor whom she feels never wants to acknowledge her and who disrespects her regularly. Sarah doesn't see her actions as threatening or disruptive but merely an appropriate effort to engage fully in classroom discussions and to be heard. According to Sarah, the younger students never have anything to say or contribute to the discussion.

The principle of nondiscrimination does not require the institution to ignore any of these relevant facts in determining an appropriate resolution between the professor and student if the learning outcomes of the institution's conflict and conduct management programs are clearly established and demand consideration of those factors. Establishing desired learning outcomes leads to the creation of conflict resolution and conduct management tools that are informed by congruent student learning theories. Inconsistent pursuit of the desired learning outcomes then becomes a test for whether disparate treatment is occurring.

Using a spectrum of conflict resolution options does not forego any of the procedural safeguards provided to students through the formal pathway of adjudication, as long as the pathways are managed by educated, well-developed, and highly skilled professionals capable of tailoring a forum that effectively meets the desired learning outcomes for the individual student and protects him or her against discriminatory conduct. The conflict resolution and conduct management program that is educationally grounded can comply with the institution's nondiscrimination obligations under two conditions.

First, all the participants must choose to participate in the selected alternative conflict resolution pathway and must do so in good faith. Pathways that empower participants to engage in their own conflict resolution methods only work if the individuals are developmentally capable of meaningful participation and learning. If students benefit from the effective resolution of their conflict or conduct issue from the chosen alternative pathway, then they have received what they need from the process and will have been treated fairly. If students choose not to participate in an alternative conflict resolution pathway, then the traditional hearing model should be the default process. By maintaining the traditional hearing model as part of the overall program, the students have the same protections against nondiscrimination that have always existed at that institution.

Second, student affairs educators must build trust in the administration of the conflict resolution and conduct management program. There must be clarity and transparency in the purpose and process of the spectrum of pathways in order to avoid a perception of disparate treatment that may result when the community experiences differing processes and outcomes. Students must be confident that regardless of the chosen pathway, they will be provided with a full and fair opportunity to be heard and respected, that they will be safe in the process and not further harmed, that a resolution will be reached in a timely manner, and that the resolution will be effective. The conflict resolution educator or conduct administrator must be sophisticated in understanding student learning theories in general, and ethical development specifically, to appropriately identify the student's readiness for a transformative experience. The professional also must command a full understanding of his or her own ethical development and social identities to avoid engaging in stereotyping and other biased decision making. That is, the effective educator requires a strongly developed internal foundation.

Returning to the case of Sarah, having the option of a facilitated dialogue or mediation allows the institution to appropriately address the conflict in a forum that views her as an equal participant rather than an alleged wrongdoer. The less-formal pathways for conflict resolution where the desired outcome is win-win provide Sarah and the professor space to engage in thoughtful reflection about their interaction. More traditional interventions such as hearings encourage participants to justify their behaviors while positioned for a win-lose outcome. To implement a conflict resolution and conduct management program without engaging in discriminatory conduct, the student participant must choose to participate in good faith. The traditional hearing process should be available for students who are incapable of participating in alternative conflict resolution methods in good faith. The conflict resolution educators must be skilled, seasoned, and knowledgeable practitioners committed to the institution's stated approach to instill trust and confidence in the community.

It is important to recognize the limits of alternative conflict resolution methods rooted in student learning theories when issues of violence and power inequality are present and undermine the shared interest in safety. Clearly, disruptive student behaviors that negatively affect the ability of the community to function and that jeopardize the safety of the student or other community members require swift and effective institutional response. While alternative conflict resolution methods should not necessarily be relied on to manage students in crisis, it is always advisable to rely on student learning concepts to shape an institutional response that creates an opportunity for making meaning, albeit at a later time or away from the institution.

## Practical Application

In this chapter we have attempted to present a collaborative conversation between student affairs professionals and in-house higher education attorneys about how to partner to create a robust conduct management program fully infused with conflict resolution pathways that meets the institution's individual needs and is educationally based. Creating learning opportunities for students in the midst of a conflict or in response to student misconduct is difficult and messy work. The urge to bring quick order to the mess through strict adherence to rules and process should be resisted. Operating in a socially just framework of thick theory is not tidy, yet we challenge colleagues to rely on the well-developed theories of moral, ethical, and psychosocial development to be comfortable in the mess long enough to lay the foundation for the development of young adults who are learning to internalize the values of integrity, judgment, compassion, personal responsibility, accountability, and respect.

This chapter reviews the conditions students learn best under and emphasizes the value of active student learning, the power of students to create their own meaning cognitively and affectively, and the role of institutions, educators, and peers to influence that learning. Conflict incidents offer a presenting issue that often represents the crisis or disequilibrium required to affect change (Erikson, 1968; Light, 2001; Sanford, 1962). These contexts for incident resolution and conduct management go well beyond simply addressing the presenting conflict. Instead, it prepares educators to leverage conflict as a tool that can enable students to integrate and differentiate in a way that helps them to form the internal foundation and function as global citizens with competence and character. While this may present a compelling case for framing all student conflict work to align with these purposes, serious consideration must first be given to readiness at the personnel, unit, divisional, and institutional levels.

While the law is flexible enough to support the institution's vision for managing student conflict and conduct issues, student affairs professionals and lawyers must undertake a realistic evaluation of their institution's, division's, conduct and conflict office's, and personnel's readiness to embrace a sophisticated and complex approach to student learning in the context of student conflict and conduct management. To determine readiness requires individuals and organizations to behave as reflective practitioners, carefully considering on a regular basis what they know, how they know it, and how they may leverage this understanding in future situations (Schön, 1983). For example, student affairs educators must be honest about their ability and capacity to explore and deliver a spectrum of conflict resolution practices. In-house counsel must be willing to challenge the traditional legal view that fairness equals sameness and sameness equals amnesty from legal action. The institution should be clear and transparent about its desired learning outcomes for the student conflict and conduct management program.

We conclude with the following assessment questions to help explore readiness and fit for each community and practitioner as they approach conflict work.

### *Professional Staff Level*

What is the current capacity of your campus's conflict resolution and conduct management educators to engage in an educationally based approach that is sophisticated enough to protect the students and the institution from harm? Are staff members

- educated in current theory and research regarding student learning processes and outcomes, as well as moral and ethical development?
- advanced in their own development of internal foundation to instill reasoned, ethical, and principled decision making in their work?
- at a level of professional maturity to deal with the ambiguity and messiness inherent in nontraditional, alternative models?
- supported by bench strength, motivation, creativity, and diversity to employ a range of resolution strategies and work meaningfully with students?
- competent in assessment to measure impact?
- ready with a demonstrated track record of making sound judgments?

## Unit Level

What is the current capacity of your functional unit to engage in an educationally based approach that is sophisticated enough to protect the students and the institution from harm? Does the unit

- employ best practices in its current work?
- have a mission, vision, strategic plan, and evaluation methods that can support this broadened approach to the work?
- have educated and experienced staff to carry out this approach?
- have sufficiently strong relationships with key campus partners (such as general counsel, intergroup relations, and public safety) to build partnerships for this work?
- demonstrate functioning in a status quo or change management phase, assuming the current work is being done well within its established framework?
- have resources at a level that can accommodate approaches that may bring greater effectiveness but perhaps not greater efficiency?

## Student Affairs Divisional Level

What is the current capacity of your division to engage in an educationally based approach that is sophisticated enough to protect the students and the institution from harm? Is divisional work

- informed by the most current theory, research, and best practices?
- conceptually and tangibly supportive of a student learning approach to its work or is it more activities/services oriented?

- articulated and measured as learning outcomes?
- grounded in valuing active student learning interventions?
- in a status quo or change management phase?

## Institutional Level

What is the current capacity of your institution to engage in an educationally based approach that is sophisticated enough to protect the students and the institution from harm?

- What is the institution's culture and approach to student conflict and conduct management?
- What is the scope of conflict resolution and conduct management services currently offered on your campus?
- How broad or narrow is conflict resolution work currently defined?
- Is the current campus approach perceived as effective in achieving the desired student learning outcomes? If yes, how so? If not, why?
- Where are potential partners, colleagues, competitors, and naysayers?
- What is the institution's risk tolerance level for potential litigation, actual litigation, public attention, and critical analysis from key constituencies and stakeholders that may result from moving beyond the comfort of your current practice?
- Is the institution in a status quo or change management phase?
- Does the institution have the capacity to withstand scrutiny and support its educational aims?
- Do the current policies and practices of key partners (e.g., general counsel, intergroup relations, public safety) support or undermine active student learning interventions?
- What is the current scope and capacity of the institution's student support services to sustain a broad range of conflict resolution offerings (i.e., counseling and psychological services, services for students with disabilities, sexual assault prevention and awareness centers, health services)?
- How can student conflict resolution educators use knowledge about the power of active, engaged learning to shape interventions? In other words, how can student conflict resolution educators leverage this assessment tool to operationalize their work?

## Conclusion

This chapter challenges the false dichotomy that pits educational intentionality against legal compliance. We put forward the *compatible to competing* continuum and recognize that one does not have to sacrifice the individual good for the community good but may invest meaningfully in both. Leveraging conflict situations for the greater good of student learning can also serve to protect the interests of the community. It is only from an informed, studied perspective about the aims of student learning that a different lens may be applied to conflict issues and the developmental role they offer.

Institutions will need to determine for themselves if they are positioned to frame their work within this broader learning perspective. The most vital element to engaging in any student-related work is authenticity. Rather than place a value judgment on preferred models and approaches, the decision about direction will need to be based on an assessment of how any organization can live into its best self. And this best self may be fluid over time depending on organizational and staff readiness. In the end, clarity about the purpose of the work and intentionality around its delivery will allow conflict resolution educators to engage in their own good work with competence and character.

As we weigh how educators may facilitate opportunities for learning offered in these transitional moments and years, we are reminded of John Dewey's notion that the mind is a verb not a noun, a process not a structure (Dworkin, 1959). How might we prompt the processes for students' full engagement in their own learning? And as educators, how might we treat our own minds like verbs to remain open to the array of approaches for encouraging the development of competence and character through the vehicles of behavioral incidents and conflict situations? If we have the capacity to remain cognizant of the ultimate purpose of our work, form will follow function. Ernest Boyer (1987), as head of the Carnegie Foundation for the Advancement of Teaching, said this of higher education:

> The aim of the undergraduate experience is not only to prepare the young for productive careers, but also to enable them to live lives of dignity and purpose; not only to generate new knowledge, but to channel that knowledge to humane ends; not merely to study government, but to help shape a citizenry that can promote the public good. (p. 297)

Envisioning student conflict resolution and management not as an end in itself (managing behavior) but as a tool for affecting student growth and development to prepare students as productive, purposeful, knowledge-generating, humane citizens of the world is a worthy purpose for student affairs educators. It creates the avenue for developing good workers to do good work. Various conflict resolution methods can be designed to provide participants with the opportunity to learn how to be good citizens in a just community. This, in the end, transforms the *what* of conflict work to the *so what* of student learning.

## Notes

1. Some key reports include but are not limited to Association of American Colleges and Universities (AAC&U, 2002, 2007), ACPA (1996), NASPA and ACPA (2004), ACPA et al. (2006), American Association for Higher Education (AAHE), ACPA, and NASPA (1998), Leskes and Miller (2006), U.S. Department of Education (2006), and the Spellings Commission Report (2006).

2. Recognizing that it is a "well settled rule that the relations between a student and a private university are a matter of contract" (p. 157).

3. Holding that "we are confident that precedent as well as a most fundamental constitutional principle support our holding that due process requires notice and some opportunity for hearing before a student at a tax-supported college is expelled for misconduct" (p. 158)

4. Holding that "in being given an opportunity to explain his version of the facts at this discussion, the student first be told what he is accused of doing and what the basis of the accusation is" (p. 582).

5. Holding that "there need be no delay between the time 'notice' is given and the time of the hearing" (p. 583).

6. Holding that in addressing student misconduct, public universities should exercise "at least the fundamental principles of fairness by giving the accused students notice of the charges and an opportunity to be heard in their own defense" (p. 157) when there are no issues of immediate threat to others.

7. Holding that "where a State must act quickly, or where it would be impractical to provide predeprivation process, postdeprivation process satisfies the requirements of the Due Process Clause [of the Fourteenth Amendment]" (p. 1812).

8. Colleges and universities receiving federal funds are prohibited from discriminating against beneficiaries of those federally funded programs based on an individual's race, color, or national origin (Title XI of the Civil Rights Act of 1964), sex (Title IX of the Civil Rights Act of 1964), age (Age Discrimination Act, 42 U.S.C. § 6104), disability (Section 504 of the Rehabilitation Act of 1973, 29 U.S.C. §794 and the Americans with Disabilities Act, 42 U.S.C. § 12101). In addition, Title IV of the Civil Rights Act of 1964 prohibits public colleges from religious discrimination in the admissions process. In addition, state laws and municipal ordinances prohibit discrimination in the provision of educational services on additional classifications such as religion, veteran's status, sexual orientation, height, or weight.

## References

Alwin, D., Cohen, R., & Newcomb, T. (1991). *Political attitudes over the life span: The Bennington women after fifty years.* Madison: University of Wisconsin Press.

American Association for Higher Education, American College Personnel Association, and National Association of Student Personnel Administrators. (1998). *Powerful partnerships: A shared responsibility for learning.* Washington, DC: American Association for Higher Education, American College Personnel Association, and National Association of Student Personnel Administrators.

American College Personnel Association. (1996). *The student learning imperative: Implications for student affairs.* Washington, DC: American College Personnel Association.

American College Personnel Association & National Association of Student Personnel Administrators. (2004). *Learning reconsidered: A campus-wide focus on the student experience.* Washington, DC. American College Personnel Association & National Association of Student Personnel Administrators.

American College Personnel Association, Association of College and University Housing Offices-International, Association of College Unions International, National Academic Advising Association, National Association for Campus Activities, National Association of Student Personnel Administrators, & National Intramural-Recreational Sports Association. (2006). *Learning reconsidered 2: Implementing a campus-wide focus on the student experience.* Washington, DC: American College Personnel Association and National Association of Student Personnel Administrators.

Association of American Colleges and Universities. (2002). *Greater Expectations: A new vision for learning as a nation goes to college.* Washington, DC: Association of American Colleges and Universities.

Association of American Colleges and Universities. (2007). *College learning for the new global century.* Washington, DC: Author.

Astin, W. A. (1993). *What matters in college: Four critical years revisited.* San Francisco: Jossey-Bass.

Baxter Magolda, M. B. (1998). Developing self-authorship in young adult life. *Journal of College Student Development, 39*(2), 143–156.

Baxter Magolda, M. (1999). Engaging students in active learning. In G. S. Blimling, E. J. Whitt, & Associates (Eds.), *Good practice in student affairs: Principles to foster student learning* (pp. 21–43). San Francisco: Jossey-Bass.

Baxter Magolda, M. B., & King, P. (2004). *Learning partnerships: Theory and models of practice to educate for self-authorship.* Sterling, VA: Stylus.

Bishop v. Woods, 426 U.S. 341 (1976).

Blimling, G. S., Whitt, E. J., & Associates. (1999). *Good practice in student affairs: Principles to foster student learning.* San Francisco: Jossey-Bass.

Board of Curators of the University of Missouri v. Horowitz, 435 U.S. 78 (1978).

Boyer, L. E. (1987). *College: The undergraduate experience in America.* New York: Harper & Row.

Cafeteria & Restaurant Workers v. McElroy, 367 U.S. 886 (1961).

Chickering, A. W., & Reisser, L. (1993). *Education and identity* (2nd ed.). San Francisco: Jossey-Bass.

Dixon v. Alabama State Board of Education, 294 F.2d 150 (5th Cir. 1961).

Dworkin, M.S. Ed. (1959). *In Dewey on education selections*. Classics in education no. 3. New York: Teachers College Press.

Erikson, E. (1968). *Identity: Youth in crisis*. New York: Norton.

Feldman, K., & Newcomb, T. (1969). *The impact of college on students: An analysis of four decades of research* (Vol. 1). San Francisco: Jossey-Bass.

Fischman, W., Solomon, B., Greenspan, D., & Gardner, H. (2004). *Making good: How young people cope with moral dilemmas at work*. Cambridge, MA: Harvard University Press.

Freire, P. (1997). *Pedagogy of the oppressed* (Rev. ed., Myra Bergman Ramos, Trans.). New York: Continuum. (Original work published 1970)

Gardner, H. (2006). *Multiple intelligences: New horizons*. New York: Basic.

Gardner, H., Csikszentmihalyi, M., & Damon, W. (2001). *Good work: When excellence and ethics meet*. New York: Basic.

Giedd, J. N. (2004). Structural magnetic resonance imaging of the adolescent brain. *Annals of the New York Academy of Sciences*, 1021, 77–85.

Gilbert v. Homar, 520 U.S. 924 (1997).

Goss v. Lopez, 419 U.S. 565 (1975).

Hardiman, R., & Jackson, B. W. (1992). Racial identity development: Understanding racial dynamics in college classrooms and on campus. *New Directions for Teaching and Learning*, 52, 21–37.

Harwood, M. (2008). Teaming up to reduce risk. *Security Management*, 66–78.

Jones, S., & McEwen, M. (2000). A conceptual model of multiple dimensions of identity. *Journal of College Student Development*, 41, 405–414.

Kegan, R. (1982). *The evolving self: Problem and process in human development*. Cambridge, MA: Harvard University Press.

King, P. M., & Kitchener, K. S. (1994). *Developing reflective judgment*. San Francisco: Jossey-Bass.

Kohlberg, L. (1976). Moral stages and moralizations: The cognitive-developmental approach. In T. Lickona (Ed.), *Moral development and behavior: Theory, research, and social issues* (pp. 31–55). New York: Holt, Rinehart and Winston.

Kolb, D. A. (1981). Learning styles and disciplinary differences. In A. W. Chickering & Associates (Eds.), *The modern American college* (pp. 232–255). San Francisco: Jossey-Bass.

Kuh, G., Schuh, J., & Whitt, E. (1991). *Involving colleges: Successful approaches to fostering student learning and development outside the classroom*. San Francisco: Jossey-Bass.

Kuh, G. D., Schuh, J. H., & Whitt, E. (2005). Never let it rest: Lessons about student success from high-performing colleges and universities. *Change: The Magazine of Higher Learning, 37*(4), 44–51.

Laney, J. T. (1990). Through thick and thin: Two ways of talking about the academy and moral responsibility. In W. W. May (Ed.), *Ethics and higher education* (pp. 49–66). New York: American Council on Education, Macmillan.

Leskes, A., & Miller, R. (2006). *Purposeful pathways: Helping students achieve key learning outcomes.* Washington, DC: Association of American Colleges and Universities.

Light, R. J. (2001). *Making the most of college: Students speak their minds.* Boston, MA: Harvard University Press.

Lipka, S. (2009, March 27) Part 1: Discipline goes on trial at colleges. *The Chronicle of Higher Education, 55*(29).

Lipka, S. (2009, April 6) Part 2: Colleges sharpen tactics for resolving academic-integrity cases. *The Chronicle of Higher Education, 55*(31).

Lipka, S. (2009, April 13) Part 3: With "restorative justice," colleges strive to educate student offenders. *The Chronicle of Higher Education, 55*(32).

Markus, H., & Nurius, P. (1986). Possible selves. *American Psychologist, 41,* 954–969.

McIntosh, P. (1992). White privilege and male privilege: A personal account of coming to see correspondences through work in women's studies. In M. Andersen & P. Hill Collins (Eds.), *Race, class and gender* (pp. 76–87). Belmont, CA: Wadsworth.

*Morrisey v. Brewer,* 408 U.S. 471 (1972).

National Research Council. (2000). *How people learn: Brain, mind, experience, and school.* Washington, DC: National Academy Press.

Palko v. State of Connecticut, 302 U.S. 319 (1937).

Pascarella E. T., & Terenzini, P. T. (1991). *How college affects students.* San Francisco: Jossey-Bass.

Pascarella E. T., & Terenzini, P. T. (2005). *How college affects students: A third decade of research* (Vol. 2). San Francisco: Jossey-Bass.

Perry, W. G. (1970). *Forms of intellectual and ethical development in the college years.* New York: Holt, Rinehart, and Winston.

Pope, R. (2000). The relationship between psychosocial development and racial identity of college students of color. *Journal of College Student Development, 41,* 302–312.

Regents of the University of Michigan v. Ewing, 474 U.S. 214 (1985).

Reyna, V. F., & Farley, F. (2006). Risk and rationality in adolescent decision making: Implications for theory, practice, and public policy. *Psychological Science in the Public Interest, 7,* 1–44.

Robinson, T. (1993). The intersections of gender, class, race, and culture: On seeing clients whole. *Journal of Multicultural Counseling and Development, 21*(1), 50–58.

Sanford, N. (1962). Developmental status of the entering freshman. In N. Sanford (Ed.), *The American college* (pp. 253–282). New York: Wiley.

Schlossberg, N. K. (1989). Marginality and mattering: Key issues in building community. In D. C. Roberts (Ed.), *Designing campus activities to foster a sense of community* (pp. 5–15). San Francisco: Jossey-Bass.

Schön, D. A. (1983). *The reflective practitioner: How professionals think in action.* New York: Basic.

Soong v. University of Hawaii at Hilo, 825 P.2d 1060 (Haw. 1992).

Stoner, E., & Lowery, J. (2004). Navigating past the "spirit of insubordination": A twenty-first century model student conduct code with a model hearing script. *Journal of College and University Law, 31*(1), 1–65.

Tatum, B. D. (1997). *"Why are all the Black kids sitting together in the cafeteria?" And other conversations about race.* New York: Basic.

Taylor, K. B. (2008). Mapping the intricacies of young adults' developmental journey from socially prescribed to internally defined identities, relationships, and beliefs. *The Journal of College Student Development, 49*(3), 215–234.

Taylor, S. H. (1998). The impact of college on the development of tolerance. *NASPA Journal, 35*(4), 281–295.

Tenerowicz, L. (2001). Student misconduct at private colleges and universities: A roadmap for "fundamental fairness" in disciplinary proceedings. *Boston College Law Review, 42*, 653–694.

Terenzini, P. T., Pascarella E., & Blimling, G. (1996). Students' out-of-class experiences and their influence on learning and cognitive development: A literature review. *Journal of College Student Development, 37*, 149–162.

Upcraft, M. L. (1994). The dilemma of translating theory to practice. *Journal of College Student Development, 35*, 438–443.

U.S. Department of Education. (2006). *A test of leadership: Charting the future of U.S. higher education.* Washington, DC.

Washington v. Glucksberg, 521 U.S. 702 (1997).

Winters, K. C. (2008, February). *Adolescent brain development: Implications for understanding youth.* Paper presented at the Annual National Conference on Law and Higher Education, Clearwater Beach, FL.

Zuniga, X., Ratnesh, B., Nagda, A., Chesler, M., & Cytron-Walker, A. (2007). Intergroup dialogue in higher education: Meaningful learning about social justice. *ASHE Higher Education Report Series, 32*(4).

# 3

# WHY OBJECTIVITY
# IS NOT ENOUGH

The Critical Role of Social Justice
In Campus Conduct and Conflict Work

*Ryan C. Holmes, Keith Edwards, and Michael M. DeBowes*

Judicial affairs administrators, probably more
than anyone else on campus, are central to the
task of building what Boyer calls a just community and a disciplined community. Programs
must be designed that are proactive attempts to
combat campus racism and sexism with the
idea of creating a community where each individual is respected, but individuals also accept
their obligations to the community.

*Gehring, 1998, pp. 265–266*

D onald Gehring, founder of the Association for Student Judicial
Affairs (renamed the Association for Student Conduct Administration in 2008) provides perhaps one of our earliest glimpses into
what it means to view student conduct work through a social justice lens.
His wise reflection on the role of student conduct administrators in building
campus community captures the essence of balancing the rights of the individual and the responsibility of community. These are the forces that challenge higher education every day and frame the theoretical and practical
applications of social justice.

In the contemporary student conduct office, practitioners regularly
encounter issues that can be more fully understood and accounted for by
using social justice as an additional lens. For example, consider an international student who is alleged to have violated the college's plagiarism policy
and is referred to the student conduct office for adjudication. Through the

trained lens of *student rights* we consider at the outset how to notify the student of the charge properly, what judicial options to provide, how to conduct an agreement or adjudication process under a well-defined policy, and what outcomes may result from this process. Adding a *social justice* lens invites deeper reflection on a case-by-case and systemic level. In this case, should the student's understanding (or lack of understanding) regarding U.S. standards of academic honesty have any impact on the decision to find the student in violation/not in violation of college policy? What influence, if any, should an international student's visa status have on a hearing officer's decision to suspend (or not suspend) an international student for plagiarism?

By way of a systemic example, consider the case of two students who desire mediation because they cannot decide who should move out of their residence hall room. One states her religious beliefs are jeopardized because her roommate openly identifies as being a lesbian. The student rights lens lets us consider whether a room is available and under what conditions a student is allowed to move. It further prompts us to consider which, if either, student has been wronged, and perhaps which student presents the better rationale for staying in the room while the other student is made to move. The administrator who adds a social justice lens will consider additional questions. Should a mediator's sexual orientation be a factor in determining that mediator's suitability to resolve the dispute? Should the mediator have prior training in facilitating resolutions in which social identities, such as sexual orientation, play a major role in the conflict? To what extent should the institution consider the physical and psychological safety of the student who identifies as lesbian in deciding whether a move is warranted? Further, does the institution unfairly burden this student if it requires her to participate in roommate mediation?

Questions such as these are not only important to consider for our students and the systems we work in, but we cannot explore fully the lens of social justice without turning that lens upon ourselves. Such introspection may produce considerable dissonance in light of our historical training and experience. Student conduct and conflict resolution professionals are routinely tapped to provide leadership for an array of complex situations in which a student's behavior is in conflict with an institutional policy, standard, or member of the community. Professional oversight of adjudication and other dispute resolution processes is naturally expected to be fair and impartial to ensure equitable educational outcomes for all involved parties. However, the notion that professionals may remain impartial in the face of their own socialization and background may not be realistic or productive, as larger societal dynamics cannot be separated from the humans involved in the implementation of these procedures.

In this chapter, we explore foundational concepts of social justice as a necessary framework for understanding the individual experience of oppression, the systemic ways in which we perpetuate injustice in our communities, and the personal and professional implications of considering our role in student conduct work through a social justice lens.

## Foundations of Social Justice

Although higher education personnel in general and student affairs educators specifically, may be very familiar with terms such as *diversity* and *multiculturalism*, differentiating between those familiar concepts and social justice may be difficult. Is social justice simply the new en vogue term, or is there a substantive difference between these ideas and how they are applied to the student affairs profession? What implications do these concepts have for dispute resolution practitioners in the higher education community?

Social justice is a fundamentally different approach that extends diversity and multiculturalism (Adams, Bell, & Griffin, 2007). Social justice includes addressing the differences among us such as race, gender, and sexual orientation while also valuing cultural differences and learning how to communicate within and across these differences. What separates social justice from diversity and multiculturalism is that social justice explicitly examines the power structures in society related to these differences, as these power structures result in privilege and oppression. Furthermore, social justice includes an action component that moves beyond the recognition of power structures in an effort to create a more just and equitable society (Freire, 1970/2000; hooks, 1994). Social justice is not a new concept. The use of the term does not mean that diversity educators and multicultural advocates have ignored power differences or failed to work for equality. It simply makes the objective of a more just and equitable society transparent.

## Social Group Identities

Social justice begins with understanding our different social groups and how our membership or perceived membership in these groups results in benefiting from or being the target of systems of oppression (Hardiman, Jackson, & Griffin, 2007). These social groups include but are not limited to race/ethnicity, gender, sexual orientation, class, age, ability, and religion. What separates these social groups from other human differences such as hair color or eye color is that there are social structures in place that benefit some and burden others depending on their identity or perceived identity within these social groups. For instance, although a person with green eyes can be mean to another with brown eyes, and that prejudice could be very hurtful, it is not demonstrative of oppression because there are no social structures in society that grant systematic benefits to people with green eyes and reinforce that personal meanness toward brown-eyed people structurally in our U.S. culture. The reason a racist comment or homophobic joke is oppressive rather than just mean is because our society is structured in a way that overtly and covertly supports, encourages, and reinforces prejudices against people of color and gay, lesbian, bisexual, and transgender (GLBT) individuals or those perceived to be GLBT.

How we identify, or are perceived to identify, within each of these social groups may provide benefit or oppression. Those individuals occupying dominant social group identities (e.g., men, Whites, and middle and upper-class people) experience privileges they did not earn as a result of the system that is in place (Johnson, 2001). These unearned privileges generally come in two forms, either *unearned entitlements*, which everyone should have, or *conferred dominance*, which no one should have (McIntosh, 2000). For example, a man's freedom to walk at night without being afraid of being raped is an example of an unearned entitlement because it is a right all of us should have. However, because of the sexual violence in society stemming from systemic sexism, generally only men experience this freedom. Because the systems in place work to their advantage, individuals with privilege are often unaware of how they benefit from the system. They often feel guilty when they first begin to realize that their achievements may not be entirely the result of their talents or hard work (Kendall, 2006). Those who have subordinate social group identities (e.g., GLBTs, Muslims, and people of color) are the targets of oppressive social structures. Because of systems working against them, members of subordinate groups are often more cognizant of the ways in which oppression operates in their lives (Tatum, 2003).

As individuals we each have a variety of social group identities (Jones & McEwen, 2000). Some of these multiple or intersecting identities may be more salient to us than others depending on whether we experience oppression as a result of our identities, our personal experiences throughout our lives, or the context that we are in at a given moment. Most of us have at least one dominant group identity and at least one subordinate group identity. Our multiple identities intersect in ways that influence how we experience our social group memberships and the corresponding privilege or oppression associated with these memberships (Andersen & Collins, 2001).

For example, how a Black lesbian experiences racism is complexly different from how a Black heterosexual man would experience racism. Although individuals may find that one aspect of their identity is generally or situationally more salient than others, it is important to note that these forms of oppression are deeply intertwined. Accordingly, competing in the "Oppression Olympics" is a zero-sum game: Prioritizing certain forms of oppression over others is not helpful in advancing social justice for all (Martinez, 1998).

Throughout our lives each of us has received messages that have informed how we view ourselves and others related to our social group identities (Harro, 2000). Our experiences through this cycle of socialization begin at birth with the message we receive from those who love and care for us, including parents and teachers. Those early messages are reinforced consciously and unconsciously by social institutions such as schools, religious institutions, and media. This socialization results in the inevitable development of individual biases and prejudices based on lifelong socialization in an oppressive society. Well-intentioned efforts by professionals who may self-identify as allies and try to convince others (and themselves) that they have transcended their own oppressive socialization because they are well-meaning, work in higher education, or have been through numerous diversity workshops can actually do harm despite their best intentions to be neutral, objective, and fair (Edwards, 2006). Once we acknowledge the inevitability of our own oppressive socialization, we can move beyond pain, denial, guilt, and defensiveness. This enables us to be more conscious of our oppressive socialization and the messages we continue to be exposed to in our lives.

## Systems of Oppression

These systems of oppression function on individual, institutional, and cultural levels through conscious and unconscious behaviors and attitudes (Figure 3.1) (Hardiman et al., 2007). For example, on the individual level, a man may be sexist toward a woman through his thoughts and actions and may consciously and intentionally try to put her down, sexually objectify her, or talk over her in a meeting as a way to be sure her ideas do not get heard. Similarly, a man could also objectify a woman or ignore her without being conscious of his actions or intending to do harm as a result of the messages he has received throughout his life about the role and status of women in society.

It is not just individual actions that perpetuate oppression. Social institutions such as education, media, criminal justice, government, business,

## FIGURE 3.1
### Multiple Dimensions of Oppression

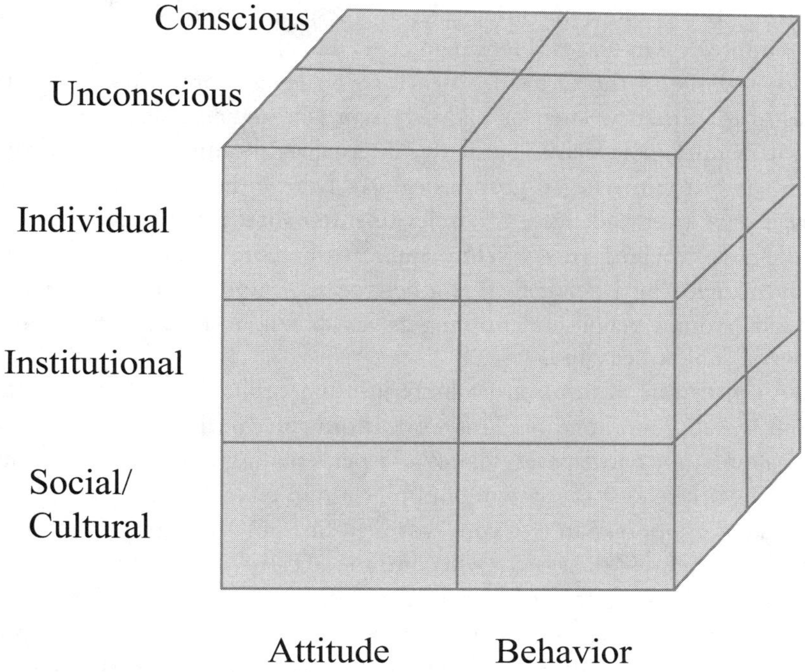

*Note:* Hardiman, Jackson, & Griffin (2007). Reprinted with permission.

health care, and religion are key aspects of systemic oppression. For instance, systemic sexism is perpetuated when businesses pay women 77.8% of what they pay men across industry. Systemic racism can be seen in how that wage gap is even greater for African American women and Latinas (Institute for Women's Policy Research, 2009). The system is also supported by broad cultural values and beliefs held by certain and powerful communities within society (e.g., marriage is between a man and a woman, a woman's place is in the home, and Arab men are probably terrorists), though it is important to realize that these beliefs are not supported by all. The system is interconnected with each level reliant on and reinforcing the others (Hardiman et al., 2007). The complexity of this system is what makes oppression so pervasive, deeply ingrained in our society, and difficult to work against personally and systemically. Chapter 1 in this volume personalizes these complex dynamics as they work to create the climate on today's college and university campuses.

One of the most pernicious aspects of this system of oppression is that even members of the subordinate group collude with the system that oppresses them, often unconsciously, as a result of being socialized by the same oppressive messages (Hardiman et al., 2007). This internalized oppression can come in the form of a woman who gives more credibility to the ideas of men than women or a Jewish man who remains silent in the face of anti-Semitic comments. Similarly, internalized dominance occurs when members of the privileged groups begin to believe the oppressive messages they receive over and over. Examples of internalized dominance include a White person who favors a White applicant because he or she thinks that applicant will "be a better fit," or a heterosexual mother who doesn't want her kids around people indentifying as gay or lesbian because she is afraid they will molest her child.

All of us can work toward a more just and equitable society, regardless of our social group identity. This work is difficult and requires doing more than simply not participating directly in perpetuating oppression. We must actually work against the system of oppression in place. Tatum (2000) likens the system of oppression to a conveyor belt. She notes that remaining still is insufficient because the system will continue to carry us along without active resistance. Working toward social justice, then, involves actually turning around and moving against the flow of the system. Just as going in the opposite direction on an airport's moving walkway could have its costs, being an advocate for social justice can have its costs as well. Kendall (2006) describes an ally as being willing to place oneself in front of a train so that a member of the subordinate group does not have to take the hit one more time. In fact, history is full of subordinate group members and dominant group members who have taken steps to fight injustice and have experienced the costs and the joys of such work (Takaki, 1993; Zinn, 2003).

## Social Justice in Higher Education

Institutions of higher education (IHEs) are not only influenced by the system of oppression, but they also serve as key institutions in perpetuating and maintaining oppression (Kivel, 2002). For instance, most IHEs have legacies of educating White upper-class men (Lucas, 2003). Beyond historical discrimination, many IHEs still perpetuate oppression in subtle and not so subtle ways (Tierney, 1993). Higher education has traditionally taken a social services approach to social justice, seeking to provide additional assistance to those who are targets of oppression (Kivel, 2000). Because oppression continues to exist in our society in many forms, this social services approach is important and necessary.

Traditional approaches to diversity and multiculturalism in higher education have primarily focused on how members of the subordinate groups experience oppression and how members of the dominant group perpetuate oppression through their actions and beliefs. However, providing additional services is not sufficient to achieve social justice. IHEs must also work to alter existing social structures and campus systems in ways that produce justice and equity for all, thus negating the need for a social services approach. This means that administrators have a responsibility not only to develop their own critical consciousness and provide additional services to those who have historically and currently experience oppression, but they must also work to ensure their colleges and universities no longer perpetuate oppression and that they educate students to have the awareness, knowledge, skills, and commitment to work toward social justice (Edwards, 2006).

## Social Justice in Student Conduct and Conflict Resolution

It is important to build a common language as we begin to discuss the implications for using a social justice lens to view student conduct and conflict resolution. Though there are many definitions of conflict, one of the more accepted is from Wilmot and Hocker (2001), which states that "conflict is an expressed struggle between at least two interdependent parties who perceive incompatible goals, scarce resources, and interference from others in achieving their goals" (p. 21). Moreover, conflict resolution, for the purposes of this chapter, is defined as "a marked reduction in social conflict" (Schellenberg, 1996, p. 9). In examining these definitions from a social justice perspective, it becomes evident that there is a glaring need for examination of current frameworks.

The conflict definition is powerful in that perception alone allows conflict to manifest itself. In the context of the college campus, one only needs to feel as though he or she is at odds with others sharing the same space or sense that the institution's systems are oppressive for the foundation of conflict to be set. And, though conflict may be seen as negative in many cases, conflict also has benefits to those directly involved as well as to others acting to help resolve the conflict. The most upfront benefit is education. Colleges and universities are charged with meeting students where they are and providing a learning experience. For this to happen, students must feel a sense of trust and authenticity when interacting with the structures and the professionals charged with fostering teachable moments.

Despite our best efforts, students may perceive traditional adjudication processes as oppressive, even if the experience of oppression is not based on the social group dynamics previously discussed. The common model of adjudication may not always be equipped to bring about effective resolution of conflict when the institution's principles and the student's behavior are in discord with each other. Adjudication, by its very design, may be inherently adversarial if respondents perceive their interests and the college's interests to differ. This is the case despite statements in institutional policies that they strive to be inclusive of the needs and interests of all community members, including the student who has allegedly violated college policy. It bears noting that many policies still fail to be inclusive of all values and cultures on campus.

Adjudication of complaints in the higher education setting generally involves a process whereby a decision maker (or decision-making body) must engage in an inquiry process that may result in "fact finding, rule interpretation, and choice of sanction" (Baker, 2005, p. 28). While a student may understandably perceive his or her interests and the college's to differ when the student has willfully engaged in a violation of college policy, adjudication may lend itself well to these conflicts when such an approach is likely to stimulate reflection within the respondent. However, traditional adjudication processes are limited to the extent that they are not always the most appropriate avenues or the most appropriate first pathways to address conflict, particularly when underlying issues result from oppressive social structures within and beyond the institution. Furthermore, adjudication processes may disenfranchise complainants and reinforce oppression, particularly when the adjudication process dismisses the significance of the complainant's identities, experience of oppression, or the impact of the respondent's behavior on the complainant.

Rule violations alone are not always the most salient presenting issues in campus judicial complaints. Referring such matters to adjudication may overlook the root causes of a dispute and miss important educational opportunities that our processes are designed to produce. Further, students may engage in conduct that flies in the face of contemporary community standards or notions of civility without crossing the threshold necessary to activate an adjudicatory process. In these circumstances, additional pathways of conflict resolution are not only helpful but arguably necessary to address issues that adjudication-based systems may not be equipped to manage.

The environments we work in create spaces for authentic reflection, dialogue, and learning among stakeholders who interact with our processes. As student conduct and conflict resolution administrators, we are entrusted with significant institutional power. That power necessitates that we are clear instruments of justice if we intend to transform, rather than replicate, the oppressive social systems that lurk within our institutions. Using a social justice lens to inform our practice can enhance our effectiveness as educators as well as improve the quality of life for members of the diverse communities in which we operate.

We must, therefore, be willing to wrestle with the complexities and contradictions that are inherent in our work. Our constituents will rightfully expect us to remain fair and objective in our decision making and facilitation, yet the inevitability of our biases is an issue we must grapple with. In traditional adjudication, we give due diligence to making fact-driven assessments about whether respondents are in violation or not in violation of our policies, yet we cannot ignore or dismiss the societal dynamics informing our assumptions, approaches, biases, perspectives, and judgments. In the adjudication and conflict resolution processes like mediation, we must consider how oppression dynamics operate, both overtly and covertly, in the presenting conflict, the disputants, and the resolution facilitators. This is not meant to be critical of past and existing efforts but rather to recognize that systems change necessitates critical self-evaluation and a willingness to explore new skill sets.

The very nature and design of our work can appear to be at odds with the oppressive societal dynamics that contextualize our experiences, though promoting social justice and achieving fair outcomes need not be mutually exclusive endeavors. Reconciling dissonance as practitioners is well within our reach if we are willing to engage in serious introspection and learning. We can discipline ourselves to be mindful of the diverse needs and range of experiences and perspectives among the students, faculty, and staff we work with, but we must also look inward at our own experiences. We must take inventory of our own socialization and the attendant narratives that inform our practice while being mindful that conscious and unconscious messages are constantly influencing us.

For some, such notions or expectations may seem benign or natural while others may regard such statements as radical departures from commonly accepted professional norms. However, we believe effective practice can only be realized through the development and integration of multicultural competencies. These competencies must extend beyond previous diversity awareness trainings. Pope, Reynolds, and Mueller (2004) define multicultural competence as the "awareness, knowledge, and skills that are needed to work effectively across cultural groups and to work with complex diversity issues" (p. xiv). Student conduct and conflict resolution professionals cannot avoid such issues nor assume that the issues have remained the same over the past decade. We have a responsibility to foster this dimension of competence in the context of new systems and a more globalized student population if we are to fully realize the transformative potential of our roles and advance social justice on campus.

## Neutrality Versus Multipartiality

Workshop participants at a national conference taking part in an exercise were given three sheets of paper. One sheet featured a list of five administrators with details about their upbringing, race, socioeconomic status, and view of student conduct. On the second sheet, participants were given a list of unique conduct cases. The third sheet invited participants to independently match administrators with cases based on which best suited the other. Upon completion of the task, participants were divided into small groups to create a group list of best fit. Remarkably, though the groups' lists differed slightly, the reasoning used in determining the best fit between administrator and case was the same. All participants believed that the administrators' personal characteristics and social group identities should be the deciding factor in matching a case to an administrator more than his or her skill sets or views of student conduct.

The exercise has real campus implications. Despite the fact that we espouse neutrality in our adjudication systems and their administrators, systems are systematically tempted to match administrators to cases based on the administrator's social group identity. Racially charged incidents are often spearheaded by administrators or student organizations appearing to share the identity of the complainant. GLBT colleagues or organizations are also called upon when the target of negative speech or behavior is thought to identify as GLBT. The intent may not be negative when this occurs, either in a real incident or in the preceding exercise. Nonetheless, we do make systematic decisions based on social group identity. This is not to say that the social group identity of either the administrator or the participant is irrelevant. But it does imply that the competencies and trust are not being built within all staff to ably respond to and account for issues engendered by social group identity. It is the professional responsibility of practitioners, from various identity groups, to continue to build multicultural competencies so that the burden of creating a socially just process does not fall on a specific group while potentially marginalizing others (Pope, Reynolds, & Mueller, 2004).

Facilitator neutrality, whether in adjudication or conflict resolution practices, is traditionally seen as central to a successful and fair process (Olshak, 2001; Warters, 2000). Though superficially attainable, when viewed through the social justice lens, neutrality is not only unachievable, but it can also limit the learning of those involved in the conflict. Colleges and universities are merely microcosms of the larger society. As long as there is bias in society, bias will inevitably find its way into processes in higher education. Wing and Rifkin (2001) found that the physical setup of a session, the questions asked or not asked, and the facilitation of the process spoke volumes about the facilitator's values, as well as consciousness levels regarding social justice and oppression. Since this is the case, if the process facilitator tries to maintain neutrality, he or she may unwittingly be drawn into the identity of one or more participants or may not offer true empathy toward another. Parts of a participant's story may not be heard or understood depending on the awareness and skill level of the facilitating professional. This can also give the process an artificial feeling in which the genuineness of the session, or the participants present, is questioned.

In contrast to absolute neutrality, multipartiality involves "critically analyzing a conflict from multiple vantage points" (Gadlin & Sturm, 2007, p. 4). Multipartiality allows for the facilitator to speak to areas of struggle and/ or oppression in the midst of conflict for all to examine in real time. This method can aid participants not just in resolving a conflict but in learning from the situation while increasing their future communication skills. Furthermore, it allows for the facilitator to be a more active participant in the process as an educator who is capable of providing a teachable moment and is not simply the keeper of the process.

## Conclusion

As college and university campuses continue to become more diverse and global, so must the knowledge base, skill sets and creativity of practitioners. Particularly with the increase of technological mediums, student affairs professionals with student conduct and conflict resolution responsibilities will continue to encounter more complex situations in which the current response methods will be viewed as increasingly antiquated. Student conduct and conflict resolution professionals are charged with upholding the policies, standards, and values of colleges and universities; nevertheless, educational moments can be lost if students perceive administrators, peers, and/or systems to be oppressive or outright adversarial. At this point in U.S. history, equality remains an aspirational standard. It now requires institutional practices and structures to strive for equality as the norm for all students. We can no longer afford to care only for symptoms, we must tend instead to the systems that perpetuate those symptoms and their unique expression in each individual.

Resolving campus disputes without recognizing the underlying belief systems of participants leaves much to be discovered while potentially allowing students to believe that all needed learning was gained in the process. If we fail to take social justice perspectives into account we risk replicating a banking approach to education (Freire, 1970/2000), in which learning is dictated and students function merely as receptacles, not partners, during teachable moments. Instead, conduct violations and conflict situations offer a tremendous opportunity to foster meaningful learning and development through partnership with students. For professionals to be good guides to students through their journey (Kegan, 1994), we must continue to strive for personal growth and understanding within ourselves. If we fail to consider social justice theory in the design and implementation of our resolution processes, we risk replicating and reinforcing the oppressive societal dynamics that surround our work. If we are sincere in our efforts to promote learning, development, and change within our students and our respective campus communities, incorporating a social justice ethic into our practice will help us facilitate, rather than impede, social justice on our campuses and work toward a more just and equitable society for us all.

# References

Adams, M., Bell, L. A., & Griffin, P. (Eds.). (2007). *Teaching for diversity and social justice: A sourcebook* (2nd ed.). New York: Routledge.

Andersen, M. L., & Collins, P. H. (2001). *Race, class, and gender: An anthology* (4th ed.). Belmont, CA: Wadsworth.

Baker, T. J. (2005). *Judicial complaint resolution models for higher education: An administrator's reference guide.* Horsham, PA: LRP Publications.

Edwards, K. E. (2006). Aspiring social justice ally identity development. *NASPA Journal, 43*(4), 39–60.

Freire, P. (2000). *Pedagogy of the oppressed* (Rev. ed., Myra Bergman Ramos, Trans.). New York: Continuum. (Original work published 1970)

Gadlin, H. & Sturm, S. P. (2007). Conflict resolution and systemic change. *Journal of Dispute Resolution, 1,* 1–63.

Gehring, D. D. (1998). What does the future hold for student judicial affairs? Just discipline? In B. G. Paterson & W. L. Kibler (Eds.), *The administration of campus discipline: Student, organizational and community issues* (pp. 255–267). Ashville, NC: College Administration Publications.

Hardiman, R., Jackson, B. W., & Griffin, P. (2007). Conceptual foundations for social justice education. In M. Adams, L. A. Bell, & P. Griffin (Eds.), *Teaching for diversity and social justice* (2nd ed., pp. 35–66). New York: Routledge.

Harro, B. (2000). The cycle of socialization. In M. Adams, W. J. Blumenfeld, R. Castañeda, H. W. Hackman, M. L. Peters, & X. Zúñiga (Eds.), *Readings for diversity and social justice: An anthology on racism, antisemitism, sexism, heterosexism, ableism and classism* (pp. 15–21). New York: Routledge.

hooks, b. (1994). *Teaching to transgress: Education as the practice of freedom.* New York: Routledge.

Institute for Women's Policy Research. (2009). *The gender wage gap: 2008.* Retrieved May 6, 2009, from http://www.iwpr.org/pdf/C350.pdf

Johnson, A. G. (2001). *Privilege, power, and difference.* New York: McGraw-Hill.

Jones, S. R., & McEwen, M. K. (2000). A conceptual model of multiple dimensions of identity. *Journal of College Student Development, 41,* 405–414.

Kegan, R. (1994). *In over our heads: The mental demands of modern life.* Cambridge, MA: Harvard University Press.

Kendall, F. (2006). *Understanding white privilege: Creating pathways to authentic relationships across race.* New York: Routledge.

Kivel, P. (2000). *Social service or social change? Who benefits from your work?* Retrieved May 15, 2005, from http://paulkivel.com/articles/socialserviceor socialchange.pdf

Kivel, P. (2002). *Uprooting racism: How white people can work for racial justice* (Rev. ed.). Gabriola Island, British Columbia: New Society Publishers.

Lucas, C. J. (2003). *American higher education: A history.* New York: St. Martin's Press.

Martinez, E. (1998). *De colores means all of us: Latina views for a multi-colored century.* Cambridge, MA: South End Press.

McIntosh, P. (2000). White privilege and male privilege: A personal account of coming to see correspondences through work in women's studies. In M. L. Anderson, & P. H. Collins (Eds.), *Race, class, and gender: An anthology* (4th ed., pp. 95–105). Belmont, CA: Wadsworth/Thomson Learning.

Olshak, R. (2001). *Mastering mediation: A guide for training mediators in a college and university setting.* Horsham, PA: LRP Publications.

Pope, R. L., Reynolds, A. L., & Mueller, J. A. (2004). *Multicultural competence in student affairs.* San Francisco: Jossey-Bass.

Schellenberg, J. A. (1996). *Conflict resolution: Theory, research, and practice.* Albany, NY: SUNY Press.

Takaki, R. T. (1993). *A different mirror: A history of multicultural America.* Boston: Little, Brown.

Tatum, B. D. (2000). Defining racism: "Can we talk?" In M. Adams, W. J. Blumenfeld, R. Castañeda, H. W. Hackman, M. L. Peters, & X. Zúñiga (Eds.), *Readings for diversity and social justice: An anthology on racism, antisemitism, sexism, heterosexism, ableism and classism* (pp. 79–82). New York: Routledge.

Tatum, B. D. (2003). *"Why are all the Black kids sitting together in the cafeteria?" And other conversations about race.* New York: Basic.

Tierney, W. G. (1993). *Building communities of difference: Higher education in the twenty-first century.* Westport, CT: Bergin & Garvey.

Warters, W. C. (2000). *Mediation in the campus community: Designing and managing effective programs.* San Francisco: Jossey-Bass.

Wilmot, W. W., & Hocker, J. L. (2001). *Interpersonal conflict.* New York: McGraw-Hill.

Wing, L., & Rifkin, J. (2001). Racial identity development and the mediation of conflicts. In C. L. Wijeyesinghe & B. W. Jackson III (Eds.), *New perspectives on racial identity development: A theoretical and practical anthology* (pp. 182–208). New York: New York University Press.

Zinn, H. (2003). *A people's history of the United States, 1942–present.* New York: HarperCollins.

# 4

# PROVIDING A SPECTRUM OF RESOLUTION OPTIONS

*Jennifer Meyer Schrage and Monita C. Thompson*

The relationship between justice and care can
be a relationship of compatibility rather than
hostility.

*Tronto, 1993, p. 167*

T he most basic function of conduct administrators is to assist in ensuring a safe and just campus climate while also caring for students. If our systems do not evolve to be accessible to all individuals on campus, as educators we fail to model the very core of our developmental work with students—an ethic of justice and care. The previous chapters set the stage for the need to confront the current challenges of tradition and provide innovative practices in the field of student conduct. These chapters demonstrate that community, educational interests, legal rights, and diverse needs are all associated with modern college students and their need for opportunities to resolve conflict in a variety of ways.

In this chapter we propose that an answer to the call for innovation is an expansion of Stoner and Lowery's (2004) Model Student Conduct Code to include a broader Spectrum of Resolution Options for responding to conduct and conflict on campus (Schrage & Thompson, 2008). First, we explain the principle concept that inspired the Spectrum Model. We then provide an overview of the spectrum and its pathways. Next, we examine how the Spectrum Model improves learning and climate and respects social justice and cultural competence. We then discuss practical application considerations and highlight the necessary system changes associated with the spectrum approach.

## The Starting Point

We introduced the Spectrum Model at the 2008 Donald D. Gehring Academy for Student Conduct Administration as an outgrowth of Schrage's unpublished essay titled "Magic Real Estate." We developed the Spectrum

Model (Schrage & Thompson, 2008) to challenge educators to design more inclusive incident response procedures in a way that preserves what Schrage calls the *magic real estate* associated with a conflict. Magic real estate describes the space between an incident and the selected resolution pathway. Often, it is in this space that the greatest potential exists for use of educational, effective, creative, flexible, restorative, and socially just resolution methods. Here, the incident remains in pure form a simple conflict. No formal set of structures or standards yet exists to restrict the space for the stories of those involved to be shared and honored. The parties are simply individuals in a dispute, rather than complainant and respondent, or accused and victim. This space is large enough for many perspectives and various framings of issues. Finding a third truth through mediation, or other forms of conflict resolution, remains an option.

Once a disputant moves beyond this magic real estate and decides to bypass other informal venues to file a complaint under a formal conduct code process, the stakes are higher. Rather than a conflict, the incident is now framed as an alleged violation. As is appropriate, a set of due process measures and related systems are triggered. Issues are framed, allegations are made, the story is told and a win-lose scenario unfolds. The respondent or accused begins the process by responding to another's narrative. From the start, it is more likely to be a defensive, competitive, punitive, and restrictive forum. In the end, all parties will be less likely to have gained a full and authentic perspective and understanding of the other's experience.

The spectrum approach assumes that a majority of incidents on campus can be managed through *alternative* (also referred to as *appropriate*) conflict resolution methods where parties are presented with a menu of options and a review of their rights before being asked to articulate their story. The need for formal resolution by adjudication for certain disciplinary incidents will always exist. Often legalistic and highly structured, however, such a venue need not be a first resort, but should be reserved for cases with the potential for the most significant consequences against a student. This is not contrary to the Model Student Conduct Code's premise that long before a conduct incident becomes formalized and processed through the rigors of an adjudication model, students should have ready access and multiple points of entry to individuals and processes that support resolution of conflict at the least formal levels (Stoner & Lowery, 2004). This understanding of the spectrum's framework is critical to understanding and implementing the model.

## Overview of the Spectrum Model

The Spectrum of Resolution Options Model (Schrage & Thompson, 2008) offers a variety of pathways for conflict management as part of a continuum (see Figure 4.1). Rather than a one-size-fits-all approach, the spectrum provides educators appropriate flexibility in working with students, faculty, and staff as they seek to resolve an incident. Further, this flexibility can come into play at any point in the institutional process prescribed for managing a conflict or conduct incident, as explained later in this chapter.

The formalism currently associated with the conduct process respects an important guiding principle: Student conduct administration must not be arbitrary. Yet, student affairs educators continue to explore and develop procedures in an effort to find the ideal balance between implementing fair process and maintaining learning outcomes. Between arbitrary case management on the one hand and legalistic procedures that inhibit learning and inclusion on the other stands the Spectrum Model.

The Spectrum Model is an intentional, deliberate, and thoughtful educational approach aimed at increasing access and improving student learning. It provides a framework for student affairs educators to return to individualized incident management that is focused on learning, student development, and the unique needs of involved parties. This model provides language and

## FIGURE 4.1
### The Spectrum of Resolution Options

*Note.* Figure developed by Schrage & Thompson, 2008.

guidelines to further campus conversations that might develop more progressive and diverse conduct and conflict resolution processes. This model draws from multiple pathways, skill sets, and tools that may already be part of the toolbox on many campuses in informal ways.

The types of incidents that can occur on campus are as unique as the individuals involved. The solutions provided for resolution should also be as sophisticated as the people and the problems involved in the conflict. Therefore, the pathways of the spectrum follow those often outlined in the fields of conflict and law, and rightly range from informal to formal in an effort to resolve issues at the lowest levels possible. These pathways include

1. No Conflict Management
   Administration intentionally refrains from initiating involvement in a campus conflict.
2. Dialogue
   Students engage in a conversation to gain understanding or to manage a conflict independent of administrator intervention or third-party facilitation.
3. Conflict Coaching
   Students seek counsel and guidance from administration to engage a conflict more effectively and independently.
4. Facilitated Dialogue
   Students access administration for facilitation services to engage in a conversation to gain understanding or to manage a conflict. In a facilitated dialogue, parties maintain ownership of decisions concerning the conversation or any resolution of a conflict.
5. Mediation
   Students access administration to serve as a third party to coordinate a structured session aimed at resolving a conflict and/or constructing a go-forward or future story for the parties involved.
6. Restorative Justice Practices (such as conferences, circles, and boards)
   Through a *diversion program* or as an addition to the adjudication process, administration provides space and facilitation services for students taking ownership for harmful behavior and those parties affected by the behavior to jointly construct an agreement to restore community.
7. Shuttle Diplomacy
   Administration actively negotiates an agreement between two parties that do not wish to directly engage with one another. This method may be an alternative to a formal adjudication process or part of the process associated with the conduct code.

8. Adjudication (Informal Resolution)
   Using the code process outlined in conduct policy, administration meets with the accused student to resolve the incident. An informal resolution is achieved when the student accepts responsibility and agrees to fulfill ordered sanctions. A discipline record is kept of any code violations.
9. Adjudication (Formal Resolution)
   Using the code process outlined in the conduct policy, administration facilitates a formal process that includes a hearing. A third party (panel or staff member) determines whether a conduct code violation occurred and issues sanctions in the case. A discipline record is kept of any code violations.

An introduction to the varied conflict management pathways is provided in the chapters that follow. In chapter 16, a working model of the spectrum approach used at the University of Michigan is presented for practitioners to consider as they craft their own version of the model to meet institutional needs and campus culture. Several additional examples from schools around the country are found in chapter 17.

## The Continuum

The Spectrum Model (see Figure 4.1, p. 67) is conceptualized as a continuum from which pathways are selected from least to most formalized. On the left end of the spectrum, there is minimal structure or little to no third-party involvement (no conflict management, conflict coaching, or dialogue). For disputants in these pathways, their primary objective centers on simply being heard rather than finding a violation of policy. In such cases, a disputant may request no formal intervention by campus staff but rather conflict coaching to initiate and engage in a dialogue that is independent of formal involvement by administrators. The advantage to students using processes in this area of the spectrum is that they can feel empowered to resolve conflicts on their own while learning and practicing important life skills. As educators, our goals include student development and learning; giving students the option to take leadership and control over their own lives, especially in difficult situations that do not rise to a significant violation, allows for growth and development. In addition, if the conflict is not resolved at this level, students have the option of involving administrators through more formal pathways along the spectrum.

Moving to the center of the spectrum, the response becomes more structured and involves third party facilitators (facilitated dialogue, mediation, or restorative justice practices). Candidates for these pathways will be involved in incidents that call for more structure to decide how to move forward. Parties, however, may each articulate a priority commitment to maintain a healthy relationship with friends, colleagues, or a student group. In such cases, constructing a mutually beneficial agreement through mediation or a restorative justice circle to resolve conflict is more desirable than triggering a formal process that risks an adversarial experience, leaves the conflict unresolved, and may result in a discipline record. Since many conflicts have an impact beyond the disputants (often witnessed by others or they affect a particular student community), using restorative practices can allow for all those affected to participate in the community-building process.

On the right end of the spectrum, pathways are highly structured and prescribed. Adjudication presents two useful pathways, including the informal resolution by agreement and the formal resolution by hearing. Parties accessing these pathways and/or the incidents involved call for a more conventional and restrained process and seek/or include formal and documented findings. Parties using adjudication likely desire minimal direct contact with one another and are less concerned with a future relationship. Pathways on this end of the spectrum are most familiar to student affairs educators as they represent the fundamentals of student conduct practice.

From one end of the spectrum to the other, each individual pathway offers valuable and relevant conflict resolution tools for today's student affairs educator. This model does not show a preference for one pathway over another. Rather, the spectrum reminds educators of the full continuum of options available and encourages practitioners to use all of them. Effective educators tailor their response to campus conflict by considering individual needs of the parties involved, including their developmental phases, cultural norms, learning styles, and social identity lenses. The Spectrum Model offers more options to support this intentional response. The model also provides flexibility for administrators and parties involved by allowing for a change of course in the resolution process.

## Supporting Just and Restorative Learning Outcomes Through the Spectrum

In addition to understanding each pathway offered on the spectrum menu, practitioners must appreciate that best practice implementation of the model requires use of a social justice and restorative justice orientation. This means that in addition to student learning, the model stands on a foundational assumption that the purpose of the conduct and conflict resolution process is (a) ensuring a just and inclusive campus for all community members by use of all available appropriate, creative, and flexible resolution methods, and (b) building and restoring the people and communities involved in and affected by harmful conduct and conflict. The model requires a paradigm shift away from punishment and a narrow win-lose framework. This paradigm shift is grounded in the theoretical principles reviewed in chapter 2 by Taylor and Varner, and bolstered by ongoing research in the field of education.

In 2000 the Conflict Resolution Education Network with the sponsorship of the U.S. Department of Education, published research concerning the benefits of conflict resolution education in schools (Jones & Kmitta, 2000). The study focused on the K–12 environment and revealed substantial positive outcomes for students and educators. Research proved that adding conflict resolution education increases academic achievement and performance, and assists classroom learning by improving interpersonal and intergroup relations and climate. The research concluded that conflict resolution teaches communication skills and self-control and increases self-esteem. It further decreases aggressiveness, discipline referrals, suspension rates, and violent behavior (Jones & Kmitta).

Using a spectrum approach with multiple resolution pathways is one important form of providing conflict resolution education on a college campus. Providing the option to draw from a continuum of conflict resolution methods on the front end provides students (and staff and faculty) with a moment to reflect and reframe an incident as they consider creative and constructive win-win scenerios to a conflict. This differs from traditional adjudication models that by nature characterize one party being right and the other wrong. It further improves student engagement throughout a process by empowering parties to drive decisions around resolution and restoration following a conflict.

## Making All Students Matter

The educational benefits of conflict resolution as a learning and modeling experience through the spectrum have important implications for diverse campus populations. Participants in a conflict resolution process have an opportunity to improve their capacity for empathy, understanding of others' perspectives, increased appreciation for diversity, and practicing tolerance (Jones, 2002). Increasing these competencies within the larger student population will likely improve the campus experience for often marginalized communities. Just as important, offering a spectrum of resolution options positively affects all student communities on campus by improving access.

In sum, the Spectrum Model improves access to just and relevant conflict resolution for all students by

1. Countering potentially oppressive institutional systems by offering pathways that do not involve the formal process or rules that were crafted by and reflect the values of the dominant campus culture(s) but are not respectful of the needs of some communities.
2. Expanding methods and venues for conflict engagement to be more inclusive of the conflict cultures of various communities and identities on campus.
3. Providing methods and venues that allow participants to go beneath the surface of an incident to consider the context of the conflict and oppressive dynamics that may have contributed to the incident.

## Oppressive Systems and the Campus Conflict Resolution Process

In chapter 3, Holmes, Edwards and DeBowes present an overview of social justice concepts and the potential implications for conduct and conflict work. Hardiman, Jackson, and Griffin (2007) also provide an overview of the foundations for social justice education. These works offer provocative considerations for the field of conduct administration and challenge student affairs educators to consider the well-documented proposition that culture is defined by standards and norms that benefit those with the most power and privilege in society. In fact, Hardiman, Jackson, and Griffin assert that "social institutions such as . . . education . . . are major participants in a system of oppression" (p. 40) by codifying oppression in laws, policies, practices and norms. Even more compelling, the authors propose that

> society's cultural norms and patterns perpetuate implicit and explicit values that bind institutions and individuals. . . . In an oppressive society, the cultural perspective of dominant groups is imposed on institutions by individuals and on individuals by institutions. These cultural norms include philosophies of life, definitions of good and evil, beauty, normal, health, deviances, sickness, and perspectives on time, just to name a few. (p. 40)

Bearing all this in mind, if the campus conduct code is meant to embody institutional values, and the practices and processes associated with the code reflect such values, we must stop and ask, "Whose values are they?" Who was at the table when that list of values was decided? Who was not? For many campuses, the conduct code may indeed be a living and breathing policy authored by their community and evolved over time to reflect the current cultures and populations on campus. For others, this is not the case.

Hardiman, Jackson and Griffin (2007) provide a sobering reminder of our responsibilities as developers of education policy. Ongoing resources must be committed to campus conduct and conflict management programs to allow staff to devote time and energy to creating and sustaining inclusive, relevant best practice procedures that meet the changing needs of their unique communities.

## Accounting for Various Conflict Cultures and Social Identities

The spectrum approach deconstructs the real or perceived institutional system of oppression by providing relevant and accessible options that ensure that all students matter, and that they feel they matter in salient ways. In chapter 1, we learned that campuses are more diverse than ever before, and with an increasingly diverse campus comes a variety of social identities, conflict styles, and cultural norms. Further, the intersectionality of many social identities and multiple cultures within one individual increases the need for flexible conflict engagement methods tailored to the needs of individuals. By providing a diverse array of approaches, the spectrum promises improved and broader student engagement in the conduct and conflict resolution process.

Because it meets parties where they are, rather than demanding that they conform to a uniform, structured, often adversarial disciplinary process, the spectrum approach minimizes marginalization. The spectrum affirms identities and cultural communities that reside in today's higher education institutions. It acknowledges perceptions and experiences by providing a range of options and is therefore more inclusive.

Figure 4.2 illustrates how social identity and culture are relevant to conduct and conflict resolution pathways. As discussed in chapter 1, some individuals may gravitate toward more informal venues. Others may find comfort in process and structure. For marginalized communities, pathways that do not represent or reinforce the power of the larger institution may be more attractive—especially if they or those within their community place less trust in the system because of prior individual experiences of discrimination in the institution. Contrast this experience with students whose life journey has garnered positive encounters that have reinforced their perception that they will be heard and understood. For the latter, speaking in a formal hearing and the traditional procedures associated with the adjudication process may be more comfortable.

Figure 4.2 illustrates how individual cultural values may inform pathway selection. In a case where both parties in a conflict come from a culture that traditionally values harmony or community over the individual, adjudication or related formal procedures will be less relevant than mediation or a restorative justice pathway. Alternatively, if notions of justice within an individual's culture center on formal findings of violations and sanctions, filing a complaint and obtaining affirmation through a code process may provide solace.

Adding to the complexity of effective conflict resolution programming is the likelihood that identity and culture will also intersect and matter in different ways depending on the incident or conflict at issue. As it relates to the implementation of the spectrum, it is important to consider that the broad dichotomies offered by Figure 4.2 are general guidelines rather than rules that can lead to inaccurate assumptions.

## FIGURE 4.2
### Social Justice Analysis of Conflict Resolution

| Informal ⟵⟶ Formal | |
|---|---|
| Emphasis on community/harmony | Emphasis on individual/rights |
| "Disputants" | "Accuser" v. "Accused" |
| High context cultures | Low context cultures |
| Parties control outcome | Outcome controlled by third party(s) |
| Party focused | Results focused |
| Less punitive | More punitive |
| Counter narrative | Master narrative |
| Resonates with marginalized communities | Resonates with dominant culture |
| Challenges status quo | Maintains status quo |

*Note.* Figure developed by J. M. Schrage & M. C. Thompson

## The Value of Stories

Adjudication under a conduct code often imposes formality and procedure that inhibits storytelling. Additionally, the threat of a code violation, a discipline record and sanctions are all in play as parties seek to resolve conflict within the formal code process. With such dynamics, it is unlikely that parties will have an opportunity to consider, explore, or voice the larger context of their conflict. For many students, especially those in marginalized communities, this removes what may be to them the core of the conflict. It labels what is most relevant as irrelevant. Offering a spectrum of resolution options offers participants venues and methods that allow for deeper analysis of issues and for a larger conversation to occur.

## Application of the Spectrum Model and System Changes

Facilitators must also consider how social justice concepts inform implementation of the Spectrum Model. In other words, in striving to be more accessible and inclusive, we must not only be self-conscious about *what* we offer students but also be intentional about *how* we do it.

### *Considering Oppression Dynamics in the Implementation of the Spectrum Model*

Offering a variety of conflict resolution pathways in conjunction with adjudication does not guarantee access and inclusion (Figure 4.3). Research has revealed notable gaps when it comes to diversity (Baker, French, Trujillo, & Wing, 2000). Conflict resolution educators do not focus sufficiently on the needs of diverse populations or issues of class and socioeconomic status when it comes to shaping curriculum. They indicated that programs do not pay adequate attention to structural issues and bias within the conflict resolution systems themselves. However, programs that do focus on bias issues in systems can improve intergroup relations and promote more just campus communities (Baker et al.)

Oppression dynamics influence the conflict resolution experience, regardless of the pathway selected (Wing & Marya, 2007). In implementing the spectrum, practitioners should consider the following strategies in how they facilitate and in determining what pathways should be offered.

1. Use multipartiality or "favor all" (help all participants with their needs so that all stories may be told).

FIGURE 4.3
**Balancing Injustice**

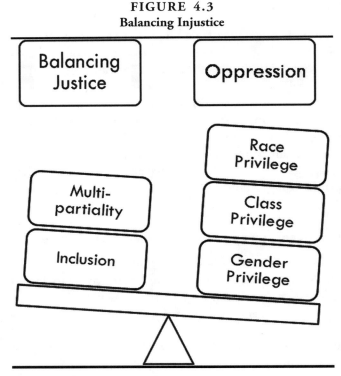

*Note.* Developed by J. M. Schrage.

2. Notice and seek to understand the asymmetry that exists between parties.
3. Consider the momentum or distraction the facilitator's social identity brings to the process.
4. Take responsibility for actively equalizing power, when necessary.
5. Make social identity available as a topic.
6. Understand that context is always relevant.
7. Emphasize creating a safe space. (Wing & Marya, 2007)

When facilitators do not understand or respect these guiding strategies, the informality that dialogue, mediation, or a restorative justice circle offers can actually result in, rather than respond effectively to, marginalization. On the surface, an issue may appear to be resolved, when in fact, the needs, voice, and/or issues of one or more parties involved was unintentionally silenced by the process (Wing & Rifkin, 2001). This can happen when momentum is given to one story based on the influence of the facilitator (and his or her identity) or when one party dominates the "airtime" in the process (Wing & Marya, 2007). For example, consider the person who is selected to speak first. Research indicates that over 80% of mediation agreements are built around the first speaker's narrative of the issues (Rifkin, Millen, & Cobb, 1991). Where resources and competencies deny the opportunity to fully embrace the above strategies, parties (especially marginalized communities) may actually fare better in a formal resolution process with basic due process rights and structure (e.g., protected speaking time) offered by this venue. As conflict resolution is infused more broadly in response models, educators must remain intentional in exploring these issues.

Another consideration for facilitators using the social justice lens in implementation of the spectrum approach is the spate of First Amendment challenges to social justice initiatives and programs in the past few years. While efforts were centered on promoting a safe and inclusive campus community, programs were criticized with allegations of jeopardizing individual process rights. The 2007 University of Delaware controversy involving allegations of "thought reform" in association with a residence life social justice curriculum offers important lessons for student affairs educators (Lukianoff, 2007). Intentional and careful program development that is vetted broadly to avoid "group think" and ensure the process is community owned is important. Also, facilitators must be mature and highly competent, and even then they must be provided with thorough oversight and guidance.

While the spectrum's use of the social justice lens triggers appropriate caution, the approach also offers plenty of reinforcement and protection of First Amendment rights on campus. By applying a spectrum approach not all cases and conflicts must go through the conduct code process. Incidents involving allegations of bias that fall short of harassment may be addressed in a space that is party driven and purely educational, such as mediation or facilitated dialogue. Such pathways can involve no threats of discipline or related measures that may chill free speech rights.

## *A Party-Driven Process*

Practitioners using the model should understand that parties to a conflict and not the potential existence of a technical code violation drive pathway selection. For example, parties accusing one another of what they are calling harassment may be offered and may select mediation as the most appropriate pathway for resolution. Important ethical and legal considerations must inform the program coordinator's facilitation of such a case. However, the existence of a potential violation would not disqualify the case from resolution via a pathway that does not involve the conduct code's adjudication process—assuming both parties agree to that approach. In other words, forcing an incident to fit a policy definition or formal process is not always necessary or effective, especially if that is not desirable for or in the best interest of the parties.

This party-driven approach assumes all parties, including faculty and staff, are required to take an active role in the resolution of their complaint or conflict or request for services for a case to proceed. The parties, not the conduct office staff, drive the resolution process.

Parties are not the only ones who benefit from the options provided by a spectrum approach. Without a spectrum of resolution pathways, administrators find themselves with insufficient processes to fully resolve campus conflicts or offer an effective educational moment to the students involved. Free speech concerns might make a disciplinary process inappropriate and leave a harmed or targeted party with no recourse. Even worse, such limitations might result in marginalization when a harmed party is disciplined because the conduct code classifies his or her behavior as a violation, and yet campus policy remains silent on the harmful behavior of the other party involved in the incident. Thus, while parties are empowered to choose their own resolution pathways and drive the processes designed to result in win-win outcomes, administrators are equally equipped with processes tailored to the needs of all parties, and responsive to the unique characteristics of each student and conflict.

## How to Incorporate the Spectrum Pathways

The Spectrum Model may be incorporated into a campus conduct and conflict resolution program in a variety of ways. First, the spectrum pathways may be offered as a prelude to the conduct code process. The pathways may also be offered as part of a diversion from the code process after it has been triggered. Finally, the spectrum pathways may be added to the menu of sanction options offered at the conclusion of a conduct case.

### Prelude to the Process

The spectrum pathways may be offered as services prior to the filing of a complaint or at the initiation of the disciplinary process. Using this approach requires staff to implement robust, focused, and careful intake procedures following an incident or in response to a request for services. As with magic real estate (p. 66), appreciating the concept of *structural determinism* is central to using the spectrum as a prelude to the adjudication or disciplinary process.

## The Intake Process—How Response Procedures Structurally Determine Outcomes

To take full advantage of magic real estate, the spectrum approach asks institutions to evaluate current intake processes to consider whether systems unnecessarily structurally determine that most conflicts will be resolved in a formal adjudication process. Borrowed from critical race theory, the concept of structural determinism may be explained as the unintentional or intentional collusion with oppression in society by system administrators who ignore dynamics that often result in a disparate impact on certain groups and set up unearned benefits and outcomes for other participants (Delgado, 1995). In this context, structural determinism applies to the obvious or hidden dynamics at play in incident response policy and procedures that force all or most incidents into a formal adjudication process—and leave the responding student with a disciplinary record. In Figure 4.4 a pattern or flow for all cases to follow is proposed as the remedy to systems that unintentionally eliminate the opportunity to increase access by using the alternative conflict resolution pathways offered in the Spectrum Model.

As noted in the first phase in the figure, practitioners must implement thoughtful intake to take full advantage of the magic real estate. The purpose of this intake phase is not to hear the complaint or discuss the incident but rather to educate parties initiating services on the availability of spectrum

### FIGURE 4.4
**Deconstructing Structural Determinism in Student Conduct Practice**

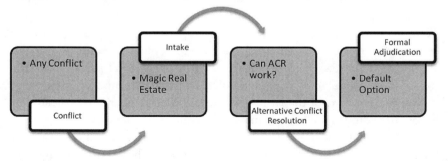

*Note.* Developed by J. M. Schrage.

pathways. Parties initiating contact must first complete a "listening session" with a staff member to learn about the menu of conflict resolution options. Parties are also encouraged to consider and identify their true objectives and explore the options that best meet those objectives. At this phase, parties are also provided with resources (e.g., counseling) outside the conduct office should they wish to immediately discuss the incident with someone who can provide support, advice, or advocacy. During this intake phase, participants are also advised of their process rights. Parties that agree to an alternative pathway in place of triggering the discipline process directly enter those pathways. If such efforts are unsuccessful or if all parties do not agree to the use of the pathway, parties may always return to filing a complaint that triggers the adjudication process. Part of preserving this space as a valid option is the commitment to confidentiality. Information shared in an attempted but unsuccessful mediation or other pathway cannot later be used or quoted in the adjudication process.

To understand the importance of the intake phase, consider the following scenario.

> The director of the Conduct and Conflict Resolution Office is summoned to a meeting on Monday morning to discuss strategies to address a disruptive incident that occurred in the residence halls over the weekend. A group of students was involved in an argument that resulted in a "tussle." Apparently all the disputants made allegations of harassment against one another. Members of the group individually report that there has been ongoing tension and disputes throughout the year. The group is made up of some students who are members of the Arab Student Association and others who are members of the Jewish Student Association.

Using this scenario, first consider the potential outcomes of a conflict management process that *begins* with a staff member and/or one of the parties naming the incident as a formal code violation that results in sending a *charge letter* to each student involved. Compare the likely outcome of this adjudication approach with a process that first provides all parties (staff and students) with individual sessions to offer a variety of venues to engage and resolve this conflict. In the latter approach, it is more likely that parties may bypass the adjudication option and instead directly enter a pathway such as a facilitated dialogue, mediation, or restorative justice circle that encourages fuller examination of the issues and provides a timely response to the conflict. If unsuccessful, parties maintain the right to enter adjudication.

## A Diversion From the Discipline Process

In addition to or instead of using the spectrum as a prelude to adjudication, pathways may be introduced as part of the discipline process through a diversion clause in the conduct policy. This would mean that a traditional application of the disciplinary process would proceed, with the caveat that parties may at any time in the process choose to attempt an alternative spectrum pathway. As with the prelude approach, if parties opt for less-formal conflict resolution but are unable to resolve the conflict in the alternative pathway, the case may return to the adjudication process. Consider the usefulness of a diversion approach in the following example.

> A resident assistant (RA), a student who identifies as Lesbian, has created a bulletin board on her floor for National Coming Out Day. The board is severely vandalized. The RA is advised by police that a video recording of the evening in question reveals that two male students on her floor were responsible for destroying the board. The RA contacts the Conduct and Conflict Resolution Office for services.

After an intake session with the conduct office, the RA may decide that the incident calls for articulating the complaint in writing as an allegation under the conduct code, but she will leave open the possibility of setting aside the complaint to participate in mediation. She does this because it feels safer, and she can engage these students within a context that makes the alleged policy violation central to the conversation. The students receive a charge letter and then participate in their own intake process. Following the intake, both students request a restorative justice circle as an alternative pathway. The students want to take ownership for what happened and restore the harm rather than pursue the case through adjudication. The RA is delighted and feels that the formal finding of a code violation is less important than a timely opportunity to participate in the restorative justice circle. She sees the alternative pathway as a safe option because she knows that she can return to adjudication if the students are not authentically taking ownership for their behavior.

## A Sanctioning Tool

Finally, the Spectrum Model may be incorporated in the campus conduct process by simply adding the pathways as options in the sanctioning stage of adjudication. The nature of an incident may require a formal structure to process it fairly and for findings to be documented. At the end of the process, however, parties and facilitators may determine that the process has not fully resolved the conflict. In such a case, the staff or students serving as hearing officers or panelists may suggest participation in one of the less-formal spectrum pathways. The following case suggests how the Spectrum Model may be applied at the sanctioning stage.

> Early one evening a campus security officer witnesses a male student standing in the inner quadrangle of the residence hall courtyard burning a personal item. By the time the security officer approaches the student, the item is no longer burning. The student (an international student) explains that he was performing a ritual out of respect for a family member who passed away. The security officer reports the incident to the housing department. Because this appears to be a violation of a fire regulation, the matter is referred to the Office of Student Conduct and Conflict Resolution for handling.

A campus demanding strict enforcement of fire codes because of past experiences involving safety risks to students may need to fully adjudicate the case and make formal findings. However, the hearing officer may also recognize the need for involved parties to understand and appreciate the perspective of the international student. As a result, a facilitated dialogue or mediation may be recommended for the parties to jointly construct a set of plans to ensure space is available for spiritual or related rituals of all cultures, and that students (especially international students) are provided with an orientation that educates this population about relevant, but possibly unfamiliar, policies.

### Special Program Development Considerations

Responsible innovation requires educators to be thoughtful and intentional with program development. Important legal and ethical boundaries must be identified and observed as institutions consider how best to incorporate the Spectrum Model on campus.

Introducing the model or its pathways without a deliberate review of how it complements or contradicts current institutional policies, practices, and positions will make programs unsustainable and vulnerable to challenges. Educators interested in implementing the spectrum pathways must consult with their community, leadership, and legal counsel in exploring the value and applicability of the model in their campus's context.

### Conclusion

The Spectrum of Resolution Options is offered as a living model. As campus populations continue to evolve, educators must be receptive to new and innovative administrative conduct practices. Assessment plays a key role in this model as it informs and supports an ever improving "Theory to Practice to Theory" helix approach to program implementation and management (S. H. Taylor, personal communication, 2009). Olshak devotes chapter 14 to the topic of assessment for conflict resolution programs. An assessment program model implemented at the University of Michigan is also provided as an example in chapter 16.

There must be room for continued transformation. Increased use of technology by our students provides one example of the dynamic nature of this work. While human contact (whether face to face or through shuttle diplomacy or a third party) is the current concept, we anticipate that technology will eventually provide an additional avenue for conflict resolution. This idea is discussed further in chapter 11. The pathways of the Spectrum Model must, and will, evolve to meet these and the other changes.

In its rather short history, conduct administration has served student affairs well by creating and maintaining a space for colleagues to learn, develop, and then contribute to and challenge student conduct practices. Indeed, the Spectrum Model is proposed as an invitation to the profession to begin a robust national dialogue on how best to meet current and future needs of our diverse campus populations while remaining committed to justice for our students and their care—the primary and eternal values that provide a solid foundation for our work together.

## References

Baker, M., French, V., Trujillo, M., & Wing, L. (2000) Conflict resolution education: How it does not meet the needs of diverse populations. In T.S.Jones and D. Kmitta (Eds.), *Conflict resolution education research and evaluation.* Washington, DC: United States Department of Education and the Conflict Resolution Education Network

Delgado, R. (1995). *Critical race theory: The cutting edge.* Philadelphia: Temple University Press.

Hardiman, R., Jackson, B. W., & Griffin, P. (2007). Conceptual foundations for social justice education. In M. Adams, L. A. Bell, & P. Griffin (Eds.), *Teaching for diversity and social justice* (2nd ed., pp. 35–66). New York: Routledge.

Jones, T. S. (2002). *Proven benefits of conflict resolution education research.* Retrieved January 4, 2009, from http://www.mainelaw.maine.edu/mlce/ppt/benefits_of_CRE.ppt

Jones, T. S., & Kmitta, D. (Eds.). (2000). *Does it work? The case for conflict resolution in our nation's schools.* Washington, DC: Conflict Resolution Education Network.

Lukianoff, G. (2007). *University of Delaware requires students to undergo ideological reeducation.* Retrieved May 15, 2008, from http://www.thefire.org/index.php/article/8555.html

Rifkin, J., Millen J., & Cobb S. (1991, Winter). Toward a new discourse for mediation: A critique of neutrality. *Mediation Quarterly, 9*(2), 151–165.

Schrage, J. M., & Thompson, M. C. (2008, June). *Using a social justice model for conflict resolution to ensure access for all students.* Paper presented at the Donald D. Gehring Academy for Student Conduct Administration, Salt Lake City, UT.

Stoner, E. N., & Lowery, J. W. (2004). Navigating past the "spirit of insubordination": A twenty-first century model student conduct code with a model hearing script. *Journal of College and University Law, 31*, 1–77.

Tronto, J. (1993). *Moral boundaries: A political argument for the ethic of care.* New York: Routledge.

Wing, L., & Marya, D. (2007, May). *Social justice mediation.* Training session presented at the Social Justice Mediation Training, University of Michigan, Ann Arbor.

Wing, L., & Rifkin, J. (2001). Racial identity development and the mediation of conflicts. In C. L. Wijeyesinghe & B. W. Jackson III (Eds.), *New perspectives on racial identity development: A theoretical and practical anthology* (pp. 182–208). New York: New York University Press.

# PART TWO

## PATHWAYS WITHIN THE SPECTRUM MODEL

# 5

# MOVING TOWARD A HEALTHIER CLIMATE FOR CONFLICT RESOLUTION THROUGH DIALOGUE

*Tosheka Robinson*

[Dialogue] moves its participants along the learning curve to that uncomfortable place of relearning and unlearning. It can move people to wonderful new levels of knowledge; it can transform relations; it can change things.

*Wink, 2005, p. 42*

Since the 17th century, the American college has evolved from using a teacher-based curriculum to one that includes research, public service, continued education, and entertainment (Bogue & Aper, 2000). As the American college has progressed, so too have expectations of higher education. In alcohol education presentations and student advocacy workshops that I facilitate with students, I often ask participants why they want to attend college. More often than not, the response is not simply to get a good education but to get a better job, to be able to make more money, and to have more opportunities upon graduation. This student response is also reflected in the Association of American Colleges and Universities (AAC&U, 2002) national panel report, "Greater Expectations: A New Vision for Learning as a Nation Goes to College," in which students said they expect a college degree to prepare them for future careers. When it comes to the workforce, employers expect college graduates to be skilled and prepared for their profession. The general public expects degree holders to become productive members of society, and faculty hope for intellectual engagement (AAC&U). One strategy for meeting these expectations is to prepare students not only to handle the day-to-day tasks on the job but also to successfully manage interpersonal conflicts.

It is important for institutions of higher education to create spaces for the campus community to engage in dialogues so students are better prepared to collaborate with future colleagues, work with teams, and resolve personal conflicts. By understanding, coaching, and modeling dialogue while implementing student conduct programs that foster dialogue and skill building, student affairs administrators will be able to better support students in this area of interpersonal development. This chapter provides an overview of methods of communication and strategies that can assist administrators in helping students understand and learn conflict resolution skills, explore the educational value of conflict, and demonstrate the power of dialogue. It further summarizes the work that various institutions are doing in the area of intergroup dialogue.

## Student Learning and Development Supports the Use of Dialogue

Student development theories assist student affairs administrators in providing quality education for those pursuing higher education (Robinson, 2005). When it comes to conflict resolution skills, psychosocial and cognitive-structural theories should be considered. Both support student development in regard to relating to others and their thinking process (Evans, Forney, & Guido-DiBrito, 1998). In chapter 2, Taylor and Varner explore in depth how alternative forms of conflict resolution are supported by student development theories. By understanding the developmental needs of their students, institutions can create effective programs that foster the intellectual growth of students and provide return on students' investment in higher education (Robinson, 2005).

The AAC&U (2002) provides an overview of college learning that "acknowledges the multiple purposes of higher learning in a complex society" (p. 9). According to the authors, students, faculty, policy makers, community members, and the business community all have a separate set of expectations. A RAND Institute study notes that "the business community identified highly valued cognitive and social skills they desired among employees including: the ability to work effectively in groups with others of diverse backgrounds, openness to new ideas and perspectives, and empathy with other workers' perspectives" (Hurtado, 2004, p. 23).

To support the expectations of respective stakeholders in higher learning, colleges and universities must "place new emphasis on educating students in becoming intentional learners" (AAC&U, 2002, p. 21). The AAC&U defines intentional learners as integrative thinkers who can pull from a variety of knowledge to make decisions. Dialogues, and the skills gained through dialogues, provide and support an environment for intentional learning to thrive. Being aware of the difference between debate and discussion in comparison to dialogue will provide a clear vision of its value in relation to conflict resolution.

## Understanding Dialogue

Understanding dialogue requires an appreciation of the differences among debate, dialogue, and discussion.

### Debate

"Debate is like a contest in which there are winners and losers" (Schirch & Campt, 2007, p. 7). Debate participants listen and identify flaws in their opponent's overall position (Schirch & Campt). Indeed, there are forums where this type of communication is appropriate and requires specific skills to be successful. Take, for example, debate competitions, debate team practice, or political debates. "Debates in the classroom are used for students to use evidence-based thinking on issues, develop verbal presentation skills, and strengthen abilities to influence others by defending one's position and countering different positions" (Ratnesh, Nagda, & Gurin, 2007, p. 37). Although appropriate in certain situations, debating to resolve a conflict may cause more conflict. Neither party involved is coming from an authentic place of listening or an openness of gaining new perspective.

### Discussion

"Discussion may be used for deliberative decision making or be more conversational to foster self-awareness and self-critique and may consist of affiliating with others through an appreciation of diversity of perspectives" (Ratnesh et al., 2007, p. 37). As the midpoint between debate and dialogue, discussion only partially provides the space to effectively manage conflict. Similar to debate, in a discussion viewpoints are analyzed and compared (Symphony Orchestra Institute, 2005). Although a discussion is less combative in comparison to a debate, it is still a process of persuading others (Winchell, 2004). In the presence of persuasion, the opportunity to listen and learn from other participants is low. When it comes to dealing with conflict, a discussion only permits surface conversations that tend to avoid searching beyond the symptom of a larger issue. In the end, relationships have remained the same, viewpoints have not been discussed in-depth, and depending on the winner and loser, frustrated feelings still exist (Symphony Orchestra Institute).

## Dialogue

"Dialogue works best when participants listen for what might be correct, true, and insightful about what others have stated" (Schirch & Campt, 2007, pp. 7–8). Unlike debate where participants listen with the purpose of finding flaws, in dialogue, listeners find ideas they can agree with and combine them with their own for the purpose of building "a larger truth than any side has on its own" (p. 8). "In addition, the purpose of dialogue, unlike debate, is not to declare winners and losers at the end of the day, but rather to engender deeper and broader understandings and insights, oftentimes leading to action, among all participants" (Schoem, Hurtado, Sevig, Chesler, & Sumida, 2004, p. 7). In dialogue, "there are only people who are attempting, together, to learn more than they now know" (Freire, 1970/2005, p. 90). Different from a discussion, dialogue goes beyond the surface of issues. It "is an open-ended process that allows all participants to gain new or deeper ways of thinking, to build relationships with others, and to work effectively on collaborative projects" (Ratnesh et al., 2007, p. 37). As such, dialogue provides the most effective mode of communication when resolving a conflict.

Wilmot and Hocker (2001) explain that conversational dialogue deepens the level of collaboration. As Wilmot and Hocker (2001) describe, dialogue allows participants to

1. Explore different assumptions
2. Develop an objective view and description of the conflict
3. Give up persuasion in favor of exploration of different perspectives
4. Look critically at all sides to the controversy
5. Express hope and belief in the goodwill of the other person and your intention to work out your differences (p. 257)

With the learning opportunities that are associated with dialogues, supporting students' conflict resolution skills will equip them with the tools they need to become successful during and after attending an institution of higher education. Making it possible for students to practice conflict resolution skills will create a culture of students who are able to manage basic and low-level conflicts on their own.

As one example of putting a dialogue process in play, Arizona State University's (2008) Wellness and Health Promotions, in collaboration with Counseling and Consultation, offers a two-part awareness and skill-building training session as a product of the Campus Care Suicide Prevention Grant.

One of the messages throughout both sessions was that assisting students while they are stressed (low risk) leads to less-distressed (crisis) students, which leads to fewer suicide attempts. In referring to these training sessions, when it comes to the development of conflict resolution skills, the idea is very much the same. Colleges and universities that support student development and awareness in the area of conflict resolution to resolve low-level conflicts will potentially reduce the amount of higher-level conflicts.

## Value of Conflict

At Utopia University, there is no conflict. Upon their arrival at the university, students read through the policies and the student code from front to back and understand their rights and responsibilities. Once in class, all students are excited to work on group projects because everyone does his or her equal share of the work, meets deadlines, and shows up for group meetings on time. Parents of students at Utopia University call faculty and staff members to compliment them on the great job they are doing assisting students as they build character and develop integrity. In addition, at Utopia University student affairs administrators are consistently met with open doors when it comes to requesting additional funding to provide services to students.

Unfortunately, for many faculty and staff members, Utopia University exists only in daydreams. It is inevitable that in our day-to-day life we will face conflict. Conflict is unavoidable. Wilmot and Hocker (2001) define conflict as being, "an expressed struggle between at least two interdependent parties who perceive incompatible goals, scarce resources, and interference from others in achieving their goals" (p. 41). Although navigating through conflict is a reality, many of us have been socialized to believe that conflict is negative and should be avoided at all costs. However, "working through conflicts is not automatically assumed to lead to a breach in the relationship; in fact, it is exactly because of working through conflicts that a deeper sense of community is developed" (Ratnesh et al., 2007, p. 40).

Consistently avoiding conflict is costly. Avoidance strategies keep a student from learning how to manage conflict effectively. "When conflicts emerge in the group, they are not taken as a sign of failed dialogue; rather, they are opportunities for deeper learning" (Ratnesh et al., p. 40). Whether through university housing or student leadership programs, learning how to manage conflict supports college and university efforts to meet the expectations set forth by the campus community and fulfills the purpose of higher education. As the AAC&U (2002) states, "Responsible learners appreciate others, while also assuming accountability for themselves, their complex identities, and their conduct" (p. 23). By acknowledging interpersonal conflict and supporting conflict resolution skills, colleges and universities create healthy campus climates for students to pursue their educational and personal goals and prepare them for life after college.

## Strategies for Fostering Dialogue on Campus

Similar to the prevention strategies used by health educators, colleges and universities can implement strategies to create an environment of support for the use of dialogue to manage conflict within the campus community. The strategies that provide the "four crucial building blocks to dialogue: suspending judgment, deep listening, identifying assumptions, and reflection and inquiry" (Ratnesh et al., 2007, p. 37) include, but are not limited to, modeling, coaching, and implementing dialogue programs on campus. Modeling dialogue for an intentional learner creates an atmosphere where conflict is less taboo and viewed as a natural part of everyday life. "They adapt the skills learned in one situation to problems encountered in another: in a classroom, the workplace, their communities, or their personal lives" (AAC&U, 2002, pp. 21–22).

As a student advocate, I provide students with resources in the hope of empowering them to take care of their own issue or concern. If students use the resources provided and are still faced with adversity, only then will I step in on the student's behalf to assist in overcoming the barrier(s). This is comparable to coaching students to use dialogue when dealing with conflict. Not all situations call for a formal intervention through the conduct office or alternative dispute resolution processes. At times, teaching students how to resolve the conflict using dialogue skills may be enough. However, if the student has tried to address the situation on his or her own and is faced with communication barriers, it may become necessary to have third-party involvement.

## Intergroup Dialogue Programs

Colleges and universities can also implement formal programs that support the development of dialogue skills. For example, intergroup dialogue programs integrate all four building blocks of dialogue. Not only do intergroup dialogue programs provide many transferable skill-building opportunities, the skills gained "are necessary for workers, students, and leaders in communities that are rapidly becoming demographically diverse in order to develop fair and culturally sensitive policies, or simply to better serve clients from diverse communities" (Hurtado, 2004, p. 23). Intentional learners are able to see themselves in a diverse world and are able to draw on differences and similarities to experience more connectedness to the community (AAC&U, 2002, p. 22).

"Intergroup Dialogue is a form of democratic practice, engagement, problem solving, and education involving face-to-face, focused, facilitated, and confidential discussions occurring over time between two or more groups of people defined by their different social identities" (Schoem et al., 2004, p. 6). In intergroup dialogue, community building and addressing social justice is the foundation for constructive management of conflict. As intergroup dialogues focus on issues of social justice, conflicts among participants will appear. When managed properly, conflicts offer the opportunity for community development and deep relationships to be formed. In an intergroup dialogue program, participants are provided a safe space to engage in dialogue covering issues that many have been told were rude or inappropriate to discuss or have never had the opportunity to engage in without fear of judgment. "After experiencing intergroup dialogue, participants typically think and see the world differently, increase personal and social awareness of different group experiences and forms of oppression in society, and build confidence in working through difference with others" (Hurtado, 2004, p. 22). A student enrolled in an intergroup dialogue course that I had the pleasure of cofacilitating noted that his experience in the course was unlike any other that he had taken at the university and he was confident that the relationships developed in class would continue to grow once the class was over.

Understanding what intergroup dialogue is and its possibilities is only part of program implementation. In order to create a successful intergroup dialogue program, important factors should be considered.

1. Dialogue is a process, not an event.
2. Dialogue is about relationship building and thoughtful engagement about difficult issues.
3. Dialogue requires an extended commitment.
4. Dialogue takes place face-to-face.
5. Dialogue takes place best in an atmosphere of confidentiality, and issues of sponsorship and context are important to its success.
6. Dialogue may often focus on race, but it also addresses multiple issues of social identity that extend beyond race.
7. Dialogue focuses on both intergroup conflict and community building.

8. Dialogue is led by skilled facilitators.
9. Dialogue is about inquiry and understanding and the integration of content and process.
10. Dialogue involves talking, but taking action often leads to good talking, and dialogue often leads to action (Schoem et al., 2004, pp. 6–14).

In the age of text messaging and social networking Web sites, our students are becoming more inclined to resolve conflicts through the typed word than through face-to-face dialogue. And when the receiver reads the typed word, much is left to interpretation, which can result in escalating the conflict. In an intergroup dialogue opportunity that includes the elements listed above, a space is created for students to normalize having dialogues about difficult topics. Students have the opportunity to practice and develop dialoguing skills that are transferable outside the classroom.

## Intergroup Dialogue Program Examples

Being able to benchmark current programs is helpful in developing new intergroup dialogue programs. The nine college and university programs in Table 5.1 participated in the intergroup dialogue project that is outlined in the Multi-University Intergroup Dialogue Research Project Guidebook (n.d.). The goal of the project was to evaluate the effects of randomly assigned students participating in the intergroup dialogue courses to determine if students learn "how to talk with and listen to students from different backgrounds, discern commonalities as well as differences in these interactions, work cooperatively across differences, and normalize and learn how to negotiate intergroup conflicts" (n.d., p. 2) in comparison to the students that were not randomly selected to participate.

Although the findings from the Multi-University Intergroup Dialogue Research Project were not yet published at the time this chapter was being written, research has been conducted to measure the impact of intergroup relations programs. In monitoring the attitude changes of intergroup dialogue participants, they reported "increased communication skills, ability to manage conflicts, growth in perspective-taking skills and complex thinking" as outcomes that have been identified in multiple studies (Hurtado, 2004, p. 30). The results of these evaluations support the development of students' interpersonal relations and conflict resolution skills.

In addition to the institutions listed in Table 5.1, the University of Illinois, Urbana-Champaign, Program on Intergroup Relations (n.d.), National

## TABLE 5.1
## College and University Programs That Participated in the Multi-University Intergroup Dialogue Research Project

| | |
|---|---|
| Institution | Arizona State University |
| Program | Intergroup Relations Center |
| Mission | "To build individual and institutional capacity for understanding difference and for engaging respectful relationships. . . . In individuals, we promote awareness and appreciation of self and others. . . . Institutionally, we provide leadership and resources that facilitate the University's responsiveness to diversity and equity in its policies, practices, and structures" (Arizona State University, 2007). |
| Offerings | • Undergraduates—Social justice events, difficult dialogues, interreligious dialogues, social justice campaigns, InVision Retreat, courses, and internships<br>• Graduates—Diversity Training Institute<br>• Faculty/Staff—Diversity Scholar Series, faculty cross-talks<br>• For the community—Healing Racism Forums, Tempe Talks, East Valley High School Diversity Summit |
| | |
| Institution | Occidental College |
| Program | Intergroup Dialogue Program |
| Mission | "The Intergroup Dialogue Program (IDP) at Occidental provides students with several unique opportunities to engage diverse democracy—personally, critically, and constructively. Courses are designed to include a blend of social psychological readings, respectful dialogue, experiential activities, and reflective writing. As a curricular initiative IDP seeks to enhance students' knowledge, understanding, and awareness about diversity and social justice while nurturing the development of constructive intergroup relations and leadership skills. In short, IDP seeks to provide diverse students with educational experiences that prepare them to participate in and foster an inclusive society" (Occidental College, n.d.). |
| Offerings | • Intergroup dialogue courses through the psychology department<br>• Peer facilitation |
| | |
| Institution | Syracuse University |
| Program | Intergroup Dialogue at Syracuse University |
| Offerings | • Intergroup dialogue academic courses<br>• Intergroup dialogue in the residence hall |
| | |
| Institution | University of California, San Diego |
| Program | Intergroup Relations Program |
| Mission | "The Intergroup Relations Program fosters the knowledge and practice of effective intergroup relations. We provide programs and services that enhance the capacity of individuals and groups to engage respectfully across differences" (University of California, San Diego, 2007). |
| Offerings | • Intergroup dialogue courses<br>• Offers 1- to 5-hour workshops |

## TABLE 5.1 (Continued)

| | |
|---|---|
| Institution | University of Maryland, College Park |
| Program | Words of Encouragement: An Intergroup Dialogue Program |
| Mission | "Words of Engagement: An Intergroup Dialogue Program is an initiative of the Student Intercultural Learning Center (SILC) of the Office of Human Relations Programs. It brings together groups of students from various social identity groups with a history of tension or conflict between them. Facilitated by trained and experienced facilitators, participants confront those tensions in order to build bridges across groups" (University of Maryland, College Park, 2008). |
| Offerings | • Facilitator training and opportunities<br>• Social Justice From Classroom to Community Workshops<br>• Dialogue courses |
| Institution | University of Massachusetts, Amherst |
| Program | Social Justice Education |
| Mission | "Social Justice Education is an interdisciplinary program of study with a focus on social diversity and social justice education particularly as they apply to a diverse range of educational systems and higher education. The master's concentration focuses on reflective practice; the doctoral concentration focuses on research informed by reflective practice. Our goals are to generate knowledge about social justice education and to apply new knowledge to the design and delivery of effective social justice educational programs" (University of Maryland, College Park, 2008) |
| Offerings | • Courses |
| Institution | University of Michigan, Ann Arbor |
| Program | Program on Intergroup Relations |
| Mission | "The Program on Intergroup Relations (IGR) is a social justice education program on the University of Michigan's Ann Arbor campus. As a joint venture of the College of Literature, Science, and Arts and the Division of Student Affairs, IGR works proactively to promote understanding of intergroup relations inside and outside of the classroom. Multidisciplinary courses offered by IGR are distinguished by their experiential focus, teaching philosophy, and incorporation of dialogical models of communication. On this site you will find information on academic and co-curricular initiatives, program history and philosophy, and resources related to social justice education" (University of Michigan, Ann Arbor, 2007). |
| Offerings | • CommonGround Workshops<br>• Intergroup relations courses<br>• Certificate of merit<br>• Summer youth dialogue<br>• Facilitator opportunities |
| Institution | University of Texas, Austin |
| Program | Intergroup Dialogue |

**TABLE 5.1 (Continued)**

| | |
|---|---|
| Mission: | "Intergroup Dialogue explores identities defined by gender, race, ethnicity, religion, sexual orientation, socioeconomic class and ability, with a specific focus on one particular identity. Students have the opportunity to examine and discuss reading materials that address issues and experiences relevant to the groups in the Dialogues. Participants and facilitators explore similarities and differences among and across groups, and strive toward a deeper understanding of individual and group identity" (University of Texas, Austin, n.d.). |
| Offerings | • Intergroup dialogue course<br>• Facilitation training and opportunities |
| Institution | University of Washington |
| Program | Intergroup Dialogue, Education and Action (IDEA) Center |
| Mission | "We create spaces here that sow seeds to be carried with us. We create here spaces to hear and feel stories of courage, compassion and healing. These spaces, within us and with each other, are spaces of hope and possibility. The mission of the Center has now expanded to supporting campus and community efforts geared toward addressing issues of oppression, empowerment, and alliance building for social justice" (University of Washington, 2009). |
| Offerings | • Undergraduate and graduate intergroup dialogue courses<br>• Facilitation training and opportunities<br>• Coalition building |

Coalition for Dialogue & Deliberation (2008), and Everyday Democracy (formally Study Circles Resource Center; n.d.) are also great resources when creating formal intergroup dialogue programs.

## Conclusion

Paulo Freire (1970/2005) said, "Without dialogue there is no communication, and without communication there can be no true education" (pp. 92–93). The expectations of higher education include delivering graduates who are prepared to enter and successfully perform in a given career, and to be socially responsible members of society. Teaching students the ability to effectively resolve conflicts is central to delivering on each of these expectations. Colleges and universities must continue to support the development of the intentional learner and his or her ability to listen and learn from multiple perspectives to create new truths (AAC&U, 2002).

When it comes to conflict resolution, the skills gained through dialogue provide students with opportunities "to deal comfortably with conflict, social differences, and sociohistorical legacies that shape their daily interactions" (Schoem et al., 2004, p. 1). As not every conflict calls for a third-party facilitator, dialoguing skills and intergroup dialogue programs will provide students with tools to successfully resolve conflicts. As colleges and universities educate students on how to capitalize on the opportunities that come with conflict and shift the negative worldviews associated with conflict, respective campuses can only benefit. These efforts support student development, which will lead to a healthier campus climate. In the end, we are reminded that "our societal task is not to end or resolve all conflicts, but to examine and understand conflict so communities can live together productively, even harmoniously, with conflict" (Schoem et al., 2004, p. 15).

## References

Arizona State University. (2007). *Intergroup Relations Center.* Retrieved December 20, 2008, from http://www.asu.edu/provost/intergroup/programs/

Arizona State University. Wellness and Health Promotions. (2008). *Campus care suicide prevention awareness & skill building.* Presented at training sessions for student affairs staff at Arizona State University, Tempe.

Association of American Colleges and Universities. (2002). *Greater expectations: A new vision for learning as a nation goes to college.* Washington, DC: Author.

Bogue, E. G., & Aper, J. (2000). *Exploring the heritage of American higher education: The evolution of philosophy and policy.* Phoenix, AZ: Oryx Press.

Evans, N. J., Forney, D. S., & Guido-DiBrito, F. (1998). *Student development in college: Theory, research, and practice.* San Francisco: Jossey-Bass.

Everyday Democracy. (n.d.). *Everyday democracy ideas & tools for community change.* Retrieved December 29, 2008, from http://www.everydaydemocracy.org/en/index.aspx

Freire, P. (2005). *Pedagogy of the oppressed* (Rev. ed., Myra Bergman Ramos, Trans.). New York: Continuum. (Original work published 1970)

Hurtado, S. (2004). Research and evaluation on intergroup dialogue. In D. Schoem & S. Hurtado (Eds.), *Intergroup dialogue: Deliberative democracy in school, college, community, and workplace* (pp. 22–36). Ann Arbor: University of Michigan Press.

Multi-University Intergroup Dialogue Research Project Guidebook. (n.d.). Retrieved December 20, 2008, from http://sitemaker.umich.edu/migr/files/migr_guidebook.pdf

National Coalition for Dialogue & Deliberation. (2008). *National Coalition for Dialogue & Deliberation.* Retrieved December 29, 2008, from http://www.thataway.org/

Occidental College. (n.d.). *Intergroup dialogue program.* Retrieved December 28, 2008, from http://departments.oxy.edu/dialogue/

Ratnesh, B., Nagda, A., & Gurin, P. (2007). Intergroup dialogue: A critical-dialogic approach to learning about differences, inequality, and social justice. *New Directions for Teaching and Learning* (111), 35–45.

Robinson, T. (2005). *A freshman year experience seminar: Using interactive theatre as a vehicle for global and social responsibility.* Unpublished manuscript, Arizona State University, Tempe.

Schirch, L., & Campt, D. (2007). *The little book of dialogue for difficult subjects: A practical, hands-on guide.* Intercourse, PA: Good Books.

Schoem, D., Hurtado, S., Sevig, T., Chesler, M., & Sumida, S. H. (2004). Intergroup dialogue: Democracy at work in theory and practice. In D. Schoem & S. Hurtado (Eds.), *Intergroup dialogue: Deliberative democracy in school, college, community, and workplace* (pp. 1–21). Ann Arbor: University of Michigan Press.

Symphony Orchestra Institute. (2005). *Dialogue.* Retrieved December 27, 2008, from http://www.soi.org/reading/goodpractice/dialogue.shtml

Syracuse University. (n.d.) *Intergroup dialogue at Syracuse University.* Retrieved December 28, 2008, from http://intergroupdialogue.syr.edu/

University of California, San Diego. (2007). *Intergroup relations program, intergroup dialogue courses.* Retrieved December 28, 2008, from http://www.ucsd.edu/portal/site/ucsd/menuitem.e25088fc289ee30b4bb91c8ad74b01ca/?vgnextoid=8a33e143556ca110VgnVCM100000c7b410acRCRD

University of Illinois, Urbana-Champaign. (n.d.). *Program on intergroup relations.* Retrieved December 28, 2008, from http://www.intergrouprelations.uiuc.edu/

University of Maryland, College Park. (2008). *Words of engagement: An intergroup dialogue program.* Retrieved December 28, 2008, from http://www.ohrp.umd.edu/WE/index.html

University of Massachusetts, Amherst. (n.d.). *Social justice education.* Retrieved December 28, 2008, from http://www.umass.edu/sje/

University of Michigan, Ann Arbor. (2007). *Program on intergroup relations.* Retrieved December 28, 2008, from http://www.igr.umich.edu/

University of Texas, Austin. (n.d.). *Intergroup dialogue.* Retrieved December 28, 2008, from http://uts.cc.utexas.edu/~igdialog/

University of Washington (2008). *Intergroup Dialogue, Education and Action (IDEA) Center.* Retrieved December 28, 2008, from http://depts.washington.edu/sswweb/idea/

Wilmot, W. & Hocker, J. (2001). *Interpersonal conflict* (6th ed.). New York: McGraw-Hill.

Winchell, P. (2004). *The power of dialogue.* Retrieved December 27, 2008, from http://www.theinvisibleschool.org/04_publications/articles1.html

Wink, J. (2005). *Critical pedagogy: Notes from the real world* (3rd. ed.). Boston: Pearson Education.

# 6

# THE ART OF
# CONFLICT COACHING

Transferring Interpersonal and Group Conflict
Resolution Skills to a One-on-One Setting

*Nancy Geist Giacomini*

Once used to bolster troubled staffers, coaching now is part of the standard leadership development training for elite executives and talented
up-and-comers at IBM, Motorola, J. P. Morgan,
Chase, and Hewlett Packard. These companies
are discreetly giving their best prospects what
star athletes have long had: a trusted adviser to
help reach their goals.

*Inner Power International, n.d.*

This chapter provides a brief history of conflict coaching as applied to the college and university setting, along with practical application tools and techniques that allow system administrators and educators to build upon existing skills to frame the conflict coaching process. The relatively straightforward nature of coaching tailored for students wishing to understand, manage, and de-escalate conflict in their lives, together with the ease in which students can be scheduled and introduced to this process in just one or two sessions with a competent coach, makes this resolution pathway particularly appealing to busy administrators.

A number of campuses that introduced campus conflict resolution programs under the umbrella of a formal mediation program over the years have begun to expand their services to include coaching. In chapter 17 Robert Hosea provides one notable example of a well-developed conflict coaching effort at Nova Southeastern University. The model, which grew out of the institution's formal mediation program in student affairs, served over 50 students in a single academic year and has now been developed as a training-to-delivery model for the residence life staff. I acknowledge his contributions to the field and thank him for informing this chapter as well.

Conflict coaching is considered best practice when provided as one of several conflict resolution options students can choose from (Jones & Brinkert, 2008). The position of conflict coaching along the spectrum of possible resolution options identifies the process as one of the less-formal means for addressing conflict (Schrage & Thompson, 2008). In fact, coaching to understand the nature and management of conflict is a valuable option across the spectrum as a process to help students master skill sets helpful in their development as young adults.

Coaching can help a student resolve his or her own conflict issues at the lowest levels, handle an active conflict in a timely way, and engage another person who has not opted for formal resolution. Or, the student may find that a coaching session serves as an entry point to a more comfortable and successful mediation opportunity. Coaching can be relevant during or after a formal disciplinary referral when it becomes apparent that conduct is interwoven with conflict. It can also serve as an educational outcome of an adjudication process.

Regardless of when conflict coaching is offered or chosen to help manage conflict, the process is comparatively simple and inexpensive to learn, implement, schedule, and evaluate, particularly if a coach has the requisite skill sets including an understanding of the nature of conflict; problem-solving, listening, questioning, and cross-cultural communication skills; and an appreciation for the developmental and social group pressures of students seeking services.

## A Brief History of Conflict Coaching on Campus

I was introduced to conflict coaching in higher education years ago during a small professional development gathering at Temple University. As a new student affairs professional and freshly trained mediator I was eager to expand my own skills while supporting a student-government-driven mediation initiative at the University of Delaware where I served as assistant dean of students. At this gathering I was introduced to the Thomas-Kilmann Conflict Mode Instrument (Thomas & Kilmann, 1974), which I later used to provide coaching on campus as well as bolster annual mediation and conflict

resolution training offered by the Association for Student Conduct Administration (ASCA). The instrument is a quick individual pencil-and-paper or
interactive computerized assessment to help an individual identify his or her
favored (and sometimes surprising) modes of managing conflict, including
avoiding, accommodating, compromising, competing, and collaborating.
Some conflict coaching programs use this tool as part of the coaching process. Other program administrators have drawn from the instrument and
training guide to present residence hall and group programs on conflict.

Now, years later, I am pleased to acknowledge the contributions of Temple University to the practice of conflict coaching while presenting coaching
as another important and unique process in a conflict resolution spectrum.
Temple University in Philadelphia, Pennsylvania, was one of the first North
American institutions whose administrators actively practiced conflict coaching on campus. These practitioners are credited with coining the term *conflict coaching* in 1996 (Brinkert, 1999). Not unlike the experience of many
institutions,

> the campus conflict resolution program [at Temple University] was experi-
> encing a low demand for mediation and, consequently, conflict coaching
> was developed under the co-leadership of professors Joseph P. Folger and
> Tricia S. Jones. . . . Conflict coaching remains a central conflict resolution
> service offered on Temple's campus and, year-to-year, is consistently put
> into practice more often than mediation. (Jones & Brinkert, 2008, p. 7)

At the time of my introduction to conflict coaching, the process was
considered cutting edge certainly in higher education but also across other
fields. Today, coaching has taken off as a lucrative field in and of itself and
is being embraced as a management tool for some of the most elite and
highest-level executives in business, leadership, and human resource development. Coaching is also growing as an avenue for personal growth, goal
attainment, and success in life as well as in a career. Coaching is not counseling but a structured one-on-one opportunity to gain insights and skills
needed to overcome specific obstacles in one's path.

Higher education has taken a gentler pace in embracing coaching techniques as a formal process option for students, yet the steadfast voices of
Temple's pioneers continue to lead the charge for taking conflict resolution
skills learned in mediation, restorative justice, communication, conflict management, and facilitation training and using them to expand conflict management menus in a one-on-one coaching setting. Jones and Brinkert (2008)
provide a timely must-read for professionals seeking a comprehensive history, primer, and resource guide to applying conflict coaching skills on campus, and in this chapter I draw heavily upon their groundbreaking program

as well as the work of colleagues, including Cinnie Noble (see http://www .cinergycoaching.com), to present a meaningful overview.

Perhaps even more than other conflict resolution processes, coaching in general has achieved significant and growing acceptance across fields. Jones and Brinkert (2008) outline a number of "drivers," or markers that suggest that conflict coaching practices will be on the rise for many years to come; these include

- The continued concern with conflict management in a complex service economy
- The strong commitment in many areas of society to productivity and ethically manage conflict
- The continued need for a one-on-one ADR [alternative dispute resolution] process
- The need for a process that has a strong and tailored skills emphasis
- Increasing market recognition and demand
- Increasing interest in the use of conflict coaching as a way to integrate and promote existing ADR processes
- The likely emergence of conflict coaching as a recognizable executive coaching specialty
- Continued support and direct involvement from organizational communication professionals who see value as an add-on or alternative to consulting, training, other types of coaching, etc.
- Continued development of conflict coaching curricula in graduate and undergraduate programs. (pp. 8–12)

Not cutting edge anymore, conflict coaching as a viable pathway option with its own unique skill sets and tools must reasonably be considered a staple menu item for student affairs professionals. If campuses are not offering this service, they are in fact limiting their own ability to empower students to resolve interpersonal conflicts they will face throughout their lives at the lowest and most effective levels.

It bears noting that many institutions do offer one-on-one opportunities for students to learn about and address conflict in other venues already. Good examples are found in residence life programs, health and counseling services, academic advisement programs, and through student organization advisers. Conflict coaching goes one step further by institutionalizing the coaching process, making the services more visible, and embedding a sustainable, supervised program in the campus culture while protecting the quality and effectiveness of coaching sessions. Further, coaching endeavors to help transform students' skill sets and build their confidence so they can become better equipped to develop personal strategies for managing all manner of conflict in their lives.

## The Appeal of Conflict Coaching on Campus

Jones and Brinkert (2008) support a model that values the context in which a student experiences and interprets conflict that is very much in keeping with student development and social justice theoretical approaches advanced in this book. Moreover, their model allows for efficiency in terms of abbreviated, conflict-specific dialogue that may not require more than an hour or two of administrative time, is educational and transformative in orientation, and promotes the model as an ancillary process that supports rather than replaces additional conflict resolution options along a process menu not unlike that promoted in this book. Finally, it brings a process formerly used to better the skills of people in high-level career positions to every student. In so doing, coaching services place skills and new opportunities for self-insight into the hands of all students, regardless of their aspirations, backgrounds, or career choices.

Conflict coaching is explored in this volume as another valuable menu option in the spectrum of processes that student conduct professionals may offer students when their conduct belies underlying conflict management issues. Campus conflict coaching has been successfully applied in cases of roommate misunderstandings; relationship conflicts; failed communication with family, professors, and administrators; poor anger management; and personal goal setting (Hosea, personal communication; Jones & Brinkert, 2008). Coaching does not strive to be counseling nor does it replace the value of guidance already received from academic advisers, residence life staff members, group advisers, and spiritual leaders. Instead, conflict coaching is a unique skill set that student conduct administrators can often and effectively incorporate into their work with students in conflict.

Conflict coaching is appealing to student conduct administrators for many reasons. For one, it is comparatively easy to administer. Unlike scheduling multiple parties to participate in a facilitated session, restorative justice circle, mediation, or a formal adjudication process, conflict coaching typically requires just two people, the administrator as coach and the student in conflict, for often no more than one session with follow-up as requested. Coaching is also appealing over other spectrum processes including mediation, because while it is often difficult to get all necessary stakeholders in a conflict to the table, at least while respecting the preferred, voluntary nature of mediation, one party is often willing to try conflict coaching with or without the other party.

Sometimes students will individually schedule a coaching session at the outset of a conflict. In other instances, it can be a successful backup plan for administrators when a mediation or other facilitated, voluntary dialogue is scheduled and one party is a no show. Conflict coaching also offers trained administrators a chance to practice their conflict management skills throughout the year more readily than they might while waiting for formal mediation programs to be developed and normalized on campuses more used to adjudication models.

One of the biggest complaints of freshly trained mediators is the lack of opportunity to readily apply and practice their newly honed skills. This in turn often results in a loss of confidence and technical abilities over time. Keeping these skills alive through practice in conflict coaching sessions benefits not only the students involved but is professionally and personally rewarding for administrators as well.

## Basic Steps, Techniques, and Transferable Skills in Conflict Coaching

Much of this chapter invites student conduct administrators to draw upon their present interpersonal tools as well as revisit principal theories that explain and support student development and social identity. Professionally, administrators must ask themselves whether present student conduct work in managing campus conduct and conflict is effective in accomplishing the stated institutional, programmatic, professional, and personal goals.

In addition, conflict coaching invites students to consider their personal repertoire of resolution responses when faced with conflict in their academic and personal lives. For many students, simply working with an experienced coach to review and consider the nature of a particular conflict, conflict in general, and response modes available to deal effectively with conflict provides ample tools and the confidence to deal directly with an issue. Coaching allows students to see, sometimes for the first time, that they can de-escalate and manage conflict effectively in their own lives.

Jones and Brinkert (2008) provide insightful principles to help inform the growth of conflict coaching tailored for colleges and universities. As expanded by the authors, these principles include the following:

- A flexible model is vital
- Both direct and indirect clients should be considered in the coaching experience
- A relational and systems orientation to conflict coaching is essential
- Coaching is a contingent activity
- Conflict coaches should be knowledgeable about conflict theory and research as well as competent in conflict analysis
- Coaching aims to foster client empowerment with the coach combining expert and facilitative approaches
- Conflict coaching is not appropriate for all cases
- Conflict coaching should follow a principle of efficiency
- Conflict coaching should follow a high ethical standard
- Conflict coaching requires quality control, assessment, and monitoring
- Conflict coaching should be seen as part of a larger system of conflict management
- Conflict coaching must be sensitive to various cultural contexts (pp. 12–17)

The Comprehensive Conflict Coaching (CCC) model (Jones & Brinkert, 2008) has been built from the Macquarie University Problem Solving for One model advanced by Tidwell (as cited in Jones & Brinkert, 2008). From this model, Temple University's Conflict Education Resource Team (CERT) developed its own conflict coaching model infused with a stronger emphasis on teaching students about conflict styles (Jones & Brinkert).

In its latest evolution, the CCC model provides a stepped, nonlinear model of conflict coaching, respecting that the model is fluid and allowing for tailoring to meet individual needs. The model further emphasizes the importance of assessing learning throughout the process so that the client can best identify "benchmarks of success to determine progress along the way" (Jones & Brinkert, 2008, p. 39).

As detailed in Jones and Brinkert (2008) stages of the CCC model include

- Preparation for coaching
  - Initial conversation
  - Assessing the client's coachability
  - Assessing the coach's ability
- The coaching process
  - Stage One: Discovering the story
    - Initial story

- Refine the story
- Test the story
  - ○ Stage Two: Exploring three perspectives—identity, emotion, and power
  - ○ Stage Three: Crafting the best story
  - ○ Stage Four: Enacting the best story

Readers trained in mediation may notice similarities between this model and basic stages found in problem-solving-style mediation models. They may also appreciate the value that conflict coaching places on storytelling, and the importance of helping people in conflict tell and retell their conflict stories to fully explore, evaluate, and reframe a situation for better conflict management.

Another noteworthy model is the CINERGY model of conflict coaching. Cinnie Nobel, attorney-mediator and certified coach provides the following information and invites readers to view her publications and resources by visiting http://www.cinergycoaching.com (see articles link). Readers will also find valuable related resources at http://www.mediate.com under the "Coaching" section.

Noble combined conflict management and coaching principles in the CINERGY model. The stages are as follows:

- Clarify the goal
- Inquire about the situation
- Name the elements of conflict
- Explore the choices
- Reconstruct the situation
- Ground the challenges
- Yes, the commitment (C. Noble, personal communication, January 22, 2009)

The essence of Noble's model is consistent with the philosophy of the International Coach Federation, including the basic premise of self-determination. Through developing the skill of artful questioning and conducting the sequential CINERGY process, coaches trained in this model help people identify their goals and what they want to do differently. Coaches assist individuals to gain insights and other perspectives on their conflicts to be able to then, choose ways of responding and interacting that are aligned with their goals. From there, the individuals explore how those choices will play out in reality, before committing to a plan of action.

Noble's model has been used widely in public and private organizations in the United States, Canada, Ireland, and Australia, both as a peer coaching program and as an additional technique for coaches, conflict management practitioners, and others who work with people in conflict (C. Noble, personal communication, January 22, 2009).

The CINERGY model does not typically use an assessment tool like the Thomas-Kilmann Instrument (1974) unless an individual is seeking conflict coaching to improve his or her overall conflict competence rather than resolve a specific conflict. For competency building, the CINERGY model incorporates the Conflict Dynamics Profile developed by Eckerd College and found at http://www.conflictdynamics.org, to help individuals better understand their "constructive and destructive responses to conflict" (C. Noble, personal communication, January 22, 2009).

With or without mediation and coaching programs in place, many colleges and universities naturally practice some brand of less-formal or institutionalized coaching and mediation thanks to the good efforts of a residence life staff, counselors, academic advisers, and so on. Learning and practicing a conflict coaching process is a natural fit for educators, administrators, and students already grounded in student development theory and trained in communication, multiculturalism, and conflict resolution skills.

What makes a more intentional and structured conflict coaching process unique is its specific agenda to support and empower a student to explore the nature and modes of conflict, provide the tools needed to help a student effectively face and manage everyday conflict, and improve the confidence and language needed to begin confronting and resolving all manner of conflict at low levels. It is further unique in that it is designed as an individual, short-term process that values the unique skill sets, context, social identities, and developmental levels of each student in his or her individual journey to understand and address conflict competently.

## Organizations and Resources That Support and Inform Conflict Coaching

Higher education has struggled to develop or identify just the right professional niche to support the unique nature of campus conflict resolution processes. This is not to discredit the supportive and growing resources found in top student affairs organizations, including the Association for Student Conduct Administration (ASCA), the Association for College Personnel Administrators (ACPA), and the Student Affairs Administrators in Higher

Education (NASPA), nor the broader-based Association for Conflict Resolution (ACR), but to acknowledge that higher education educators and administrators need to develop meaningful local, national, and international forums to explore, promote, evaluate, and support conflict management efforts for colleges and universities.

In terms of conflict coaching resources in general, two international organizations of note are the International Coach Federation (ICF) and the International Association of Coaches (IAC). According to the ICF Web site, the ICF has the largest worldwide resource for business and personal coaches and is a valuable resource for individuals who wish to find a coach. It is a nonprofit organization of over 17,000 members worldwide who practice business and personal coaching. The ICF also offers a Special Interest Group on conflict coaching.

The IAC was established in 2003, and according to its Web site, has a membership of over 12,000 coaches in some 80 countries. Thomas Leonard, often credited as the founder of the coaching profession, developed the first international standards for coaching certification that "embraces universal guidelines, principles, proficiencies, standards and behaviors that make a coach a great coach, regardless of profession or geography" (IAC, n.d.).

## Conclusion

As process options and resolution tools go, conflict coaching has got a lot to offer. Coaching in and of itself has already been embraced across fields as a valuable and marketable one-on-one approach to building skills and confidence in individuals and empowering them to reach personal goals, which means the value of this process has already been accepted in the business world. Coaching on campus gets extra points in relation to social justice considerations in that it brings to every student a highly respected and often costly skill-building opportunity formerly available only to high-level managers in elite businesses (Jones & Brinkert, 2008). As modeling goes, few process options have the same potential to serve students on campus and later in their chosen fields, when the student as a young professional considers coaching as an option for further success and personal/professional growth.

Conflict coaching is also appealing in that it sells the value of personal conflict resolution skills in a nonthreatening way. Mediation and other face-to-face processes, while valuable, can be uncomfortable. Being coached one-on-one to handle a conflict effectively without the formal trappings of a scheduled sit-down, mediated session between parties is often much more comfortable for students who might otherwise simply say no to existing resolution options and ignore a growing conflict until it worsens. And personal conflicts, as we well know, often build until they negatively affect the parties involved and their communities as well.

The skills and basic conflict coaching model is not complicated nor particularly time intensive. Those already drawn to and trained in related areas, including mediation, intergroup dialogue and diversity, communication, and restorative justice, will find common themes and skill sets transferable to the coaching setting. That is not to say that conflict coaching is not grounded in its own ethical principals and structured using tailored steps, techniques, and skills particularly useful to this approach, but that many campus administrators and educators will find a common practical and philosophical language here to build on.

Readers seeking further conflict coaching information are encouraged to investigate the online and text resources mentioned in this chapter. The colleagues and organizations used as references are ripe resources for those wishing to advance the responsible and effective use of conflict coaching techniques and practices within a campus community to help students understand and resolve personal conflict.

The Association for Student Conduct Administration (ASCA) continues to nurture conflict coaching as a valuable process option for helping students manage conflict thanks in particular to the innovative contributions of Robert Hosea (2008). Hosea introduced conflict coaching as a process option in student conduct administration for the first time at the 2008 ASCA Donald D. Gehring Academy for Student Conduct Administration. He shares his coaching research and experiences from Nova Southeastern University in chapter 17.

## References

Brinkert, R. (1999, July). *Challenges and opportunities for a campus conflict education.* (CREnet) Conference, Boston, MA.

Eckerd College. (n.d.) *Conflict dynamics profile.* Retrieved January 23, 2009, from http://www.conflictdynamics.org/cdp/

Inner Power International. (n.d.). *Executive coaching.* Retrieved January 23, 2009, from http://www.innerpowerintl.com/services/executivecoaching.htm

International Association of Coaching. (n.d.). *About the IAC.* Retrieved January 20, 2009, from http://www.certifiedcoach.org/mission/about.html

International Coach Federation. (n.d.). *Why join ICF?.* Retrieved June 14, 2009, from http://www.coachfederation.org/about-ICF.

Jones, T. S., & Brinkert, R. (2008). *Conflict coaching: Conflict management strategies and skills for the individual.* Thousand Oaks, CA: Sage.

Schrage, J. M., & Thompson, M. C. (2008, June). *Using a social justice model for conflict resolution to ensure access for all students.* Paper presented at the Donald D. Gehring Academy for Student Conduct Administration, Salt Lake City, UT.

Thomas, K. W., & Kilmann, R. H. (1974). *Thomas-Kilmann conflict mode instrument.* Tuxedo, New York: Xicom.

# 7

# FACILITATED DIALOGUE

## An Overview and Introduction
## for Student Conduct Professionals

### *Jay Wilgus and Ryan C. Holmes*

Peace is not merely a distant goal that we seek,
but a means by which we arrive at that goal.
*Martin Luther King Jr.*

Resting dormant within the traditional student conduct code lies an underused, underappreciated, and understudied pathway of conflict resolution known to conflict professionals as *facilitated dialogue*. Although often used informally on our campuses, facilitated dialogue can serve student conduct professionals far more usefully when used as an essential and intentional pathway. This pathway can help students and administrators address a wide array of campus conflicts that may otherwise be left unresolved under the current judicial hearing paradigm. While particularly beneficial for multiparty conflicts that envelop our campuses several times each year, facilitated dialogue can also play an integral role in managing smaller conflicts. Facilitated dialogue is not simply a method of communicating in and through conflict but also a must-have tool for the student conduct professional.

This chapter provides an overview of and introduction to facilitated dialogue in three sections. The first section describes the basics of facilitated dialogue, including a working definition, a primer on the purpose and utility of facilitated dialogue on college campuses, and a description of the characteristics of conflict situations well suited for resolution or management using facilitated dialogue. The second section provides a reference point for the role of facilitator, including facilitator responsibilities, basic facilitation techniques, and a framework for choosing the right facilitator(s) to assist in a particular conflict. Finally, the third section reviews six key aspects of facilitated dialogue in a social justice context: multipartiality, diversity, intercultural awareness, identity awareness, power, and the creation of safe space.

This chapter is not exhaustive but rather an introduction to another option in a series of pathways that allow for the healthy resolution of conflict and conduct on campus, ranging from minimal structure to highly structured or informal to the most formal methods.

## The Basics of Facilitated Dialogue

Some terms come to common usage in American culture with widely understood and widely accepted definitions. Such is rarely the case among student affairs practitioners who endlessly debate the meaning of words like *diversity*, *sustainability*, or *community*. These words, like others, can have one meaning for the speaker and a completely different meaning for the listener. The same can be said of the term facilitated dialogue. No authoritative source provides *the* definition as it relates to conflict resolution on college campuses. There are, however, various themes and characteristics of facilitated dialogue that can be relied upon for guidance and clarity.

### *Working Definition of Facilitated Dialogue*

For the purposes of this volume, the term facilitated dialogue refers to a conversation between two or more individuals or groups in which a trained multipartial facilitator helps parties overcome communicative barriers and engage in productive conversation regarding issues of mutual concern. Facilitated dialogue describes a method of interacting whereby individuals and groups learn to communicate in, and through, conflict. Although facilitated dialogue shares many similarities with traditional problem solving (or facilitative) mediation models explored in chapter 8, it differs in that facilitated dialogue is not necessarily designed to produce or work toward a set of agreements (Folger, Poole, & Stutman, 2005). Rather, facilitated dialogue is simply about engaging parties in cooperative dialogue without concern for the end product. In some instances, dialogue may lead to a set of agreements. In others, it may simply produce robust conversation that helps parties understand each other. Either way, facilitated dialogue is an essential pathway for student conduct professionals because of its wide applicability and utility.

### *Purpose and Utility of Facilitated Dialogue on Campus*

College campuses are wonderful places to work and study. The environment typically values differing thoughts, ideas, beliefs, and perceptions. Students, staff, and faculty are almost always encouraged to appreciate various religions, philosophies, races, ethnicities, genders, abilities, ages, classes, appearances, and sexual orientations. The end result is an engaging workplace, an incredible learning environment, and the perfect breeding ground for conflict. As the natural by-product of competing thoughts, ideas, beliefs, perceptions, and backgrounds (Rabie, 1994), conflict was bound to arise on campuses for as long as higher education has existed. The resulting challenge for administrators lies not in finding a way to end campus conflict but in finding a way to transform, or reframe, conflicts into opportunities.

Facilitated dialogue can do just that by creating opportunities for peace and relationship building. It has the power to convene opposing parties and bring them to the table. It can create respect where there was none and produce harmony among enemies. It is an excellent way to transform competition into collaboration. Moreover, facilitated dialogue can serve as the broad brush needed to address expansive campus conflicts in which agreement is not as important as understanding. In that sense, it gives campus administrators an additional tool to use when they are not exactly sure which one to apply.

For example, when conflict occurs in an environment where there is a familiar tool or pathway available (e.g., a roommate conflict in the residence halls calls for roommate mediation), administrators or student staff are fairly adept at working through differences among students. However, they are frequently less comfortable with process options when conflict occurs between student groups, between a student group and the university, or in other situations that fail to fit neatly into a "systems as usual" framework. Many talented professionals have asked themselves and each other, "How should we deal with this one?" This chapter asserts that the pathway needed in many of those situations is facilitated dialogue.

## When to Use Facilitated Dialogue

Equipped with the understanding that facilitated dialogue is an essential pathway within the Spectrum of Conflict Resolution Process Options (Schrage & Thompson, 2008), campus administrators still must know which situations call for facilitated dialogue and which do not. This section is intended to explain how to do just that by describing two fact patterns that frequently arise—in one form or another—on college campuses nationwide. Consider the following two scenarios and try to determine which is better suited for traditional mediation and which for facilitated dialogue. Assume you work in the student conduct office on your campus and it's your job to determine how each of the following situations should be handled.

### Scenario Number 1: Shannon and Heather

Two freshmen roommates, Shannon and Heather, live together in a residence hall room that overlooks a beautiful valley. Heather thinks Shannon is strange because she is Goth and rarely comes out of the room. According to Heather, Shannon smells and has a weird boyfriend who regularly spends the night in their room. Heather wants Shannon kicked out of the room. In contrast, Shannon is frustrated that Heather makes her feel so unwelcome in her own room. Shannon reveals to you that she is bipolar and that she can't concentrate in her room because Heather and her friends are loud, giggly, and chatty in the adjoining living room. Heather drew several pictures on the living room wall depicting a Goth female with words like "smelly" and "sex freak," Shannon assumes the pictures portray her; Heather says it has nothing to do with Shannon. Neither Shannon nor Heather wants to move out because both of them love the view from their room. You become aware of this situation and are trying to determine what to do to address potential policy violations and the underlying conflict.

*Scenerio Number 2: The Order*

The Order, a senior honor society on campus with a history of secrecy, discriminatory, and exclusionary practices, has been present on campus for more than 100 years. In the past years, their practices have been exposed to the greater university student body and community via the campus newspaper. Many of the secret rituals associated with the group appear to mimic Native American ceremonial practices and involve similar artifacts. The secret membership and its practices have been made public and thus created a major conflict among students. Trisha, a senior who accepted membership in The Order, is also president of the Black Student Union (BSU). She has been approached by several other student leaders of Black student organizations on campus who state that they refuse to work with or support the BSU if she remains a member of The Order and demand that she resign from The Order or as president of BSU. Trisha is hurt and feels that she should not have to choose between her leadership positions (Schrage & Thompson, 2008).

A quick analysis reveals that in scenario 1 involving Heather and Shannon, the conflict arose in the residence halls where there is likely a resident adviser supervising the floor. The conflict appears to be limited to two roommates feuding over various issues, including hygiene, lifestyle, noise, respect, and drawings. In scenario 2 involving The Order, the conflict involves a larger group of people not readily identifiable and is evolving in the public eye via the campus newspaper. Trisha, The Order, BSU members, Native American students, and others presumably have a vested interest in what is going on, although each holds a very different perspective. Campus administrators might recognize this conflict as an opportunity to improve the campus climate and provide an important educational experience for students.

Unfortunately, they may also be struggling to find the right pathway to handle this delicate situation.

Scenario 1 is well suited for mediation because it involves identifiable stakeholders who need help resolving issues of mutual concern. Mediation, although much like facilitated dialogue, is a good tool to use in this conflict because Shannon and Heather need help resolving the issues between them if they are going to remain in the same room. Assuming they can agree on certain things, such as visitor hours and noise levels, they may find living together much easier and possibly even enjoyable (Boulle, 2001; Warters, 2000). Warters explores these applications further in chapter 8.

Scenario 2, on the other hand, is better suited for facilitated dialogue because it involves a larger group of stakeholders whose interests cover an array of perspectives. It is not clear whether any agreements need to be made between parties or whether they just need to understand each other's point of view. The process of convening a facilitated dialogue would help identify which stakeholders need to be at the table while uncovering underlying interests of each individual or group. In the end, scenario 2 may call for multiple facilitated dialogues (Wilkinson, 2004): one within BSU, one within The Order, one among Native American students, and yet another between BSU, The Order, and Native American Students. The one certainty is that this situation calls for quick intervention because of the turmoil it is producing across campus. A facilitated dialogue pathway provides the tools needed for campus administrators to bring this conflict into focus and begin working toward resolution.

Facilitated dialogue is a valuable, early intervention pathway to get the ball rolling in unclear scenarios. It can produce dialogue where there is conflict and get parties on the pathway to peaceful interactions. Without it, scenario 2 would likely play out in the public eye until parties either capitulated or resolved their differences in escalated ways or behind closed doors. From a social justice perspective, using facilitated dialogue in this situation increases the opportunity for all voices to be heard, and through use of multipartiality decreases the risk of certain communities' being marginalized. Unfortunately, constructing a facilitated dialogue requires more than simply pulling a single tool from the toolbox. It requires a sophisticated understanding of the facilitator's role, facilitation techniques, and more.

## The Role of a Facilitator

A facilitator in the facilitated dialogue context acts as a multipartial third party to help parties communicate. In the Spectrum Model (Schrage &

Thompson, 2008), this is the first pathway in which a third-party is brought into a conflict. It is the facilitator's responsibility to guide the dialogue in a way that overcomes communicative barriers and keeps parties moving forward productively (Hogan, 2002). Much like a mediator, a facilitator is responsible for controlling the process and allowing participants to control the outcome.

## Facilitator Responsibilities

There are literally thousands of responsibilities for the facilitator to consider in a facilitated dialogue, but the primary areas of focus (Landrum, 2003) are as follows:

- Eliciting the participants' acceptance to simple ground rules, like
  - Taking turns talking
  - Treating each other with dignity and respect
  - Avoiding name calling
- Determining who will be consistent participants and who will appear as necessary
- Establishing an appropriate meeting schedule
- Developing a list of topics for discussion and deciding how to prioritize them
- Summarizing, reframing, and recording key comments on a flip chart
- Reframing adversarial propositions or positions into open-ended inquiries designed to discover solutions
- Summarizing progress that group has made
- Sensing when interactions cease to be productive and intervening to return the group to effective dialogue or moving to another more easily manageable topic
- Structuring issues or positions in terms of underlying interests
- Organizing topics to achieve early consensus on less-difficult issues, thus giving the participants a sense of accomplishment and progress
- Preparing written minutes or summaries of each session for review and reference
- Ensuring separation between dialogue and decision making
- Creating and maintaining a safe space for all participants to improve the likelihood that all voices are heard in the process
- Noticing when participants and/or voices are being marginalized in the process and actively working to balance power in the room.

In addition, the facilitator is often responsible for one of the most difficult parts of a facilitated dialogue—convening the meeting (Carlson, 1999). This includes

- working with identifiable stakeholders to determine who needs to be at the table,
- selecting an appropriate location that feels comfortable and safe for all stakeholders, and
- inviting parties to participate in the dialogue.

If a facilitator can accomplish these things, then he or she has served the parties well. Although the facilitator need not be a certified professional, he or she must have some basic training in process design, facilitator responsibilities, facilitation techniques, cultural competence, social justice, and the nature of conflict and conflict resolution work.

## Facilitation Techniques

In addition to understanding a facilitator's responsibilities, the facilitator should also have a strong grasp of key facilitation techniques. Some key facilitation techniques include modeling, reflective listening, and displaying empathy (McCain & Tobey, 2007).

### Modeling

One of the most important things for a facilitator to do is model the behavior that he or she expects of the parties. By embodying the spirit of the session, the facilitator can subliminally teach participants how to construct and maintain a successful dialogue. The facilitator can use this method to show participants the importance of displaying an attentive body posture, giving eye contact as a show of attention, and displaying how the control of other nonverbal behaviors can aid in positive interaction between parties (Olshak, 2001). Another good modeling technique is to avoid making assumptions about what a party is thinking or saying (Cheldelin & Lucas, 2004). By letting participants explain what they mean, and attempting to gather a true understanding, the facilitator sets a tone of patience and acceptance while encouraging continued progress in the dialogue.

### Reflective Listening

Another way to avoid faulty assumptions is through reflective listening. Using this method, the facilitator can restate, question, and/or summarize information given by any party (Olshak, 2001). This can be done before a response is given to the information as a way of displaying a desire to understand rather than be heard. If attentive, participants will likely find this to be a valuable tool of communication. In addition, reflective listening can limit the amount of speech and meaning that gets lost in translation. For example, if something is seemingly misunderstood because of language barriers, inter-cultural disconnects, or contrasting identities, the facilitator can help parties understand each other by reflectively listening as participants observe the session.

## Displaying Empathy

Finally, a lot can be gained in the session if the facilitator and participants display empathy. Empathy, "showing understanding and respect for some-one else's views, values, and emotions" (McKearnan & Fairman, 1999, p. 339) can help participants see each other as helpers in a process rather than adversaries in competition. Displaying empathy does not mean that either party is agreeing with the views of the other. On the contrary, empathy means displaying understanding and respect even if you disagree. Through this method, not only can the dialogue be productive, it can also aid in main-taining equal power between parties.

Although relatively easy to conceptualize, these techniques are more dif-ficult to apply in practice—especially in conflict that involves multiple stake-holders. The following guidelines are provided to help administrators collaborate with campus and community members who may have the skills necessary to lead a productive dialogue.

## Choosing a Facilitator

Choosing a facilitator can become overly complicated if administrators make the mistake of assuming that a facilitator must possess a skill set not already commanded by most student conduct administrators. Backgrounds in com-munication, conflict resolution, diversity, and/or student development all serve a facilitator well in this process. Although certified professionals may be desirable in some situations, certification is not required. More than likely there is someone on campus who would prove an excellent facilitator for any given conflict because of his or her demeanor, positional power, communica-tion skills, or relationship to the parties. A person may also be a good facilita-tor if he or she is simply well respected among participants and can bring calmness, wisdom, and facilitation skills to the process. Moreover, there is nothing inappropriate with pairing two individuals to serve as cofacilitators to lend support, wisdom, experience, and diversity to a dialogue.

Regardless, the following characteristics should be considered in choos-ing a facilitator:

- *Multipartiality*: Everyone in the group must be comfortable with the facilitator and believe that he or she is skilled enough to ensure that all perspectives are voiced in the conversation and given equal weight, regardless of the facilitator's own background or biases. This is absolutely critical to a fair and productive dialogue. Without it conversations will barely get started. For this reason, it is critical that administrators responsible for selecting the facilitator be intentional in considering how the social identity(s) of the facilitator(s), and his or her self-awareness, may affect the dynamics of the dialogue.

- *Skill and experience*: The right facilitator should have a good understanding of responsibilities, facilitation techniques, and collaborative problem-solving principles, especially if the group anticipates a high level of conflict. Some experience with the substantive issues can also be helpful in situations where the subject matter is unique or not easily understood.
- *Cost*: In many situations a facilitator can be found among the group of individuals responsible for supervising, advising, or managing the conflicted parties. If not, and if no one else on campus is capable of serving as a volunteer facilitator, then it may be necessary to look off campus to a community partner who can be hired to facilitate a dialogue.

The selection process for the facilitator ought to result in a decision that is acceptable to all parties, but it should not interfere with the process itself. Some conflicts require immediate attention, so it would be imprudent to delay facilitated dialogue in an attempt to find the ideal facilitator. In those situations, it's wise to find the best possible person in the moment and get the parties talking.

A great facilitator need not be a highly compensated professional or the one with the most training in conflict resolution. Many student conduct professionals are perfectly capable of being excellent facilitators so long as they possess the skills and attributes described in this section. This chapter, combined with a meaningful skills-based training course in mediation or facilitation relevant to higher education (e.g., see conflict resolution offerings at the Association for Student Conduct Administration, Donald D. Gehring Academy at www.theasca.org) and an understanding of the dynamics described below, would likely be enough to prepare most aspiring facilitators to serve as a multipartial third party in campus conflicts.

## Key Aspects of Facilitated Dialogue in a Social Justice Context

In a social justice context several additional aspects of facilitated dialogue are essential for the facilitator to understand. By ignoring them, a facilitator can materially alter the outcome of a conversation or cause a vital stakeholder to disengage from the process entirely. This section examines six final aspects of facilitated dialogue that must be considered in a social justice context if the facilitator intends to serve the parties well. They include multipartiality, diversity, intercultural awareness, identity awareness, power plays among participants, and the need to create a space that feels safe for everyone involved.

## *Multipartiality*

Multipartiality (the ability to analyze a conflict using multiple viewpoints) is preferred in facilitated dialogue over impartiality (the appearance of being neutral through the duration of a process). Through multipartiality, all participants are provided a safe arena to see the conflict from fresh angles and identify areas of struggle and/or oppression, while helping improve communication skills. A multipartial facilitator can show participants that there is more than one way to view a conflict (Gadlin & Sturm, 2007). Through multipartiality, together with the absence of a personal agenda in the conflict, the facilitator can help parties feel empowered to engage fully in dialogue and have their voices heard. In serving all parties, the facilitator can restate a participant's point to ensure that it is heard and understood in a nonpositional and productive way.

Nonetheless, the concept of multipartiality does not come without challenges. One key concern is that participants can feel as though they are not getting *equal* attention, understanding, or air time. Participants may challenge or criticize the "facilitator's actions or words" (Straus, 1999, p. 308) and overall credibility. If this occurs, it is the facilitator's responsibility to legitimize such thoughts, rather than become defensive. The facilitator's ego is not nearly as important as his or her service to the group (Straus). A skilled facilitator can engage critical participants in a way that redirects the energy back into the group for the positive benefit of everyone. Further, a skilled facilitator ultimately demonstrates that all points of view are heard and honored, and all parties supported and respected. This occurs regardless of whether each participant is given exactly the same amount of speaking time or at what point in the process each participant contributes.

## *Diversity*

Facilitators working in a social justice context must have a strong working understanding of issues related to personal diversity. Far more is present in a session than what originally appears to be on the surface. This can introduce opportunities for, and challenges to, group learning and understanding

(Straus, 1999). For example, a diversity of opinions and views provides groups with various ideas and tools necessary to construct beneficial solutions to their conflict. Diversity can also help unlock participants from their respective positions, empathize with others, and cause them to be more likely to take risks and trust that progress is being made. In contrast, diversity can also be the source of arguments and other negative attitudes and expectations. A facilitator who is familiar with the role of diversity in the session will be better equipped to handle behaviors, positive or negative, as part of the dialogue process and use them for the betterment of the group.

### Intercultural Awareness

Intercultural awareness is becoming similarly important in facilitating a dialogue. As the United States becomes more culturally diverse and increasingly more integrated, colleges and universities undergo comparable changes. As such, administrators and facilitators must develop intercultural awareness and recognize the ethnocentric view communication patterns often originate from. Individuals who communicate from an ethnocentric viewpoint have the tendency to interpret and/or judge other groups and situations through their own meaning-making systems (Borisoff & Victor, 1998). This is true on a regional and national scale, and also within college environments that produce a variety of subcultures. For example, in scenario number 2 discussed on pp. 115 and 116, BSU's culture is presumably very different from The Order's, which makes communication between groups even more difficult. Areas of intercultural awareness to be accounted for include, but are not limited to, language differences, place (i.e., where a person comes from and the way he or she manipulates that environment), the way people interpret the world around them, and nonverbal communication behavior (Borisoff & Victor). Though the facilitator will not understand everything there is to know about all cultures, an increased level of intercultural awareness will allow the facilitator to use his or her role more effectively and increase the likelihood of producing a positive interaction among participants.

### Identity Awareness

The multipartial facilitator should also understand the concept of identities. Since identities, real or perceived, have the ability to offer a benefit or a disadvantage to groups of people, the facilitator ought to actively attempt to eliminate the establishment of oppressive dynamics during the dialogue. As one example, consider the role that emotion plays during a dialogue. In some settings, showing emotion can be seen as a detriment to communication, while in others it can be seen as a necessary component (Jones & Brinkert, 2008). A skillful facilitator can help parties understand that emotion may be used as an analytic tool and that it can be "another form of rationality, rather than an irrational response" (Jones & Brinkert, p. 106). In addition, a facilitator can use multipartiality to point out that it takes some people longer to process emotion and that they may perceive emotion as being uncomfortable to deal with (Jones & Brinkert). A facilitator gains credit in the eyes of all participants by using this type of approach, seeming neutral while being multipartial, and is more effective in the process.

## Power in the Session

Even though a facilitator may be extremely skilled in available techniques and possess a keen understanding of the cultural aspects involved in the process, the facilitator must constantly guard against power shifting in the session. The same group affiliations at work outside the dialogue can enter the process and support the oppression of and/or benefit to certain participants. Once inserted, though the dialogue can still survive, power can disrupt the good faith effort of parties and make them reluctant to engage in open, honest communication. If not careful, the facilitator can also be made the culprit as participants attempt to manipulate the facilitator's multipartial approach to gain favor. This can be countered only if the facilitator understands when to be an active participant and when to be invisible, placing responsibility on the participants to depend on each other more than the facilitator.

## Safe Space

Institutions of higher education are often idealized by the dominant culture as tranquil places or ivory towers (Cheldelin & Lucas, 2004). Yet, these same institutions can foster real and perceived bias toward the values and opinions of marginalized and oppressed communities. For some it is very hard to feel wholly woven into the fabric of their surroundings. This requires facilitators to have the ability to create a safe space for all participants. This can be done by selecting a neutral or multipartial site for dialogue or by assuring participants through the introduction and ground rules that things discussed in the session will be used for the session without consequence. Either way, safety is integral to the success of the session. Though facilitated dialogues may not mimic the acceptance level of larger society, they are important for institutions of higher education striving to give students the room to strengthen communication skills and develop an authentic self-identity. The safer all feel in the dialogue space, the more likely their time together will be increasingly productive.

Despite a facilitator's best skills and efforts, success is never guaranteed. There is always the risk that a dialogue could turn sour, and that risk is never more evident than in the pit of the participant's stomach as they enter the room to talk. However, if the facilitator is able to remain multipartial throughout the dialogue and create an environment that permits all voices to be heard regardless of power, then the dialogue is headed in the right direction and will likely produce a positive result for all stakeholders.

## Conclusion

Facilitated dialogue has a way of bringing people together when they are most divided and of mending wounds that are too often left to heal improperly, leaving lifelong scars. Without opportunities for dialogue, our students may needlessly suffer from unresolved conflict. The ultimate purpose of this chapter is to expand our thinking as professionals about how we conduct our affairs when the judicial hearing paradigm does not work. It further challenges us to rediscover or investigate for the first time the value of facilitated dialogue as an established pathway for best managing even our campus's most heated conflicts.

Finally, while facilitated dialogue is important in bringing productive closure to campus conflicts, its more lasting effect on students may be its ability to transform their way of thinking about "enemies" and "others" and developing conflict resolution skills to last a lifetime. A student who is able to engage others in productive dialogue in the face of conflict is ultimately a student we may proudly graduate from our institution. For he or she has become courageous enough to engage, wise enough to select the most effective resolution pathway, experienced enough to choose the best resources and tools, and skilled enough to turn conflict into peace.

## References

Borisoff, D., & Victor, D. A. (1998). *Conflict management: A communication skills approach* (2nd ed.). Needham Heights, MA: Allyn & Bacon.

Boulle, L. (2001). *Mediation: Skills and techniques.* Charlottesville, VA: Butterworths.

Carlson, C. (1999). Convening. In L. Susskind, S. McKearnan, & J. Thomas-Larmer (Eds.), *The consensus building handbook: A comprehensive guide to reaching agreement* (pp. 169–198). Thousand Oaks, CA: Sage.

Cheldelin, S. I., & Lucas, A. F. (2004). *Academic administrator's guide to conflict resolution.* San Francisco: Jossey-Bass.

Folger, J. P., Poole, M. S., & Stutman, R. K. (2005) *Working through conflict: Strategies for relationships, groups, and organizations* (5th ed.). Boston, MA: Pearson Education.

Gadlin, H., & Sturm, S. P. (2007). Conflict resolution and systemic change. *Journal of Dispute Resolution, 1,* 1–63.

Hogan, C. (2002). *Understanding facilitation: Theory and principles.* London: Kogan Page.

Jones, T. S., & Brinkert, R. (2008). *Conflict coaching: Conflict management strategies and skills for the individual.* Thousand Oaks, CA: Sage.

Landrum, M. (2003). *Facilitated dialogue: A tool for early conflict intervention.* Retrieved December 19, 2008, from http://www.mediate.com/burklandrum/pg42.cfm

McCain, D. V., & Tobey, D. D. (2007). *Facilitation skills training.* Alexandria, VA: ASTP Press.

McKearnan, S., & Fairman, D. (1999). Producing consensus. In L. Susskind, S. McKearnan, & J. Thomas-Larmer (Eds.), *The consensus building handbook: A comprehensive guide to reaching agreement* (pp. 325–373). Thousand Oaks, CA: Sage.

Olshak, R. (2001). *Mastering mediation: A guide for training mediators in a college and university setting.* Horsham, PA: LRP Publications.

Rabie, M. (1994). *Conflict resolution and ethnicity.* Westport, CT: Praeger.

Schrage, J., & Thompson, M. (2008). *The order.* Written for the 2008 Donald D. Gehring Academy for Student Conduct Administration, Salt Lake City, UT.

Straus, D. A. (1999). Managing meetings to build consensus. In L. Susskind, S. McKearnan, & J. Thomas-Larmer (Eds.), *The consensus building handbook: A comprehensive guide to reaching agreement* (pp. 287–324). Thousand Oaks, CA: Sage.

Warters, W. C. (2000). *Mediation in the campus community: Designing and managing effective programs.* San Francisco: Jossey-Bass.

Wilkinson, M. (2004). *The secrets of facilitation: The S.M.A.R.T. guide to getting results with groups.* San Francisco: Jossey-Bass.

# 8

# MODELS OF
# MEDIATION PRACTICE

*William Warters*

Man must evolve for all human conflict a method
which rejects revenge, aggression, and retalia-
tion. The foundation of such a method is love.

*Martin Luther King Jr.*

The term *mediation* refers, in the broadest sense, to conciliatory interventions by an acceptable third party who works with individuals or
groups in conflict to facilitate the development of a shared and
mutually acceptable solution to their problem(s). The problems may be relational, substantive, or (typically) some combination thereof. The actual practice of mediation in higher education (as elsewhere) varies tremendously in
terms of the characteristics of the parties served and the mediation format
and approach (Warters, 2000).

Variations may include the degree of formality or informality accorded
to the process, the openness of the process to party influence, the amount of
time parties spend face-to-face, the number and type of person(s) chosen to
intervene, and the relative emphasis placed on problem solving and settlement or some form of transformation (individual, relational, or systemic).
This chapter explores some of these variations in the context of higher education, reviews the predominant models of mediation practice, and provides a
general road map for conflict handlers interested in understanding the mediation terrain.

## Mediation in the Campus Context

Mediation emerged on campuses in the late 1970s and early 1980s, during a
time when colleges and universities were experiencing a noticeable growth in
legalism. As university enrollments and personnel expanded with the baby
boom, campus administrators developed a seemingly ever-increasing set of

rules and regulations designed to manage the changing campus environment. While previously the courts had been reluctant to get involved in campus issues, during the 1970s they began hearing more campus-based disputes, and federal courts established a variety of new guidelines relating to internal grievance procedures.

Also during this period a larger proportion of university personnel joined unions and collectively bargained over contracts. These factors, along with growing student expectations of involvement in their educational institutions and more careful monitoring of the "fairness" of procedures, began to have a noticeable impact on policy making. A *due process explosion* occurred, with many new campus policies being developed that provided detailed grievance and disciplinary procedures aimed at protecting individual rights, checking administrative discretion, and fending off possible lawsuits.

These changes began to influence people's experience of life on campus. In an article in 1978 Ryor asked, "Who Killed Collegiality?" arguing that the era of collegiality was being replaced by one of liability. Other observers (Marske & Vago, 1980) described the environment of the late 1970s as alienated and driven by a complex web of legal guidelines. Signs of this increasing legalism included the growing availability of prepaid (i.e., student-fee-funded) student legal services and new liability insurance policies provided by the American Association of University Professors (AAUP) tailored specifically to the needs of faculty.

University administrators were moving to establish in-house legal counsel, as they were no longer able to function with the occasional use of the expertise of a lawyer sitting on their board of directors. The National Association of College and University Attorneys (NACUA) experienced its greatest period of growth. Stetson University began hosting the popular annual conference on law and higher education in the late 1970s, and in 1987 the Association for Student Judicial Affairs (renamed the Association for Student Conduct Administration in 2008) was formed as an offshoot of this gathering, designed to promote and support professionalism in the increasingly complex student conduct administration field. Clearly, due process and law were on the mind of many during this period, but so were dispute-handling alternatives.

## Campus Alternative Dispute Resolution (ADR) History

Mediation, which emerged in the shadow of campus legalism, represented a relatively small voice in campus conduct management conversations in the late 1970s and early 1980s. Advocates of mediation were enthusiastic, however, and open to sharing their knowledge and resources. Campus experiments with mediation grew steadily, with a notable rise in activity in the wake of four annual national campus mediation conferences beginning in 1990. Most of the early programs primarily served students, but over time programs emerged that served staff, faculty, and community members as well. By the end of 1991, 35 campus mediation programs were visible in the United States and Canada, and 165 programs were logged as of 1998 (Warters, 1998). While a comprehensive survey has not been taken in recent years, based on the number of programs with a Web presence, program growth has continued to well beyond 250 distinct and visible programs.

## Goals of Mediation

In the 1970s in the broader society, the emergence of community and court-affiliated mediation initiatives was, at least in part, a response to popular dissatisfaction with the administration of justice (Levin & Wheeler, 1979). Policy aims for community and court-affiliated mediation programs included improving access to justice, reducing court waiting lists, and increasing consumer satisfaction with the legal system.

On campus, however, the goals were not quite so tightly linked to improving grievance handling and perceptions of campus justice systems. Campus mediation efforts included a more pronounced focus on providing opportunities for student (and staff and faculty) development and learning (Rodgers, 1983), promoting service to the community, and as tools for preventing escalated conflict. Staff and administrators have been interested in finding ways to address conflict more effectively and proactively but particularly in ways that help sustain rather than diminish the feeling of community on campus. Because of its flexibility as a conflict management approach and learning opportunity, mediation had found a place for itself on college campuses.

## Types of Mediators

As mediators become more sophisticated, and as the number of mediators and range of settings where they work increases, so has the debate about who should mediate and how and what styles are most appropriate. Mediators can play many different roles in relation to the parties. For instance, Moore (1996) identified *social network*, *independent*, and *authoritative* mediator types. A social network mediator is part of an ongoing and shared social network with parties, such as a friend, family member, colleague, elder, or religious leader. They are chosen because they have earned the trust of the parties. This kind of mediator is often sought in more collectivist cultures where community relationships remain important. The independent mediator, on the other hand, which is most common in the North American context, is perceived to have no vested interest in the conflict and is not supposed to be connected to the parties in any way. He or she is expected to be impartial and objective, standing outside the dispute, and has no decision-making power in the case and no power to enforce agreements that might be reached. This is quite unlike the authoritative mediator who has ties to the parties, has a vested interest in what happens, and often has the power to enforce agreements because of the mediator's higher rank in some authority structure of relevance to the parties. This type of mediator might be a party's supervisor or employer, for instance, who has decided that having the parties solve a conflict is likely to be better than an imposed solution.

Another interesting distinction has to do with the degree to which mediators involve themselves with social norms related to the conflict context. Waldman (1997) has identified three broad types: *norm-generating*, *norm-educating* and *norm-advocating* mediators. The norm-generating types, probably the most common, are focused on maintaining the autonomy of parties, letting them develop their own norms based on their relationship and their context (for instance, in a community mediation between neighbors). The norm-educating mediators use the mediation process to help educate parties to the relevant social or legal norms in their community (for example, divorce cases or restorative conference circles), either during the sessions or between them through consultation with external experts, but then leave it up to the parties to decide how they might be applied. Norm-advocating mediators (for example, in environmental or public policy mediations) not only work to educate parties about relevant social and legal norms, but they will advocate for their inclusion in agreements. In these cases, the mediators may even withdraw from a case if it seems as if the parties were going to agree to something that is outside the norms deemed acceptable to the mediator. There is a lot of potential overlap between these types, but they point out the wide variety of roles mediators may play in conflict situations.

## *Mediator Styles*

Observers and scholars of mediation have often characterized individual mediators as having a particular *style* of practice that is thought to be relatively consistent across cases. For example, Silbey and Merry (1986) identify *bargaining* and *therapeutic* mediator styles, Kolb (1983) notes *dealmakers* versus *orchestrators*, and Riskin (1994) designates *evaluative* versus *facilitative* styles. Rather than representing dichotomous choices, these designations are better understood as the endpoints on a continuum that stretches between a problem-solving, settlement-oriented mediator approach (often more directive) and a more relationship-oriented approach (often less directive). Kressel and his colleagues (1994) have noted that a mediator's style is typically something he or she performs "without fully recognizing the underlying coherence or 'logic' behind their style" (p. 72). The distinct models of mediation we will explore in the next section provide frameworks for practice that can be quite useful in guiding mediator behavior in a more conscious way.

Readers are advised to avoid becoming drawn into the (at times) polemical debate on models and styles. Preferred approaches are clearly influenced by the norms and conditions found in a given context, as well as the educational background, training, and level of experience of a mediator. These differences in context influence what we think works and why, and they vary considerably even within a given campus environment. Consider, for instance, the different factors and process choices a mediator may face addressing a stalled labor contract negotiation, a conflict between a supervisor and an employee over alleged sexual harassment, a tenure and promotion conflict, a roommate conflict over study habits, and a fight between two key members of the campus baseball team. Each context brings with it certain norms and behavioral expectations (labor relations, human resources, faculty governance, residence life, student activities, athletics, etc.) that can influence our choices regarding model and preferred style.

## Models of Mediation

Program administrators can now choose (either consciously or by default based on their choice of trainers) among a growing variety of relatively distinct mediation models based on different underlying philosophies and preferred formats. We will examine *Problem-solving, Transformative, Narrative, Social Justice* and *Insight* models of mediation in some detail.

Reviewing these models provides program developers with more information as they consider their own goals and the kind of work they hope to accomplish. For example, if a mediation program is being designed to serve the broader community as well as the campus and it welcomes group and town-gown conflicts, the program must be capable of managing multisided and often multiparty conflicts. Often the disputants in these cases have ongoing relationships; therefore, it would be important for the training to value and recognize that conflict is often set in a context of deep personal emotion that may be only ambiguously related to the immediate issues.

However, if a program (say, a student clinical training program) is linked to the business school or labor relations, addressing primarily contract-related disputes, the philosophy of mediators might be informed by collective bargaining characteristics, such as bipolarity and the need to reach a written settlement agreement requiring a training model compatible with this approach. Perhaps the program is designed to focus solely on students, building on the belief that mediation is a vehicle for personal development with an emphasis on future behavior. This too would affect the emphasis of training and choice of model.

## Problem-Solving Mediation

Problem-solving mediation, sometimes referred to as *interest-based mediation*, has been the default model that most mediators are exposed to in their initial training. It is grounded in the principles espoused in the widely read book *Getting to Yes* (Fisher & Ury, 1981) and is well developed in Christopher Moore's book, *The Mediation Process* (1996). Mediators come to understand that conflict parties often have positions that may appear inflexible, but with skillful questioning mediators can help uncover underlying interests that are driving them. Once interests are identified, solutions that let both parties get at least some of what they want can be devised.

The goal is to help parties reach a mutually acceptable agreement. In an interest-based mediation model, based as it is on the norms of an individualist culture, mediators are trained to separate the people from the problem and to keep the focus on the problem itself, encouraging parties to explore data and experiences related to the problem at hand. The approach to the problem is pragmatic, and settlement through bargaining and compromise is a primary goal. The result is that when mediators probe for issues underlying the conflict, they tend to focus on information related to the problem itself rather than on exploring broader issues related to the parties' identities and relationships.

## Evaluative and Facilitative Problem-Solving Styles

Within the broader problem-solving model, a couple of stylistic subtypes, *evaluative* and *facilitative,* have been the subject of much scrutiny and discussion based on a mediator-style grid developed by law professor Len Riskin

(1994, 1996). Riskin (2003) has since revised his model to use the terms *directive* and *elicitive*, but the earlier grid is more well known and quite widely used.

Evaluative mediators are characterized as enacting a more distributive version of the problem-solving approach that assumes that a primary obstacle to settlement is often a party's stubbornness and/or unrealistic assessment of the strength of his or her case under a given set of rules or laws. The mediator sees his or her job as providing parties with a more balanced and realistic positional assessment. Evaluative mediators are characterized as more prone to actively narrowing topics for discussion to legal or contract-related issues, pushing hard for settlement, giving parties their opinion of what seems fair, and working to narrow the "settlement range" in hopes that parties will agree. This style may be most prominent in contexts where parties are contending a single issue such as money (think small claims court, payment disputes, or civil court cases), and where mediators have prior experience exercising considerable decision-making authority (think former judges or business executives).

Facilitative mediators, on the other hand, are portrayed as being much less controlling of the process, leaving the choice of topics and evaluation of options clearly in the hands of the parties. Mediators focus on managing the communication process, helping parties identify and express their underlying interests and needs, assuming that this will reveal areas of overlapping interests that can be used in the crafting of an agreement, often through trade-offs or compromises. It is generally assumed that the parties, when faced with a solution that allows both to get some of what they want, will choose it over more selfish options. The importance of mediator neutrality and impartiality is emphasized as a key to success. This style preference is more common in contexts involving parties with ongoing relationships and cases with multiple tangible and intangible issues (such as divorce or interorganizational conflicts). The facilitative problem-solving style of mediation is probably the normative model offered by the majority of training programs for new mediators.

## Transformative Mediation

In contrast to the problem-solving model, transformative mediators are taught to focus on the relationships of parties involved. The model known as transformative mediation is based on the books *The Promise of Mediation* by Robert Baruch Bush and Joseph Folger (1994, 2005). The approach has its roots in the moral development theories of social psychologist Carol Gilligan (1982), and its creators see conflict mediation as an opportunity for moral growth and development of the participants. The transformative approach does not seek as its goal the resolution of the immediate problem but rather seeks the empowerment and mutual recognition of the parties involved.

Empowerment, according to Baruch Bush and Folger (1994), means enabling the parties to clarify and define their own issues and to seek solutions on their own, increasing their capacity for individual decision making. Recognition means enabling parties to see and understand the other person's point of view—to understand how they have defined the problem and perhaps why they seek the solution that they do. Empowerment and recognition processes may pave the way for a mutually agreeable settlement, but that is only a secondary effect. Baruch Bush and Folger have defined successful mediation as occurring when parties in the mediation process have been

- made aware of the opportunities presented during the mediation for empowerment and recognition;
- helped to clarify goals, options, and resources, and then to make informed, deliberate, and free choices regarding how to proceed at every decision point;
- helped to give recognition to the other wherever it was his or her decision to do so.

The primary goal of transformative mediation is enabling parties to approach their current problem, as well as later problems, with a stronger, more open view. The model seeks to avoid the problem of mediator directiveness believed to occur too often in problem-solving mediation, instead putting responsibility for all outcomes squarely on the disputants. At the college and university level, a National Consortium of University Conflict Transformation Programs has been formed that includes James Madison University's Institute for Conflict Analysis and Intervention, Hofstra University School of Law, University of North Dakota's Conflict Resolution Center, and Temple University's School of Adult Education. These programs provide a good source of information and training related to the transformative model.

## Narrative Mediation

Like transformative mediation, narrative mediation was developed as an alternative to the problem-solving model. *Narrative Mediation* by John Winslade and Gerald Monk (2000) lays out the model in some detail. The approach comes from the tradition of narrative family therapy developed by Michael White and David Epston (1990) in the mid-1980s. It is based upon the premise that we live our lives according to the stories (narratives) that we and others tell about ourselves. Drawing on a postmodern understanding of objectivity, it privileges stories and the meanings within stories over facts and causes. Postmodernism recognizes that one's point of view can never be completely objective and an account of an event is intrinsically linked to one's point of view. One's point of view, by extension, comes directly out of one's sociocultural context.

Conflict occurs through the clash of storied accounts of the people in disagreement. For the narrative mediator, it is the *conflict story* that is viewed as the problem rather than the person or parties. Mediators are interested in how the conflict story affects an individual's life more than whether the story is factual. The conflict stands between the people rather than something that is inside themselves. In the narrative mediation process, conflict parties pass through three broad and often nonlinear phases: *engagement, deconstructing the conflict-saturated story*, and *constructing an alternative story*. Engaging the parties in the process involves creation of an appropriate context for the conversation, whereas the deconstructing process involves "undermin[ing] the certainties on which the conflict feeds and invites the participants to view the plot of the dispute from a different vantage point" (Winslade & Monk, 2000, p. 72). The construction of an alternate narrative is the mediator's prime focus. Construction of the alternative account begins with the belief that a story of cooperation probably already exists and only needs to be uncovered through listening for problems and opportunities or exceptions.

Narrative mediators rely heavily on a technique known as *externalization*. The mediator speaks about the conflict as if it were an external object or third party that has a life of its own. For example, the mediator would not ask questions exploring how Jackie and/or Dave were the cause of the conflict, but rather about how the conflict has caused difficulties between them. The conflict may be named and its history and point of origin traced. The conflict may be vilified and labeled as interfering, tricky, or expensive, and the parties are encouraged to search for ways to escape from the "tyranny" of the problem.

In a new book on practicing narrative mediation, the authors provide nine hallmarks that summarize the model's approach.

1. Assume that people live their lives through stories.
2. Avoid essentialist assumptions.
3. Engage in double listening.

4. Build an externalizing conversation.
5. View the problem story as a restraint.
6. Listen for discursive positioning.
7. Identify openings to an alternative story.
8. Re-author the relationship story.
9. Document progress. (Winslade & Monk, 2008, p. 3)

Using a variety of questioning techniques the mediator generally seeks to develop a better understanding of the narratives behind the conflict and help parties jointly create a new alternative narrative rooted in cooperation and mutual respect.

## Social Justice Mediation

The social justice model of mediation, a variant of the narrative model, pays special attention to the prevention of narrative domination (one story over-shadowing or controlling others) and the replication of racial privileging or oppressive dynamics. The model was developed by Leah Wing and colleagues (see Wing & Rifkin, 2001; Wing, 2002) from the University of Massachusetts at Amherst and is now being used on a growing number of campuses. Research on mediation discourse finds that a challenge facing mediators is helping disputants tell their stories fully and in a way that doesn't involve just reacting to the accusations of the first or most recent speaker (Cobb & Rifkin, 1991). A related challenge for mediators is developing an understanding of how social structures and inequalities limit the kinds of life narratives and ways of framing situations that are possible for members of one group or another and how the mediators' own biases may be playing a part in the process.

Social justice mediation, and narrative mediation more broadly, involves recognizing that one cannot be completely neutral and requires practitioners to take a stand on issues stemming from the dominant societal discourses that create and re-create systems of oppression. Mediators trained in the social justice model spend additional time prior to their mediation skills training learning about oppression theory and core social justice and racial identity development concepts. Within the mediation training, two basic concepts that have traditionally been taught are called into question: neutrality, which means that mediators don't take sides, that they're impartial and equally distant from both parties; and symmetry, which is connected to the concept of fairness—giving each person the same amount of time to speak, for example.

In the social justice model, rather than training mediators to be impartial, mediators learn to be multipartial, able to assist both participants in telling their stories. This can result in the mediation becoming asymmetrical—for example, because of differing communication styles, some people need more time to express themselves. The social justice model also often involves a greater amount of time spent in separate sessions, in a shuttle mediation style, to prevent parties from having to defend their worldviews and react to the others rather than telling their own story fully. Another key for this approach is the availability of a multicultural pool of trained mediators who can create a comfortable and engaging environment for disputants with different experiences and cultural backgrounds. Wing and her colleagues at the Social Justice Mediation Institute have been offering training institutes to help support the spread of the approach.

## Insight Mediation

The insight mediation model (Melchin & Picard, 2008; Picard & Melchin, 2007) is the newest of those described here. It draws on the work of Canadian philosopher Bernard Lonergan (1970) and his theory of insight. The mediation model was developed by a pair of faculty colleagues from Ottawa, Canada, namely Cheryl Picard (Carleton University) and Kenneth Melchin (Saint Paul University). Mediators who practice this approach are trained to look for *direct insights* (moments of clarity, the aha!) and *inverse insights* (realizations that certain assumptions or lines of inquiry are incorrect) into what the conflict means to each party. Primary attention is given to a number of core concepts—the centrality of *learning* (and who is doing it) in conflict, *emotions* and their connection to a party's *values*, and the importance of identifying a party's underlying *cares* and *concerns* (their perceived threats).

Transformative and narrative model proponents generally maintain that probing for information about the problem just tends to keep parties locked into a conflict and that to achieve resolution a shift must be made away from the problem. In contrast, Picard and Melchin find that by focusing on the problem and by exploring the parties' concerns about the conflict, they can break through to a deeper understanding of relational issues of the problem. Insight mediators work under the assumption that conflicts are maintained by feelings of *threat* and work to help parties use the conflict to examine and understand their underlying values and perceived threats to these. Feelings of threat are linked to parties' past experiences, present behaviors, and expectations about the future. Insight mediators use a process of *linking, delinking,* and *verifying* to clarify the source of feelings and to clear up misconceptions. In comparison to the transformative model, focused as it is on the interactions between parties (looking for opportunities to foster empowerment and recognition), and the narrative model where the mediator works to coconstruct a new nonconflict story (and spends little time probing the problem story), the insight model takes parties through an in-depth exploration of the problem rather than around it.

While the insight model shares similarities with the problem-solving model, the difference, according to Picard and Melchin (2007), is that the insight model is relationship centered rather than problem centered and assumes that parties must not only explore the problem but move through and beyond it to gain understanding. Apropos of educational institutions, insight mediation is all about learning, and in particular learning by the parties (as opposed to the curious mediator, judge, or arbiter). This includes

- learning about the deeper cares and concerns of others,
- learning about values and how they are at work in conflict,
- learning about strategies for pursuing values without threatening the values of others.

The model is currently in use at the Carleton University Centre of Conflict Education and Research and taught to students in the Graduate Certificate in Conflict Resolution offered there. The developers view this model as particularly well suited to conflicts where there is an ongoing relationship. Because of the newness of the model, they are inviting researchers and practitioners to evaluate its usefulness in a variety of contexts.

## Conclusion

The opportunities that mediation of campus conflicts can open up are significant for more than just the parties in a conflict. As these models of mediation suggest, the practice of mediation on and off campus has become more nuanced, and mediators are becoming more self-aware and self-confident. In addition to helping parties in a dispute sort out their concerns, the very process of creating a mediation service and training new mediators gets right to the heart of the educational mission. As mediation researcher Kenneth Kressel (2006) aptly notes, "The ability to effectively manage conflict may well be considered one of the basic characteristics of the truly educated person. Training in mediation is an important subset of this ability" (p. 750). Program developers working on college campuses are in a great position to teach and reinforce these basic skills of conflict resolution and to offer powerful learning opportunities in some of the higher-order abilities that these models of mediation bring into view. It is work well worth the attention and dedication it requires.

## References

Baruch Bush, R. A., & Folger, J. (1994). *The promise of mediation: Responding to conflict through empowerment and recognition.* San Francisco: Jossey-Bass.

Baruch Bush, R. A., & Folger, J. P. (2005). *The promise of mediation: The transformative approach to conflict* (Rev. ed.). San Francisco: Jossey-Bass.

Cobb, S., & Rifkin J. (1991). Practice and paradox: Deconstructing neutrality in mediation. *Law and Social Inquiry, 16*, 35–62.

Fisher, R., & Ury, W. (1981). *Getting to yes: Negotiating agreement without giving in.* New York: Penguin.

Gilligan, C. (1982). *In a different voice: Psychological theory and women's development.* Cambridge, MA: Harvard University Press.

Kolb, D. M. (1983). *The mediators.* Cambridge, MA: MIT Press.

Kressel, K. (2006). Mediation revisited. In M. Deutsch, P. T. Coleman, & E. C. Marcus (Eds.), *The handbook of conflict resolution: Theory and practice* (pp. 726–756). San Francisco: Jossey-Bass.

Kressel, K., Frontera, E. A., Forlenza, S., Butler, F., & Fish, L. (1994). "The Settlement-Orientation vs. the Problem-Solving Style in Custody Mediation." *Journal of Social Issues, 50*(1), 67–84.

Levin, A. L., & Wheeler, R. R. (Eds.). (1979). *Perspectives on justice in the future: Proceedings of the National Conference on the Causes of Popular Dissatisfaction With the Administration of Justice.* Egan, MN: West Pub. Co.

Lonergan, B. J. F. (1970). *Insight: A study of human understanding.* New York: Philosophical Library.

Marske, C. E., & Vago, S. (1980). Law and dispute processing in the academic community. *Judicature, 64*(4), 165–175.

Melchin, K. R., & Picard, C. A. (2008). *Transforming conflict through insight.* Toronto, Ontario, Canada: University of Toronto Press.

Moore, C. (1996). *The mediation process: Practical strategies for resolving conflict* (2nd ed.). San Francisco: Jossey-Bass.

Picard, C. A., & Melchin, K. R. (2007). Insight mediation: A learning-centered mediation model. *Negotiation Journal, 23*(1), 35–53.

Riskin, L. L. (1994). Mediator orientations, strategies and techniques. *Alternatives to the High Cost of Litigation, 12*(9), 111–114.

Riskin, L. L. (1996). Understanding mediators' orientations, strategies, and techniques: A grid for the perplexed. *Harvard Negotiation Law Review, 7*, 1.

Riskin, L. L. (2003). Decision making in mediation: The new old grid and the new new grid system. *Notre Dame Law Review, 79*(1), 1.

Rodgers, R. F. (1983). Using theory in practice. In T. K. Miller, R. B. Winston, & W. R. Mendenhall (Eds.), *Administration and leadership in student affairs* (pp. 111–144). Muncie, IN: Accelerated Development.

Ryor, A. (1978, June–July). Who killed collegiality? *Change, 10*(6), 11–12.

Silbey, S. S., & Merry, S. E. (1986). Mediator settlement strategies. *Law & Policy, 8*(1), 7–32.

Waldman, E. A. (1997). Identifying the role of social norms in mediation: A multiple model approach. *Hastings Law Journal, 48*(4), 703, 707–710.

Warters, W. (1998). *The history of campus mediation systems: Research and practice.* Paper presented at the meeting on Reflective Practice in Institutionalizing Conflict Resolution in Higher Education, Georgia State University, Atlanta. Retrieved December 18, 2008, from http://law.gsu.edu/cncr/images/higher_ed/papers/99–1Warterspap.pdf

Warters, W. C. (2000). *Mediation in the campus community: Designing and managing effective programs.* San Francisco: Jossey-Bass.

White, M., & Epston, D. (1990). *Narrative means to therapeutic ends.* New York: Norton.

Wing, A. L. (2002). *Social justice and mediation.* Unpublished doctoral dissertation, University of Massachusetts at Amherst.

Wing, L., & Rifkin, J. (2001). Racial identity development and the mediation of conflicts. In C. Wijeyesinghe & B. W. Jackson (Eds.), *New perspectives on racial identity development: A theoretical and practical anthology* (pp. 182–208). New York: New York University Press.

Winslade, J., & Monk, G. (2000). *Narrative mediation: A new approach to conflict resolution* San Francisco: Jossey-Bass.

Winslade, J., & Monk, G. (2008). *Practicing narrative mediation: Loosening the grip of conflict.* San Francisco: Jossey-Bass.

# 9

# RESTORATIVE JUSTICE FROM THEORY TO PRACTICE

*Andrea Goldblum*

The circle meetings are full of teachable moments. Overall, they give offenders a chance to rethink where they are headed. This could turn a life around.

*Silver Gate Group, 2002*

For colleges and universities to be successful, more is needed than instructors, textbooks, and libraries. The environment or campus climate of the institution is a critical component, as it has the potential to nurture and integrate individuals as valued members of the educational community who have equal opportunities for learning. For many students, the environment is heavily influenced by the quality of relationships with faculty, staff, and other students, and the sense of community or connection. It is, however, difficult to feel connected when there is conflict or victimization that is not addressed appropriately (Reistenberg, 2003). Thus, colleges are also places of social regulation where conflict management and discipline become important aspects of the educational experience.

Most behavioral interventions by college personnel are intended to be educational in nature. But traditional disciplinary processes often have punitive or retributive components, such as suspension, expulsion, exclusion or banning, or loss of privileges. A punitive orientation may lead to increased feelings of resentment and alienation in the offenders rather than making them thoughtful or regretful about the behavior and its impact.

There are certainly situations in which students must be removed from school for their own safety and the safety of others. Suspensions and expulsions may serve to remove students who seriously disrupt the educational process and even provide a cooling-down period. But suspension and expulsion may have little educational value for the affected students except as a punitive lesson. An educational opportunity to provide guidance and intervention may be lost. The very students who are most in need of social support and education may be denied these things. And forced separations from school send the message to students that they are not welcome nor wanted. Some student conduct administrators challenged by past precedent, zero tolerance policies, three strikes you are out protocol, and risk management concerns may feel that this is appropriate. Is it our job, after all, to provide increasing support for students with a history of repeated or very serious violations that may warrant separation from the institution?

The answer is yes; first and foremost, we are in the business of student development and education. But even further, these students continue to have needs that affect the community as well as themselves. Their behavior may not stop; they may move on to other institutions and continue acting out there. They may come back to our own institution once their suspension is complete and may not have any additional support to help them be more successful than they were before they were suspended.

Broadly, Restorative Justice as a theory and practice promotes individual responsibility and community restoration, sometimes immediately, and sometimes long after an incident has affected a group. This chapter, along with chapter 10, considers the use of restorative principles as a pathway option in managing conflict and conduct on campus.

## The Case for Restorative Justice

Restorative Justice (RJ) is a set of principles and practices used in criminal justice systems around the world since the mid-1970s as a method of reforming the way societies deal with crime and other violations. RJ is based on tribal or indigenous practices for peacemaking and responding to wrongdoing, particularly the practices of the Maori people of New Zealand, the Inuits, and the native peoples of the northern Pacific coast of North America. I enjoyed codeveloping one of the first university RJ programs in the late 1990s at the University of Colorado at Boulder.

The main principles of RJ in general involve a shift in the paradigm of how we look at offenses or crimes. Instead of crimes being considered violations of laws or the state, they are considered violations of people, relationships, and community. RJ considers that these violations create obligations, the greatest of which is to identify and repair the harm. This is accomplished, to whatever extent possible, by holding offenders directly responsible to those harmed, rather than or in addition to the state. This is usually done in face-to-face encounters. RJ also gives victims and, in some cases, other affected community members a direct voice in the process and outcomes, hopefully providing a meaningful, healing, and satisfying result for all involved (Zehr, 2002).

Howard Zehr (2002), a pioneer in the field of Restorative Justice, defines RJ as "a process to involve, to the extent possible, those who are most involved in or have a stake in a specific offense and to collectively identify and address harms, needs and obligations, in order to heal and put things as right as possible" (p. 37). Zehr developed three questions that have guided RJ:

- What is the harm that has been done?
- How can that harm be repaired?
- Who is responsible for the repair?

These are in contrast to the questions implicitly or explicitly asked in criminal justice, including: What law was broken? Who broke it? How should the offender be punished?

While the focus of the criminal justice system is predominantly on the offender, and the system is designed to keep the offender and victim apart, RJ strives to balance the rights and needs of all involved in or touched by an offense. The principle is that offenders need to learn empathy and understanding about how their actions affected others. They need to accept responsibility and be accountable for their choices and actions, and to have support in making changes in their lives and in reintegrating into their communities. Victims need information about the offense; for healing to begin, they often need to know the answers to "Why did this happen?" and "Why me?" They also need a greater sense of safety; a voice in the process and a say in the outcome; validation; restitution where applicable; and a sense of justice served. The community needs an opportunity to express its concern as primary or secondary victim, and encouragement to be involved in the welfare of its members (Zehr, 2002).

Key factors in the success of RJ are voluntary engagement of the parties, acceptance of responsibility by the offender, and the underlying philosophy of RJ—reintegrative shaming. The basis of this philosophy is that disapproval of behavior can be expressed in an atmosphere of respect while providing support for the offender to reintegrate into the community without feeling like an outcast (Cameron & Thorsborne, 2001; Strickland, 2004). In other words, it is the behavior rather than the offender that is condemned.

The results of using RJ in criminal justice systems are encouraging. Research has found that victims and the affected community are more satisfied with the process and outcomes of RJ than with the criminal justice system. Offenders are also more satisfied and more likely to comply with outcomes or agreements than with sentencing conditions. They are also less likely to reoffend (Ierley & Classen-Wilson, 2003).

## Restorative Justice Models

No one model encompasses RJ particularly on a college campus. The most common programs at large include victim-offender mediation, community group conferencing, victim panels, and community accountability boards. Some of these are discussed in chapter 10. When applied in the context of the educational environment, RJ has some of the same general goals as the criminal justice system. However, there are more specific goals, including behavioral, developmental, and interpersonal. Goals of RJ programs in higher education may include

- maintaining an environment in which compliance with community standards is an outcome of understanding and a sense of community (Morrison, 2005);
- encouraging accountability and responsibility through personal reflection within a collaborative process;
- reintegrating offending students into the community as valuable contributing members;
- creating caring climates that support healthy communities, lifestyles, and choice (Amstutz & Mullett, 2005);
- creating a culture of inclusion and belonging;
- helping offending students understand the harm they may cause, as well as develop empathy for the harmed;
- listening and responding to needs of offenders and victims;
- preventing escalation of violence;
- promoting collaborative problem solving;
- promoting resiliency;
- teaching negotiation and mediation skills.

Whatever model is used, answering the following questions should be central to the process: What happened? Who has been affected and how? How can the harm be repaired? How can the offender and others make better future choices?

In some cases, RJ programs may be used as diversions from the traditional disciplinary system. In others, they may be used as sanctions, such as the use of victim panels and restoration or community restitution corps. And even when colleges do not have formal RJ programs, they can still use restorative practices and language. For example, instead of talking about policies or laws that were violated or focusing on quasi-legal processes, a discipline officer can discuss and help the student identify who was affected and what harm was caused by the student's behavior. Hearing officers can determine educational sanctions that help the student offender repair harm and make better future choices.

## Essential Restorative Justice Factors

Whatever the model, some factors are essential for RJ programs in colleges and universities to be effective. First and foremost, offending students must accept responsibility for their actions and be held accountable directly to those whom they have harmed. Victims must be given a voice in the process, and the focus of the process must be on harm rather than on rule breaking. In addition, there must be an understanding and acknowledgment that relationships are central to building a sense of community, belonging, and ownership. Conflicts should be viewed as learning opportunities, particularly in helping students learn to solve their own conflicts. The administration should ensure that the program is culturally and developmentally appropriate to the student population, and that collaborative problem solving is encouraged. Students should be empowered to change and grow through storytelling and the appropriate expression of emotions, active listening, and development of empathy (Amstutz & Mullett, 2005; Morrison, 2002).

Restorative justice practices are not appropriate in all cases. In situations in which the offender does not accept responsibility, or the perception of basic facts of a situation differ, some adjudicatory process may be more appropriate. In addition, if the offender is defensive and/or the victim may be revictimized by the process, RJ will not be effective. Finally, in cases in which there is a great power differential, processes that keep participants apart may be the most appropriate. Finally, schools that have a very authoritarian or hierarchical approach to behavior management are unlikely to find RJ approaches to their liking.

Adequate training and other resources are essential to the success of RJ programs. While some processes may take little financial resources or training, such as some uses of circles, others like community group conferencing are time and resource intensive. Programs may take quite a while to get started unless they have dedicated staff with sufficient training. It is also important for all staff involved to be trained in RJ principles and practices.

The design and components of training programs are critical to the success of RJ efforts. If inadequately trained, practitioners may have no effect on participants or even do harm through revictimization or marginilization. Aspects of training should include

- determining which situations are appropriate for RJ interventions;
- determining the appropriate people to invite and engaging them effectively in the process;
- preparing for the process;
- dealing with issues that may arise during the process;
- writing agreements that are doable, clear, realistic. and measurable;
- monitoring compliance with agreements and following up with participants;
- knowing when and how to call off a process if it is not working well;
- ensuring that facilitators can handle the strong emotions that are often an inherent part of the process (Cameron & Thorsborne, 2001).

Finally, it is important to assess RJ programs to ensure they are being appropriately used and that they meet goals in an effective manner. When applied appropriately by trained practitioners with a broad understanding of underlying principals, RJ has been shown to support students in their individual growth and ability to manage conflicts, as well as support communities by assisting students to see their interrelated roles as members of a learning community.

## Applying Restorative Principals That Support Efforts to Curb the Misuse of Alcohol and Other Drugs on Campus

Colleges cater not only to the intellectual development of students but also to their social development. And together with the many healthy and legal outlets for student social development, many colleges, including some of the most academically rigorous, have social and cultural environments in which underage and heavy drinking are accepted, even promoted. In fact, the college party scene is part of the American psyche. But, as pointed out on the Web site College Drinking: Changing the Culture (2007), "The consequences of excessive and underage drinking affect virtually all college campuses, college communities, and college students, whether they choose to drink or not." Moreover, as stated by Rev. Edward A. Malloy, president emeritus at the University of Notre Dame, "Decisions about alcohol consumption are not just individual; they can affect the common life of the university" (National Institute on Alcohol Abuse and Alcoholism [NIAAA], 2007).

William DeJong (2004) states that misuse of alcohol is the principle social problem faced by American higher education. About 83% of college students consume alcohol, and about 41% are heavy or binge drinkers (defined as consuming five or more drinks on a single occasion; NIAAA, 2008). Studies have shown that 48% of students who drink alcohol drink to get drunk (DeJong), 31% meet the criteria for alcohol abuse (College Drinking: Changing the Culture, 2007), and around 6% of students are alcohol dependent (DeJong). The risk is even higher for members of "select" communities, such as Greek organizations, intramural teams, and intercollegiate athletics. For example, 86% of males who live in fraternity houses and 80% of women who live in sorority houses are heavy drinkers (DeJong).

In addition to arrests and disciplinary action because laws and rules are being violated, the results of misuse of alcohol may include physical effects ranging from hangovers to blackouts to alcohol poisoning and even death (about 1,700 student deaths per year are alcohol related). There is also a correlation between heavy alcohol use and lower academic achievement (College Drinking: Changing the Culture, 2007).

Alcohol misuse on college campuses is not a victimless crime, as outlined in Table 9.1. The secondary impacts often involve livability or quality of life issues for other members of the university community and those who live and work close to campuses. For example, students may find their sleep or study time interrupted. Friends have to "babysit" others who are highly intoxicated to make sure they are safe. Students who are too intoxicated to make healthy choices may have unsafe, unprotected sex. Campuses, local businesses, and neighbors often have to deal with trash, vandalism, vomiting, and public urination on their properties, as well as the noise and disruption caused by loud parties. And fights and sexual assaults are often alcohol related. It is estimated that between 50% and 80% of campus violence is alcohol related (DeJong, 2004). In addition, 2.8 million college students drive while they are under the influence of alcohol, placing themselves and all around them at risk (NIAAA, 2007).

In addition to alcohol, other drugs are also an issue on college campuses, as noted in Table 9.2. Not only can drugs affect students' health and academic progress, they can also have an impact on the university community. In addition to community effects similar to those associated with alcohol, the use and sale of drugs by students may result in thefts to get money to support drug habits, assaults, other dangerous behavior from drug deals gone bad, and the presence or use of weapons that sometimes accompany the drug culture.

## TABLE 9.1
### Secondary Impacts of College Student Alcohol Use

- 60% of students had their sleep or studying interrupted by drinking or drunk students
- 48% of students had to take care of a drunk student
- 29% of students were humiliated or insulted
- 20% of women students had received unwanted sexual advances
- 19% of students were in a serious argument
- 15% of students had their property damaged

*Note.* Data taken from "Secondary Effects of Alcohol Abuse," by U.S. Department of Education Higher Education Center for Alcohol and Other Drug Abuse and Violence Prevention, 2008. Retrieved June 2, 2009, from http://www.higheredcenter.org/high-risk/alcohol/second ary-effects.

## TABLE 9.2
### Annual Prevalence of Drug Use Among Full-Time College Students

| | |
|---|---|
| • Any illicit drug | 35% |
| • Marijuana | 32% |
| • Ritalin | 3.7% |
| • Inhalants | 1.5% |

*Note.* From "Monitoring the Future: National Survey Results on Drug Use, 1975–2007, Vol. 2. College Students and Adults Ages 19–45," by L. D. Johnston, P. M. O'Malley, J. G. Bachman, & J. E. Schulenberg, 2008 (NIH Publication No. 08–6418B), Bethesda, MD: National Institute on Drug Abuse.

Colleges often depend on basic awareness programs and/or zero tolerance policies to deal with alcohol and drug misuse; however, evidence indicates that these have had little success overall (DeJong, 2004). College disciplinary systems respond to individual cases of alcohol misuse but often do not work as a deterrent and rarely work to promote cultural change. Interventions at the individual level cannot resolve problems that are part of the cultural landscape (Karp, Breslin, & Oles, 2002). In addition, efforts based on purely moral grounds are likely to be ineffective (DeJong). The most effective way to reduce alcohol and other drug problems on campuses is to change the environment that promotes alcohol and other drug misuse.

## Successful Intervention Measures

The NIAAA Task Force on College Drinking has determined that the most successful interventions are those that simultaneously target the individual student, the student body, and the college or university community; this is called the three-in-one approach (NIAAA, 2007, 2008).

Individual students who are at risk (or who have gotten in trouble) must receive appropriate screening and interventions. However, the students who are most at risk are the least likely to voluntarily use intervention services. And while mandating participation may be useful, voluntary participation is the most effective. It is therefore important to find ways to motivate students to participate.

Participation of the student body in developing intervention strategies is crucial for three reasons. First, students are more likely to be influenced by peers than by university/college administrators. Second, students are the most likely to be affected or victimized by other students' alcohol and drug-related behavior. Third, by actively involving the student body, an us-versus-them dynamic is avoided. Students are often reluctant to report that they have been affected by alcohol or other drug-related behavior, either because they do not want to get peers into trouble or because they accept the inappropriate behavior and its effects as the norm. Responses to misuse must be established that encourage the positive involvement of peers.

Finally, involvement of the community reinforces behavioral norms and expectations. In addition, community coalitions using comprehensive and coordinated approaches have been key in addressing the environment that encourages misuse (DeJong, 2004).

Restorative Justice involves all three of these components, and when used as part of a comprehensive approach it can be effective in reducing the problems associated with alcohol misuse. This model can be uniquely effective in dealing with alcohol and other drug-related cases in which the offender's behavior has affected others in his or her community.

In traditional disciplinary processes, attention may be diverted from the offender's behavior to the process itself or the offender's perceptions of the fairness of the rule or law or whether "everyone else does it." RJ focuses attention directly on the offender's behavior and the decision-making process that resulted in the behavior. If alcohol or other drug use was a factor in the behavior, it is almost certain to arise as part of the discussion, both in describing the incident and in determining how the offender can make better future choices. If part of an outcome or contract focuses on alcohol or drug education, intervention, or treatment, the voluntary nature of the agreement should make the student more motivated to comply with and succeed in any program. What makes RJ effective in situations involving alcohol and drugs is the intensely personal nature of the interactions.

RJ is not appropriate for all alcohol and other drug-related cases. Very serious cases in which campus safety necessitates suspension or dismissal, like those involving drug sales, sexual assaults with alcohol, or other drug involvement, are not usually appropriate for RJ. Some RJ processes are very labor intensive; therefore, for very minor cases RJ may not be the best use of resources.

Situations in which RJ is most applicable are those in which there is a normative violation that has an impact on other individuals or the community. RJ programs have been effectively used in everything from vandalism by drunk students to out-of-control parties and even alcohol-related riots. Most often, RJ programs serve as diversions from traditional disciplinary or criminal justice systems. For example, at the University of Minnesota, when police cite students in the residence halls, they also provide information about the RJ program. The student then has three days to apply for the program (Carew, 2007). At the University of Colorado at Boulder (2007), student offenders may be referred to the RJ program by the court, by police officers, or by a judicial affairs hearing officer. The incentive for students to take part in RJ programs may be a clean disciplinary record if students successfully complete the program.

## Restorative Justice Program Models

A number of RJ program models can be used for alcohol and other drug-related incidents or cases.

### *Community Group Conferences*

Community Group Conferences are the most traditional of restorative justice models and are often called *circles*, based on the physical placement of the people involved. Community group conferences can be especially effective in dealing with alcohol and other drug-related cases that have a wider impact, or when others have been harmed. In community group conferences, the student offender is involved in face-to-face dialogue with the people who were most affected by the student offender's behavior. The circle of participants is enlarged to include supporters of the offender and the victim. Each person has an opportunity to speak, and all participants must listen. There is no back-and-forth adversarial discussion, which creates an atmosphere in which the student offender may be less defensive and more open to hearing and understanding the impact of his or her actions and the role alcohol or other drugs played.

The group discusses the incident and identifies the harm done. The members then work to come to a consensus and develop an agreement on how the offender can repair the harm and what needs to be done to help the offender make better future choices. The circle is a safe place for friends and supporters to express concern about the student offender's drinking or other drug use. The circle also provides a forum for building or rebuilding positive relationships. Because all participants have a stake in the outcome, mentoring relationships between community members and the student offender may result. This can provide additional support for the student offender to deal with substance abuse issues. Some facilitators may even have a substance abuse counselor or wellness professional present to participate in the circle to address substance abuse issues directly and personally. These participants may also provide a reality check about college students' use of alcohol and other drugs, as students surrounded by a peer group of heavy drinkers or drug users often develop a misperception of what is "normal" or acceptable behavior in the greater community.

### Community Accountability Boards

Community accountability boards are often used for violations involving quality of life or "livability" issues. They are particularly effective when a victim cannot be identified or does not want to participate in a circle, or when the community is the victim. They are also valuable when large numbers of cases require a response that is timelier and less resource-intensive than community group conferences, or if it's a single case with a large number of participants. The key is that the board members give expression to the community's norms and expectations, and offenders are held directly accountable to the community that their behavior affected.

Community accountability boards are typically composed of members of a community and an adviser. For college student offenses, such boards may comprise members of affected neighborhoods, peer students, faculty, or a mix of constituent representatives. Offenders tell their story to the board members then hear the impact of their actions from either the involved parties or from members of the board. The board determines an outcome or the student and the board members will negotiate a contract.

Outcomes from accountability boards often include community restitution in the form of service in the affected community. Many community impact boards work directly with neighborhood groups and associations or with municipal programs to sponsor and supervise such programs. For example, students who threw a party that got out of control may find themselves picking up party litter in their neighborhood.

## Victim Panels

When traditional disciplinary or intervention programs are used, it may be clear to the administrator involved that the student offender does not realize the effect of his or her actions, the scope of the impact, or the potential risk the offender posed, and needs to hear it directly from the victim. In some cases, the victim may be unknown. In other situations, a victim may not feel comfortable interacting directly with the offender or sharing how he or she was affected. Or administrators may not have the appropriate experience or skill set to be able to facilitate or mediate such an interaction. In situations like these, panels may be made up of victims of other situations that are similar; in essence, they are "surrogate" victims who can effectively communicate the victim's perspective. The goal is to help identify the harm that was caused or could have been caused by the offender's actions as well as to help the offender develop empathy. Victim panels are typically used as sanctions offenders are assigned to. Such panels have been extensively used by the courts in cases involving driving under the influence of alcohol.

## Restorative Circles

At times the line between victim and offender is blurred, such as in fights or mutual harassment. Incidents like these are more likely to occur when drinking is involved. In other situations with ongoing tension between groups of students, the conflict may erupt when fueled by alcohol. In such instances a modification of the community group conference may be used. The goal of restorative circles is to restore the sense of peace and community, to defuse tensions and conflicts, and to explore mutual responsibility and impact (University of Colorado, 2007).

## Reentry Circles

Some offenses may be so serious or have such an impact that separation or suspension from the college or university is appropriate. RJ can still be effective in the form of reentry circles following the period of suspension when a student is ready to return to campus. The process is similar to the community group conference but without the goal of developing a contract to repair harm. The goals of reentry circles are to clear the air of outstanding grievances, check in to see how everyone is doing, and assist the offender in reassimilating into the community. It is important that the affected community hear the offender accept responsibility for his or her actions, as well as for the offender to understand the scope of the impact. The offender may also share what has happened during his or her absence, including any intervention strategies used, to demonstrate that the risk of a recurrence of behavior is not likely or that the offender is committed to upholding community norms.

### Check-In Circle

The check-in circle may be useful for students who are in recovery programs. It is a group communication tool that allows group members to check in on how they are doing with sobriety and the recovery process. It differs from group therapy in that no one provides therapy or has greater power than any of the others in the circle. Members can provide mutual support, as well as share observations and concerns about each other. In addition, should a member leave the recovery program because of a relapse, the check-in circle can help that person explain what happened and help ease reintegration into the group (Reistenberg, 2005). Check-in circles can also be used in smaller communities, such as residence hall floors or living units, to ensure that any lingering concerns, hurts, resentments, and other emotions after an incident are attended to.

### Restoration Corps

Finally, in response to quality-of-life violations, students may be assigned or may agree to perform community restitution to directly repair the environmental harm. When large numbers of students are involved or such assignments occur regularly, establishing a program to manage the logistics can make this more effective and efficient. The University of Colorado at Boulder (2007) has a program called the Buff Restoration Corps, in which a volunteer takes students to clean up party debris on Saturday mornings.

## Conclusion

When used appropriately, Restorative Justice can have a truly transformative effect on individual students, including those involved with alcohol and other drug-related incidents. The process can promote better communication and increased motivation to change behavior on the part of the offender. Because of the nature of interactions in RJ processes, the consequences (which may actually differ little from those given in formal disciplinary processes) tend to be more meaningful and have a deeper and longer-lasting impact. The involvement of victims and other harmed/affected parties promotes the building of a sense of community that cares about all its members, even offenders, while it can help victims recover or heal. The following chapter explores RJ language and practices further in the context of student conduct boards and RJ conferences.

## References

Amstutz, L., & Mullett, J. ( 2005). *The little book of restorative discipline for schools.* Intercourse, PA: Good Books.

Cameron, L., & Thorsborne, M. (2001). Restorative justice and school discipline: Mutually exclusive? In H. Strang & J. Braithwaite (Eds.), *Restorative justice and civil society* (pp. 180–194). Cambridge, UK: Cambridge University Press.

Carew, E. (2007). *Residence halls get new kind of justice.* Retrieved August 15, 2008, from http://www.mndaily.com/articles/2007/09/24/72163495

College Drinking: Changing the Culture. (2007). *A snapshot of annual high-risk college drinking consequences.* Retrieved September 26, 2008, from http://www.col legedrinkingprevention.gov/StatsSummaries/snapshot. aspx

DeJong, W. (2004). The impact of alcohol on campus life. In D. Karp & T. Allena (Eds.), *Restorative justice on the college campus: Promoting student growth and responsibility, and reawakening the spirit of campus community* (pp. 101–119). Springfield, IL: Charles C Thomas.

Ierley, A., & Classen-Wilson, D. (2003). Making things right: Restorative justice for school communities. In T. Jones & R. Compton (Eds.), *Kids working it out* (pp. 199–219). San Francisco: Jossey-Bass.

Karp, D., Breslin, B., & Oles, P. (2002). Community justice in the campus setting. *Conflict Management in Higher Education Report, 3*(1). Retrieved August 15, 2008, from http://www.campus-adr.org/cmher/ReportArticles/Edition3_1/Karp3_1a .html

Morrison, B. (2002). Bullying and victimization in schools: A restorative justice approach. *Australian Institute of Criminology: Trends and Issues in Crime and Criminal Justice, 219,* 1–6.

Morrison, B. (2005, March). *Building safe and healthy school communities: Restorative justice and responsive regulation.* Presented at the meeting of Building a Global Alliance for Restorative Practices and Family Empowerment, Part 3, Penrith, New South Wales, Australia.

National Institute on Alcohol Abuse and Alcoholism. (2007). *What colleges need to know now: An update on college drinking research* (NIH Publication No. 07–5010). Washington DC: U.S. Department of Health and Human Services.

National Institute on Alcohol Abuse and Alcoholism. (2008). *Research findings on college drinking and the minimum legal drinking age.* Retrieved September 28, 2008, from http://www.niaaa.nih.gov/ABOUTNIAAA/NIAAASponsoredpro grams/drinkingage

Reistenberg, N. (2003). *Restorative schools grants final report—January 2002–June 2003.* St. Paul: Minnesota Department of Education.

Reistenberg, N. (2005). *PEASE Academy: The Restorative Recovery School.* Retrieved September 26, 2008, from http://www.safersanerschools.org/library/pease academy.html

Silver Gate Group. (2002, Spring). Restorative justice on the new frontier. *Prevention File, 17*(2), 7–9.

Strickland, R. (2004). *Restorative justice.* New York: Peter Lang.

University of Colorado at Boulder. (2007). *Restorative Justice Program academic year report*: August 1, 2006–May 11, 2007. Boulder: Author.

Zehr, H. (2002). *The little book of restorative justice.* Intercourse, PA: Good Books.

# READING THE SCRIPTS

Balancing Authority and Social Support in the
Restorative Justice Conference and the
Student Conduct Hearing Board

*David R. Karp*

The aim of education is to reveal an attainable
image of self that is lovelier than that manifested
in his or her present acts.

*Noddings, 1984, p. 193*

T he educational process can help students aspire to higher accomplishments than those troubled situations they sometimes find themselves in. Indeed, the Council for the Advancement of Standards in Higher Education (2006) argues, "Student Conduct Programs must identify relevant and desirable student learning and development outcomes and provide programs that encourage the achievement of those outcomes" (p. 3). This chapter explores the learning environment created in student conduct practices through a dissection of the scripts used in student conduct board hearings (SCBHs) and in restorative justice conferences (RJCs) to identify the educational and developmental opportunities embedded in each practice.

Prominent leaders in student conduct administration Ed Stoner and John Lowery (2004) present a template or Model Student Code of Conduct for colleges and universities with a model hearing script. While Stoner and Lowery recommend the use of an SCBH, they also allow that "a college or university may wish to institute either an arbitration or a mediation requirement prior to reaching the more formal Student Conduct Board Hearing stage. . . . In some cases a formal fact finding process is not required" (pp. 47–48). In this chapter, I will contrast one alternative process—restorative justice—with the SCBH. Each has its own model script, and the chapter explores how the process unfolds in each case.

Restorative justice is a popular variant of mediation and offers a variety of practice models (Barton, 2003; Karp & Allena, 2004; Van Ness & Strong, 1997; Zehr, 1990). On the college campus, two restorative practices are most common: the RJC and the accountability board. The restorative justice accountability board (sometimes called integrity boards and reparative boards) may be seen as a hybrid between the SCBH and the RJC. Rather than focus on the overlap, however, this chapter focuses on the differences in practice between the SCBH and the RJC, especially on issues of authority and social support and central concepts in sociology and criminology.

## Characteristics of the SCBH and the RJC

A traditional SCBH model as advanced by Stoner and Lowery (2004) often consists of a chair who oversees the hearing, ensuring that the process is followed according to plan. Although Stoner and Lowery do not specify the membership of a conduct board, they commonly include representatives from students, faculty, and/or the administration. A hearing invites participation of the *accused student* (student accused of violating the code of conduct), *complainant* (the person submitting the charge, which may be a victim of the offending behavior or a college official), *advisers* for the accused student and/or complainant, *witnesses* to the incident, and *character witnesses* on behalf of the accused student.

By contrast, the RJC has two cofacilitators who share responsibility for overseeing the process. They meet with conference participants in advance to prepare them for the conference and to assess whether the case is appropriate for an RJC. Participants typically include the *student responsible* (a student who has admitted violating the code of conduct), *harmed parties* (people who were affected by the incident), and *support people* for both the responsible and harmed parties.

## Dissecting the Scripts—Stage One

Table 10.1 presents the first stage of the RJC and the SCBH. This stage includes introductions of participants and some guidelines and expectations for the conference or hearing. The restorative script is used by Skidmore College (my institution) and is an adaptation of several published and unpublished restorative scripts (Barton, 2003; Dinnan, 2007; O'Connell, Wachtel, & Wachtel, 1998). The conduct board script is quoted verbatim from Stoner and Lowery (2004, pp. 68–76).

## TABLE 10.1
### Introduction and Ground Rules

| RJC Script | SCBH Script |
| --- | --- |
| • Welcome everybody. Before the formal part of the conference begins, I would like us to introduce ourselves and indicate briefly our reasons for being here. I am _____ and I will be co-facilitating today's conference. | *Begin tape recorder.* |
| | • Good afternoon, my name is [_____], and I will be serving as the chair of the Student Conduct Board. My role is to oversee the Student Conduct Board Hearing that will be conducted today. Please note that today's Student Conduct Board Hearing is being tape-recorded. This recording represents the sole official verbatim record of the Student Conduct Board Hearing and is the property of this institution. At this time, I will ask the members of the Student Conduct Board to introduce themselves. |
| • Thank you for attending. At today's conference, we will be focusing on the [*incident*] that happened on [*date*]. We will focus on what _____ [*first name of student responsible*] did and its impact on others. Once we have learned more about what happened, we will identify what harm was caused and how it might be repaired. We will also focus on what can be done to reassure us that the behavior will not be repeated. | |
| | • Would the Accused Student(s) introduce himself/herself (themselves)? |
| | • Would the Accused Student's advisor introduce himself/herself (*if present*)? |
| | • Would the Complainant introduce himself/herself? |
| | • Would the Complainant's advisor introduce himself/herself (*if present*)? |
| | • Would the individuals who are here today as possible witnesses introduce themselves? |
| • This conference is voluntary. We do not have to reach an agreement today, and if we do not, the issue will be referred back to the [*conduct administrator*] and handled in a different way. I am hopeful that we will reach an agreement and, if so, we will submit it to the [*conduct administrator*] for approval. It is possible, but rare, that the [*conduct administrator*] will want to make changes to the agreement. Does everybody understand this? | *If the Complainant or the Accused Student has an advisor, read the following statement:* |
| | • The role of the advisor during this Student Conduct Board Hearing is limited. It reflects that this process is not a courtroom proceeding, but is part of the institution's programs that are designed to provide a good living/learning environment for all members of our academic community. An advisor may not question witnesses or make statements before the Student Conduct Board. The only appropriate role for the advisor is to provide advice to the student who has requested his/her presence in a manner which does not disturb the proceedings of the Student Conduct Board. If an advisor fails to act in accordance with the procedures of the Student Conduct Board, he/she will be barred from these proceedings. |
| • One goal of this conference is to create an environment in which everyone can speak freely and fully about how they feel about what happened. As facilitators, our job is to ensure that everyone here has a voice. Sometimes we will have open dialogue in which everyone can participate as they wish; at other times we will go around the circle inviting | • I would like to remind everyone participating in this Student Conduct Board Hearing that falsification, distortion, or misrepresentation before the Student Conduct Board is a violation of the Student Code. Any person who abuses the Student Code System in this way may face disciplinary charges for that violation. Witnesses, other than the Accused Student and the Complainant, are present in |

**TABLE 10.1  (Continued)**

| RJC Script | SCBH Script |
|---|---|
| each person to offer their perspective. When we do, a person can always pass if they do not have anything they want to say at that time. <br><br> • Another job for us as facilitators is to create an environment of trust, so that we can speak honestly about the incident. To enable this, will everyone agree that what is said in this circle will stay in the circle—that we will not talk about what people have said here to others? <br><br> • Does anybody have any questions about the process before we begin? Please ask at any time. | the Student Conduct Board Hearing only while offering their information. <br><br> • Would all witnesses, other than the Accused Student and the Complainant, please leave the Student Conduct Board Hearing room and wait outside. You will be asked to reenter the Student Conduct Board Hearing to offer your testimony. Before we proceed, are there any questions? <br><br> • The Accused Student and the Complainant may challenge any member of the Student Conduct Board for bias if you believe that he or she cannot be fair in this Student Conduct Board Hearing. Does the Accused Student wish to challenge any member of the Student Conduct Board for bias? Does the Complainant wish to challenge any member of the Student Conduct Board for bias? [*If so, the student should be asked to explain what might prevent the member from participating fairly in the Student Conduct Board Hearing and the chair may then recess the Student Conduct Board Hearing briefly to consider and to decide the challenge.*] |

*Note.* SCBH Script from Stoner and Lowery (2004, pp. 68–76).

The introduction to the process sets a tone. At the outset, it is clear that the RJC and the SCBH differ, especially in their formality. Nevertheless, every student conduct process seeks to balance two goals that are in tension—authority and social support. One goal is to convey to participants that the process is meant to be taken seriously. The administration is concerned with conduct and wants all to know that the process may have real consequences for the participants, the response will be commensurate with the severity of the incident, and the process is not arbitrary but thoughtfully conceived and implemented. This may be defined as the goal of establishing *authority.* One of the founding fathers of sociology, Max Weber examined the basis of authority, especially legal authority, and found that it is established when it is impersonal, abstract, consistent, and rational (Trevino, 1996). It is vital to establish authority in a student conduct process, otherwise it loses legitimacy.

But another goal is to create an atmosphere of *social support* conducive to honest communication, active participation, open dialogue, and personal commitment to change. While the first goal lends itself to an austere, formal proceeding, the latter nudges toward informal and personal discussion. Social support can be defined as emotional or instrumental help that assists the person and builds relationships. One of the world's leading criminologists, Francis Cullen (1994), goes so far as to argue that "across nations and across communities, crime rates vary inversely with the level of social support" (p. 537). In other words, providing social support is an essential ingredient to responsible behavior.

The opening scripts of the RJC and SCBH offer an opportunity for participants to introduce themselves and to learn about how the process will unfold. But, the use of language here is quite important. Notice the use of nonoverlapping terms found in each of the scripts in Table 10.2.

The aggregation of these terms sets the tone for the process. Typically, conduct processes seek to avoid courtroom language; indeed Stoner and Lowery (2004) argue that "the practice of calling student discipline proceedings 'judicial' . . . [is a] 'cardinal error'" (p. 15). The SCBH reflects this ideal

## TABLE 10.2
**Introductory Scripted Language Contrasting Social Support and Authority**

| *RJC* | *SCBH* |
|---|---|
| Conference | Chair |
| Co-facilitator | Hearing |
| Incident | Tape recording |
| Harm | Official verbatim record |
| Repair | Accused |
| Reassure | Complainant |
| Behavior | Statements |
| Voluntary | Witnesses |
| Agreement | Proceedings |
| Issue | Procedures |
| Voice | Barred |
| Dialogue | Falsification |
| Circle | Distortion |
| Trust | Misrepresentation |
| Honesty | Violation |
| | Code system |
| | Disciplinary charges |
| | Testimony |
| | Challenge |
| | Bias |

when it replaces, for example, the term *defendant* with *complainant* and the term *trial* with *hearing*. However, to establish authority, it still makes use of other terms, such as *statements, witnesses,* and *testimony*. The RJC avoids such language more universally to further set it apart from a quasi-courtroom experience.

One important example of the authority/social support comparison is the difference between the role of the SCBH chair and the RJC cofacilitators. The term *chair* implies a power hierarchy, that the person in the role has an important directive role. Having cofacilitators suggests that power is devolved, and that even between the two roles, emphasis is on running a process instead of determining decisions for others.

This egalitarian decision-making model is also implied in the restorative conference by assuming all participants are present voluntarily and will remain throughout the conference. Role differentiation is emphasized in the conduct board by (a) introducing and identifying participants by their position, for example, accused student; (b) narrowly prescribing the way in which various participants can speak, for example, the adviser cannot question witnesses or make statements; and (c) excluding participants from the hearing at various points depending on their role. Such differentiation establishes a carefully crafted power structure that helps ensure authority, that the process will be undertaken efficiently and fairly, participants will be constrained to ensure civility, and that the power lies primarily with those who will remain present throughout the entire process. That is, the chair and other board members who are the only ones to obtain full information, in the end will make the decisions.

In contrast, the RJC suggests a more open but uncertain or ambiguous process. Roles are not clearly defined, fewer ground rules are established, and no tape recording is made. The emphasis is on participation, with suggestions that all will have a chance to speak, that open dialogue will occur, and that finding agreement is not mandatory but is in the hands of participants. Restorative practices sacrifice some authority in favor of building an atmosphere of trust, inclusion, and empowerment.

## Dissecting the Scripts—Stage Two

The next stage in both processes (Table 10.3) is focused on information gathering. In the RJC, the process includes narrative accounts by all participants, sharing from their perspective what happened and how they were affected by the incident. There is an opportunity for participants to ask questions of each other and react to statements others have made.

In the SCBH, the accused student states whether he or she is in violation, and the board evaluates presented evidence. At this stage, accused students, complainants, and others (except advisers) are treated as witnesses to the incident, all providing information about what happened. Board members are allowed to ask questions of witnesses, and accused students and complainants are able to ask questions as long as they are directed to the chair of the board.

The first spoken statement in the restorative conference illustrates the most important difference between models: The case was referred to the RJC because the student responsible has taken responsibility for what happened (and is offered an opportunity to resolve the incident via an RJC diversion program) and/or *admitted* to violating the code of conduct (therefore participating in the RJC as part of the *sanction* phase of the disciplinary process). In contrast, the conduct board is convened with the emphasis of determining whether the student is in violation. The SCBH has a *due process* focus, making sure that facts are revealed carefully and accurately. In keeping with the value of authority, the conduct board is concerned with *objectivity* and determining, through evidence, what really happened at the incident.

The RJC is less concerned with the facts, though they are not irrelevant. Instead, because the student has admitted fault, the conference is more concerned with the *subjective* experience of stakeholders in identifying how they were affected by the incident. Because of this difference, cases in which a student is professing innocence would not be referred to a restorative conference. Note again that there are hybrid models including restorative accountability boards that *are* designed to take cases that require fact finding, just like a SCBH. To avoid confusion in this chapter, I am focusing on the restorative conferencing and the conduct hearing board only to highlight the distinctions between models.

Because restorative justice focuses less on fact finding than on personal narratives, it moves proceedings in a different direction than the conduct board hearing. Often, an SCBH will be concerned not only with the question of whether the student violated the code of conduct but with which code was violated. The student might have been charged, for example, with violating code numbers 3, 8, and 11, but will argue that he or she only violated number 3. Nuanced and lengthy evidence analyses often ensue while the board investigates and then deliberates about the right assignation. The RJC is little concerned with this issue. Instead, the line of inquiry is on determining the nature of harm caused by the offending behavior. Visually, a cofacilitator tracks stated harms as they are described on a flip chart for all to view. In restorative justice, a major goal is to educate offenders about the

## TABLE 10.3
### Information Gathering: Harm Identification Versus Violation Identification

| *RJC Script* | *SCBH Script* |
|---|---|
| *Co-facilitator takes notes. When everyone has spoken, the notes are summarized and harms are listed on a flip chart. Then the group is asked for confirmation and completeness.* | • The Student Conduct Board is considering charges, which have been brought against [_____], the Accused Student, by [_____], the Complainant in today's Student Conduct Board Hearing. Under the Student Code, [_____], the Accused Student, has been charged with the following violations of the Student Code: |
| *All questions below are suggested prompts. Facilitator can modify as appropriate.* | *The Student Conduct Board Chair reads each of the violations of the Student Disciplinary Code, which the Accused Student is alleged to have violated.* |
| *To everyone:* | |
| We will start the conference by asking everyone to tell us about what happened from their perspective. We will start with the person(s) responsible and then hear from his/her supporter(s), and then hear from harmed parties and their supporters. | • Would the Accused Student please respond to each of the charges, which I have just read indicating whether you accept responsibility for violating this provision of the Student Code? |
| *To student responsible:* | *If the Accused Student does not accept responsibility for violating each of the provisions of the Student Code listed above, then the Student Conduct Board Hearing shall proceed. If the Accused Student does accept responsibility for violating each of the provisions of the Student Code listed above, then the Student Conduct Board Hearing shall proceed with the presentation of information limited to that which should be considered in the imposition of sanctions.* |
| • _____<br>[*name*], you have already admitted your involvement in this incident. Before you tell us about what happened, is there anything you would like to say? | |
| • Please tell us what happened. How did you get involved? | • At this time, we will begin the portion of the Student Conduct Board Hearing during which information is presented for consideration in determining if the Accused Student has or has not violated the Student Code. |
| • What was going through your mind at the time? | *Witnesses may be asked to swear or affirm to tell the truth at this point if the institution wishes to follow this practice.* |
| • How did you feel about what happened right afterward and how do you feel now? | • The Complainant and Accused Student will be provided the opportunity to share introductory remarks, which should not exceed five (5) minutes. You are not required to do so. If you have prepared an Impact Statement in writing or wish to make one orally, you may do so at this time. Are there any questions before we proceed with any introductory remarks? |
| • Who do you think has been affected by this? How? | |
| • Who do you think is responsible for this incident and its consequences? [*Watch out for any victim-blaming and intervene if it occurs*] | • Would the Complainant in this case like to make introductory remarks? If so, please proceed. |
| • Have you been in trouble like this before? [*If student responsible fails to reveal documented past incidents, facilitators are to raise them.*] | • Would the Accused Student in this case like to make introductory remarks? If so, please proceed. |
| | • At this time, the Student Conduct Board will hear witnesses offer testimony for consideration in determining if |

## TABLE 10.3 (Continued)

| *RJC Script* | *SCBH Script* |
| --- | --- |
| • Is there anything else you would like to say at this point?<br><br>• Thank you<br><br>*To supporters of student responsible:*<br><br>• How did you find out initially about what happened?<br><br>• What did you think when you first heard?<br><br>• What has happened since?<br><br>• How do you feel about the incident now?<br><br>• What do you see as the harmful consequences of this incident?<br><br>• Is there anything else you would like to say at this point?<br><br>• Thank you<br><br>*To primary, then secondary harmed parties:*<br><br>• Thank you for your patience.<br><br>• Please tell us what happened from your perspective and what it has meant for you.<br><br>• In what ways were you affected by this incident?<br><br>• How do you feel about the incident now?<br><br>• Is there anything you would like to ask _____ [*student responsible*]?<br><br>• Is there anything else you would like to say at this point?<br><br>• Thank you<br><br>*To harmed party supporters:*<br><br>• How did you find out initially about what happened?<br><br>• What did you think when you first heard?<br><br>• What has happened since? | the Accused Student has or has not violated the Student Code. The Student Conduct Board will begin by calling witnesses to present testimony. After the Student Conduct Board has called all the witnesses it considers appropriate, the Complainant, followed by the Accused Student, will be afforded the opportunity to call additional witnesses.<br><br>• The members of the Student Conduct Board will have the opportunity to question each witness. Witnesses called by the Student Conduct Board may be questioned by the Complainant, followed by the Accused Student, after the Student Conduct Board has concluded its questioning. Witnesses called by the Complainant and Accused Student will be questioned initially by the Student Conduct Board. Following the conclusion of the Student Conduct Board's questioning, the individual calling the witness will have the opportunity to have questions asked of the witness. Following the conclusion of this questioning, the other individual will have the opportunity to have questions asked of the witness. Before a witness is excused, the chair will ask members of the Student Conduct Board and the Complainant and Accused Student if they have any final questions.<br><br>• All questions by the Complainant and Accused Student of witnesses should be directed to the chair of the Student Conduct Board.<br><br>• Are there any questions before witnesses testify? [*Typically, the Complainant will be asked to testify first, followed by the Accused Student, and then other witnesses.*]<br><br>• At this time, the Board will hear from the Complainant. Do the members of the Student Conduct Board have any questions for this witness?<br><br>*After completion of questioning by the Student Conduct Board:*<br><br>• Does the Complainant wish to provide any additional information to the Board?<br><br>• Does the Accused Student have any questions to be directed to the Complainant? Please remember to direct your questions to the chair of the Student Conduct Board.<br><br>• At this time, the board will hear from the Accused Student.<br><br>• Do the members of the Student Conduct Board have any questions for this witness? |

## TABLE 10.3 (Continued)

| RJC Script | SCBH Script |
|---|---|
| • How do you feel about the incident now? | *After completion of questioning by the Student Conduct Board:* |
| • What do you see as the harmful consequences of this incident? | • Does the Accused Student wish to provide any additional information to the board? |
| • Is there anything else you would like to say at this point? | • Does the Complainant have any questions to be directed to the Accused Student? Please remember to direct your questions to the chair of the Student Conduct Board. |
| • Thank you | |
| *To student responsible:* | *After the Complainant and the Accused Student have testified, the following procedures will be followed for additional witnesses called by the Student Conduct Board.* |
| • _____ | |
| [*name*], you have now had a chance to hear about how the incident has affected everyone, is there anything you would like to say at this time? | • The next witness to be called by the Student Conduct Board is [_____]. Do the members of the Student Conduct Board have any questions for this witness? |
| *To everyone:* | *After the completion of the questioning by the Student Conduct Board:* |
| • Is there anything you would like to say in response? | • Does the Complainant have any questions for this witness? Please remember to direct your questions to the chair of the Student Conduct Board. |
| *Facilitators may wish to shift primary leadership at this point and have the facilitator who has been listing harms lead the review of them and the brainstorming process to find solutions.* | *After the completion of questions suggested by the Complainant:* |
| | • Does the Accused Student have any questions for this witness? Please remember to direct your questions to the chair of the Student Conduct Board. |
| • We will now summarize our list of harms. | *After the completion of questions suggested by the Accused Student:* |
| • Is there anything to be changed or added? | • Are there any final questions before this witness is excused? Thank you very much for taking the time to participate in this Student Conduct Board Hearing of the Student Conduct Board. Your participation is appreciated. Please do not discuss with other potential witnesses the information you have shared with us today. |
| | *This process is repeated until the Student Conduct Board has called each witness.* |
| | • At this time, the Complainant and the Accused Student will be provided the opportunity to make concluding remarks. You are not required to do so. Are there any questions before we proceed? Would the Complainant in this case like to make concluding remarks? If so, please proceed. |
| | • Would the Accused Student in this case like to make concluding remarks? If so, please proceed. |

**TABLE 10.3  (Continued)**

| RJC Script | SCBH Script |
|---|---|
| | • At this time, we would ask that the Complainant, Accused Student, and their advisors (*if any*) leave the Student Conduct Board Hearing room so that the members of the Student Conduct Board may determine if the Accused Student is responsible for any of the violations of the Student Code with which he/she has been charged. |
| | • After the determination regarding responsibility is made, you will be asked to return to this room. The Student Conduct Board will announce its decision regarding responsibility. If the Accused Student is found not responsible concerning all charges, the Student Conduct Board Hearing will be adjourned. If the Accused Student is found responsible concerning any charges, the Student Conduct Board will consider the following additional information related to sanctioning. |
| | A. Character witnesses on behalf of the Accused Student; |
| | B. Any prior violations of the Student Code by the Accused Student; and |
| | C. Recommendations for sanctioning from the Complainant and the Accused Student. |
| | *Turn the tape recorder off. Once the Student Conduct Board has concluded its deliberations concerning responsibility on each alleged violation, the Complainant, and Accused Student are called back into the Student Conduct Board Hearing.* |

*Note.* SCBH Script from Stoner and Lowery (2004, pp. 68–76).

consequences of their behavior, in large part because so few have considered them beyond their own personal concerns.

This stage continues the contrast between authority and social support. Facilitators use participants' names rather than addressing them by role (e.g., accused student). This signals that informality and personal recognition are more important than role differentiation. RJC facilitators invite participants to ask each other questions, while the conduct board chair asks that all questions be channeled through the board. As Stoner and Lowery (2004) note, the SCBH chair repeatedly reminds participants to direct their questions to the board to reduce the risk of conflict between complainant and accused, and maintain "a process that is calm rather than confrontational" (p. 65). This is a reasonable concern especially when accused students are denying responsibility, but less important when they have already made an admission.

One of the most notable distinctions between the two models in this stage is the introduction of the private deliberation process in the conduct board hearing. All other participants are excused while the board deliberates to determine if the student is in violation. (A second deliberation occurs when the board decides the nature of the sanction). This again highlights the value placed on authority by preventing all the participants from hearing all the information and having a voice in all the decisions. Restorative justice practitioners believe keeping all participants present throughout increases trust because they will have a full understanding of others' viewpoints and why each decision has been made.

Participants' roles are quite different in the two practices. The SCBH refers to *accused student*. The term *student responsible* in the RJC highlights the admission of responsibility. In the conduct board hearing, a student victimized by an incident is called a *complainant* and in the restorative conference, he or she is called a *harmed party*. Again the terms signal the emphasis in the SCBH that the victim's role is to present evidence (complaint) to determine responsibility, and in the RJC the role is to describe how he or she was affected by misconduct. This is further reinforced by the role of witnesses in the SCBH who also help verify the circumstances of the incident. Such people may or may not be invited to a restorative conference depending on whether they are viewed as harmed parties.

In the conduct board hearing, both complainants and accused can bring advisers, whose role as noted in Table 10.1, "is to provide advice to the student who has requested his/her presence in a manner which does not disturb the proceedings." In the restorative conference, responsible and harmed parties are encouraged to bring support people. Their role is *not* to offer counsel, but to help parties feel more comfortable and to offer their perspective on the impact of the incident. In sum, the information gathering stage of the SCBH is designed to present and evaluate evidence to determine responsibility. In the RJC, this stage is used to identify the harm caused by the misconduct.

## Dissecting the Scripts—Stage Three

Table 10.4 introduces the final stage of the processes. Both are focused on determining appropriate sanctions and agreements. In the RJC, the decision-making process concentrates on repairing harm and rebuilding trust. In the SCBH, the decision making focuses on evaluating the character of the accused student.

## TABLE 10.4
### Decision Making About Sanctions and Agreements

| *RJC Script* | *SCBH Script* |
|---|---|
| *Start a new flip chart page called "repairs" or "solutions."*<br><br>*To everyone:*<br><br>• We have all spoken about the harms caused by this incident and are now at the stage of identifying what can be done to make things right. Two basic questions will guide us forward.<br><br>   1. How can the harm be repaired?<br>   2. How can we regain confidence in _____ [*student responsible*] so that we can trust that s/he will be a responsible member of our community?<br><br>• Please remember that our focus is on finding solutions. We are not here to decide if _____ [*student responsible*] is a good or bad person, but to figure out how the harm can be repaired and trust rebuilt.<br><br>• If you do not believe we can work on solutions together, we can discuss this and, perhaps, end the conference. Would you like to continue with the conference?<br><br>• This next stage is about coming up with ideas. We will write all of the suggestions on the flipchart. Later we can decide to make changes and finalize an agreement that is satisfactory to everyone.<br><br>• During this brainstorming process, we will post all of your ideas on the flipchart. Later, we can refine them and write up the agreement.<br><br>*To student responsible:*<br><br>• Looking at this list of harms, what do you think can be done to repair each harm? | *Turn the tape recorder on.*<br><br>• This Student Conduct Board Hearing of the Student Conduct Board is now back in session. The Student Conduct Board has considered the charges against [_____], the Accused Student. The Student Conduct Board has evaluated all of the information shared with it and has determined which information was more credible, when the information was in conflict.<br><br>• Regarding the charge of [_____], the Student Conduct Board finds you [responsible] [not responsible].<br><br>*Repeat this sentence for each violation of the Student Code with which the Accused Student has been charged. If the Accused Student is found not responsible of all charges, read the following statement.*<br><br>• This Student Conduct Board Hearing of the Student Conduct Board is now concluded. Any further questions regarding the student code system or this decision of the Student Conduct Board should be directed to [_____]. Questions regarding this case should not be directed to any member of Student Conduct Board. The members of Student Conduct Board are cautioned not to discuss this matter with anyone to respect the privacy of all persons involved. Thank you very much for your participation.<br><br>*If the Accused Student is found responsible of any charge, read the following statement.*<br><br>• At this time, the Accused Student may ask the Board to call a reasonable number of character witnesses. Does the Accused Student wish to do so?<br><br>• Would the character witness please state your name and tell us the nature of your acquaintance with the Accused Student and comment on the student's character?<br><br>• Do the members of the Student Conduct Board have any additional questions for this character witness?<br><br>• Does the Accused Student wish to have any questions asked of this character witness? Please remember to direct any questions to the chair of the Student Conduct Board.<br><br>• Does the Complainant wish to have any questions asked of this character witness? Please remember to direct any questions to the chair of the Student Conduct Board. |

## TABLE 10.4 (Continued)

| *RJC Script* | *SCBH Script* |
|---|---|
| • What else can you do that can demonstrate you can be a positive member of our community? | *Repeat as necessary for each witness.* |
| | • Would the Complainant like to offer any comments for consideration in the imposition of sanctions? |
| *To harmed parties sequentially, then support persons:* | • Would the Accused Student like to offer any comments for consideration in the imposition of sanctions? |
| • Looking at this list of harms, what do you think can be done to repair each harm? | • At this time, we would ask that the Complainant, Accused Student, and their advisors leave the Student Conduct Board Hearing room so that the members of the Student Conduct Board may determine the sanctions to be recommended in this case. |
| • What else would you need to see from _____ [*student responsible*] to restore your confidence in him/her? | • The Student Conduct Board will now request information regarding the Accused Student's prior violations of the Student Code, if any. Has the Accused Student been found responsible for violating the Student Code in any prior incidents? |
| *To student responsible:* | |
| • Would you be willing to agree to these suggestions? | • After the Student Conduct Administrator considers the Student Conduct Board's sanctioning recommendations, and determines what sanctions to impose, the Accused Student and Complainant have the opportunity to return to this room. |
| *To everyone:* | |
| • What do you think of what we have come up with so far? Is this a fair and reasonable outcome? | • The decision regarding sanctions will be announced. You may choose not to attend the announcement of the sanctions. Regardless, the Accused Student and Complainant (if a student) will receive written notification of the outcome of the Student Conduct Board Hearing. |
| • Now that we have reached an agreement, we will write it up for you to sign. Each of you will get a copy of the agreement, and we will submit it to the [*conduct administrator*] for approval. | *Turn the tape recorder off. Once the Student Conduct Board has concluded its deliberations the Accused Student and Complainant are called back into the Student Conduct Board Hearing.* |
| • If the agreement is accepted by the [*conduct administrator*], then _____ [*student responsible*] will have to complete the various tasks by the deadline or he/she will not be able to register for next semester's classes [*or will have his/her diploma held if a graduating senior*]. | *Turn the tape recorder on.* |
| | • This Student Conduct Board Hearing of the Student Conduct Board is now back in session. The following sanction(s) will be imposed in this case: |
| | *Read each of the sanctions.* |
| • If after you [*student responsible*] leave, you believe that this process was conducted unfairly, you can appeal the agreement we have reached with the [*conduct administrator*]. | • This decision may be appealed within five (5) working days of receipt of written notification of the decision in this case. Appeals should be made in writing and delivered to [_____]. Decisions of the Student Conduct Board and/or the Student Conduct Administrator may be appealed on the following grounds only: |
| • While we write up the agreement, we would like you to complete an | A. The original Student Conduct Board Hearing was not conducted fairly in light of the charges and |

## TABLE 10.4 (Continued)

| RJC Script | SCBH Script |
|---|---|
| evaluation form. This will help us to know how well this process worked for you and how we can improve it.<br><br>*Pass out and collect forms. Have agreement signed and pass out copies.*<br><br>CLOSING THE CONFERENCE<br><br>*Try to end on a positive note by expressing appreciation for the hard work completed.*<br><br>• Thank you for your hard work today. In closing this conference, I'd like to go around the circle and ask each person how he or she is feeling about how things went. I'll start by saying . . . | information presented, and not in conformity with prescribed procedures giving the Complainant a reasonable opportunity to prepare and to present information that the Student Code was violated, and giving the Accused Student a reasonable opportunity to prepare and to present a rebuttal of those allegations.<br>B. The decision reached in this case was not based on substantial information.<br>C. The sanctions were not appropriate for the violation of the Student Code which the Accused Student was found to have committed.<br>D. New information, sufficient to alter a decision, is now available which was not available to the person appealing at the time of the original Student Conduct Board Hearing. For more information, please refer to the Student Code which is published in the [_____].<br><br>• Are there any final questions at this time?<br><br>• Any further questions regarding the student code system or this decision of the Student Conduct Board should be directed to [_____], the Student Conduct Administrator. Questions regarding this case should not be directed to any member of Student Conduct Board. The members of Student Conduct Board are cautioned not to discuss this matter with anyone, to respect the privacy of all persons involved.<br><br>• This Student Conduct Board Hearing of the Student Conduct Board is now concluded. Thank you very much for your participation.<br><br>*Turn tape recorder off.* |

*Note.* SCBH Script from Stoner and Lowery (2004, pp. 68–76).

The RJC begins this stage with a reminder of the twin purposes of the conference: to identify and repair harm and to restore trust in the community. The facilitator specifically discourages the group from passing judgment about the character of the student responsible. Restorative practitioners often say that the facilitators place the incident, not the student, in the center of the circle. This means that all parties consider the harm that was caused and from their particular vantage point share how they were affected and what they believe needs to happen to make things right.

The restorative justice facilitator also asks if participants wish to proceed with the conference. This is done to emphasize the voluntary nature of the conference and reaffirm the commitment of the student in taking responsibility for the misconduct. Because the decision-making process is collaborative and inclusive, it is important that all parties agree to continue. If not, then the conference will end and the case will be referred to a more formal decision-making process, such as the SCBH.

The conduct board hearing begins this stage with the introduction of character witnesses invited to speak on the accused student's behalf. The board is thus allowed to make an evaluation of the student's character and use that to inform sanctioning. Presumably, the board is expected to sort out whether the misbehavior is characteristic of the person or if the violation was out of character and not likely to be repeated.

In the RJC, concerns about the risk of reoffense are directed toward identifying how the student can demonstrate prosocial behavior rather than determining the student's character. Nevertheless, past misbehavior is revealed, the student responsible and support people share their perspectives, and participants do draw conclusions about risk. Students who pose a high risk will need to do more to restore confidence than those who pose less of a risk.

This final stage in the proceedings recapitulates the contrast between authority and social support. In the SCBH, a second private board deliberation is introduced. The accused student and complainant are excluded, and thus may not understand the rationale behind the sanctioning decision. When they are invited to return, the script does not require that any rationale be provided. Again, the board exerts authority and may undermine a sense of trust, fairness, or legitimacy. Research in criminal justice has demonstrated that restorative practices succeed better than courts in achieving this sense of trust, fairness, and legitimacy in a process or decision reached, although we do not have controlled studies comparing such outcomes between RJCs and SCBHs (Tyler, Sherman, Strang, Barnes, & Woods, 2007). We can expect, however, that parties who collaborate on an agreement are more likely to view it as fair than parties who have little to no control over the outcome.

## Sanctioning

The Model Code (Stoner & Lowery, 2004) provides a list of sanctions that reflect a variety of punishment philosophies. Table 10.5 enumerates these sanctions and their descriptions. I have added a third column which associates each sanction with a punishment philosophy (Braithwaite & Pettit,

## TABLE 10.5
### Model Code Sanctions

| Sanction | Description | Philosophy[a] |
|---|---|---|
| Warning | A notice in writing to the student that the student is violating or has violated institutional regulations. | Retribution |
| Probation | A written reprimand for violation of specified regulations. Probation is for a designated period of time and includes the probability of more severe disciplinary sanctions if the student is found to violate any institutional regulation(s) during the probationary period. | Deterrence |
| Loss of Privileges | Denial of specified privileges for a designated period of time. | Incapacitation Retribution |
| Fines | Previously established and published fines may be imposed. | Deterrence Retribution |
| Restitution | Compensation for loss, damage, or injury. This may take the form of appropriate service and/or monetary or material replacement. | Restorative Justice |
| Discretionary Sanctions | Work assignments, essays, service to the [College] [University], or other related discretionary assignments. | Restorative Justice |
| Residence Hall Suspension | Separation of the student from the residence halls for a definite period of time, after which the student is eligible to return. Conditions for readmission may be specified. | Deterrence Incapacitation Retribution |
| Residence Hall Expulsion | Permanent separation of the student from the residence halls. | Deterrence Incapacitation Retribution |
| [College] [University] Suspension | Separation of the student from the [College] [University] for a definite period of time, after which the student is eligible to return. Conditions for readmission may be specified. | Deterrence Incapacitation Retribution |
| [College] [University] Expulsion | Permanent separation of the student from the [College] [University]. | Deterrence Incapacitation Retribution |
| Revocation of Admission and/or Degree | Admission to or a degree awarded from the [College][University] may be revoked for fraud, misrepresentation, or other violation of [College][University] standards in obtaining the degree, or for other serious violations committed by a student prior to graduation. | Deterrence Incapacitation Retribution |

## TABLE 10.5 (Continued)

| Sanction | Description | Philosophy[a] |
|---|---|---|
| Withholding Degree | The [College][University] may withhold awarding a degree otherwise earned until the completion of the process set forth in this Student Conduct Code, including the completion of all sanctions imposed, if any. | Deterrence<br>Incapacitation<br>Retribution |

[a] Punishment philosophy statements by Braithwaite and Pettit (1990).
*Note.* SCBH Script from Stoner and Lowery (2008).

1990). Deterrence requires that the punishment should be swift, certain, and severe or painful enough to the student responsible, that it deters him or her as well as others from repeating the violation. Retribution specifies that punishment should reassure the community that the violation will not be tolerated and should be proportionately harsh to offset any benefit accrued by the offending behavior (e.g., an eye for an eye). Incapacitation directs that punishment should limit the student's ability to repeat the offense. Restorative justice practitioners shy away from using the term *punishment* but specify that agreements should repair the harm and rebuild trust.

Clearly, most sanctions in the Model Code focus on deterrence, retribution, and/or incapacitation. Often, one sanction can serve multiple ends. For example, paying a fine is painful enough that it can reassure the community that the student responsible is not getting away with anything and make him or her think twice about repeating the violation. Even though it involves money, however, it does not repair harm to a harmed party like restitution.

The Model Student Conduct Code (Stoner & Lowery, 2004) does not espouse any particular punishment philosophy nor does the script offer guidance to board members, except that they take into consideration comments by the accused student and the complainant in sanctioning. The model code further provides the board with options that can support their personal values, though weighted toward deterrence and retribution.

In contrast, restorative justice facilitators specifically encourage restorative outcomes and discourage other sanctions. Still, a restorative conference may arrive at deterrence or incapacitation-focused outcomes (e.g., residence hall suspension) if conference participants cannot identify actions the responsible student can take to restore trust. In this case, though, the framing of the decision is different. In the SCBH, the question for the board is: Is the misconduct severe enough to warrant suspension? In the RJC, the question to harmed parties is: What would it take for you to feel OK about the student responsible remaining on campus? Though framed differently, each may lead to suspension, but the nature of the discussion will be quite different.

In a restorative justice model, all efforts are made to avoid suspension from the institution, and the burden of responsibility to avoid suspension shifts to the student responsible. For instance, the facilitator may state that the student cannot register for the following semester's classes until all reparative tasks are completed. Thus, the student may self-suspend by failing to live up to an agreement he or she made, but the institution has not suspended the student.

## Conclusion

The restorative conference and student conduct board share a goal of creating a process that is "educational, not adversarial" (Stoner & Lowery, 2004, p. 16) and one that treats "all students with equal care, concern, honor, fairness, and dignity" (p. 15). The SCBH must be able to handle cases where accused students are denying responsibility and must make a recommendation about sanctions. The RJC is specifically designed to create a collaborative decision-making process that meets the needs of harmed parties and is limited to cases where an admission is made. In such cases, the process seeks to provide greater opportunity for learning and reflection by student offenders.

A study in the *Journal of College Student Development* by Cooper and Schwartz (2007) suggests that students tend to have difficulty with moral judgment, and argues that conduct professionals should develop practices "that would help students understand their responsibilities for living in an academic community, e.g., critical reflection" (p. 606). Given that a large number of students admit responsibility for their misconduct, restorative justice rather than adjudication through conduct boards holds great opportunity as an alternative pathway in that it aspires to the noble mission of higher education to further self-reflection and moral development in our students.

## References

Barton, C. (2003). *Restorative justice: The empowerment model.* Sydney, Australia: Federation Press.

Braithwaite, J., & Pettit, P. (1990). *Not just deserts.* Oxford, UK: Clarendon Press.

Cooper, M., & Schwartz, R. (2007). Moral judgment and student discipline: What are institutions teaching? What are students learning? *Journal of College Student Development, 48,* 606.

Council for the Advancement of Standards in Higher Education. 2006. *CAS self-assessment guide for student conduct programs.* Washington, DC: CAS.

Cullen, F. T. (1994). Social support as an organizing concept for criminology: Presidential address to the academy of criminal justice sciences. *Justice Quarterly, 11,* 537.

Dinnan, C. (2007). *Conference facilitator's script.* Waterbury: Vermont Department of Corrections.

Karp, D. R., & Allena, T. (Eds.). (2004). *Restorative justice on the college campus: Promoting student growth and responsibility, and reawakening the spirit of campus community.* Springfield, IL: Charles C. Thomas.

Noddings, N. (1984). *Caring: A feminine approach to ethics and moral education.* Berkeley: University of California Press.

O'Connell, T., Wachtel, B., & Wachtel, T. (1998). *Conferencing handbook: New real justice training manual.* Pipersville, PA: Piper's Press.

Stoner, E. N., & Lowery, J. W. (2004). Navigating past the "spirit of insubordination": A twenty-first-century model student conduct code with a model hearing script. *Journal of College and University Law, 31,* 1–77.

Trevino, J. A. (1996). *The sociology of law: Classical and contemporary perspectives.* New York: St. Martin's Press.

Tyler, T. R., Sherman, L., Strang, H., Barnes, G. C., & Woods, D. (2007). Reintegrative shaming, procedural justice, and recidivism: The engagement of offenders' psychological mechanisms in the Canberra RISE Drinking-and-Driving Experiment. *Law and Society Review, 41,* 553–585.

Van Ness, D., & Strong, K. H. (1997). *Restoring justice.* Cincinnati, OH: Anderson.

Zehr, H. (1990). *Changing lenses.* Scottdale, PA: Herald Press.

# II

# USING SHUTTLE DIPLOMACY TO RESOLVE CAMPUS CONFLICT

*Jennifer Meyer Schrage and Michele Goldfarb*

Research and practice can only be made more effective by an increased awareness of the larger context of injustice and by translating that into "best practices" which address power imbalances and considerations of the variety of entry points for transformation.

*Wing, Bowland, Guinee, Abdul-Hadi Jadallah, & Roy, 2008, p. 3*

Offering a Spectrum of Resolution Options provides campus communities with a variety of methods for conflict management. It is important that this menu of resolution pathways offers parties relevant and accessible options that suit their unique objectives. Campus conduct administrators assist students with a broad range of issues, and often there are significant and sensitive personal, developmental, ethical, and even legal issues at play in any given conflict.

Shuttle diplomacy is one menu option on the spectrum that may resonate with parties when all other options are ill suited to address the individual needs of those involved in the conflict. Shuttle diplomacy is a valuable tool for administrators when there is a legitimate concern that a student may reject other services because more informal methods such as mediation and dialogue do not "feel safe" or appropriate, and yet the formal structure and confrontational nature of adjudication may be intimidating or overwhelming for one or more parties involved. Therefore, shuttle diplomacy is placed in the middle of the Spectrum of Resolutions Options visual model (Schrage & Thompson, 2008).

In this chapter we define shuttle diplomacy as it relates to the spectrum. We then explore application methods and the issues to consider in using this conflict management technique.

## Defining Shuttle Diplomacy

Shuttle diplomacy is a form of assisted negotiation. Simply put, negotiation is a bargaining process between parties to solve a problem (Warters, 2000). Several forms of negotiation have developed in the field of conflict resolution but most assume that parties can and will negotiate directly with one another. Negotiation does not require use of a third-party facilitator. However, negotiation frequently focuses on positions and a narrow and limited set of objectives rather than on managing the conflict in a way that helps develop a future for the parties. Moreover, often this narrow form of negotiation cannot address the complexity of the people and relationships involved. Shuttle diplomacy (as the name suggests) was developed and initially used primarily in international relations and has since come to refer to a method whereby a third party serves as an intermediary between two parties who do not wish to interact directly (Fisher, Ury, & Patton, 1991).

The spectrum offers a campus application of shuttle diplomacy. It is a specific conflict management technique for the college environment. In this pathway, a campus administrator or another trained professional serves as a third-party facilitator for parties in a dispute. This method is used when one or more of the parties expresses that he or she does not wish to interact directly with the other party(s). The facilitator therefore shuttles between the parties to assist in negotiating an agreement. Typically, the tone of this negotiation is pragmatic and focused on specific issues. Usually it begins with a presentation to the intermediary of one party's positions for the other party to consider. A shuttle diplomacy case may involve some bargaining; however, the method's intentionally narrow objectives often provide for speedy resolution within a span of one or two sessions.

Comparing shuttle diplomacy to the other spectrum pathways can assist in gaining an understanding of this method. Shuttle diplomacy is similar to mediation in that the resolution is party driven and cannot be imposed by the facilitator. It differs from mediation, however, in that its focus is generally not about crafting an agreement that seeks to ensure a "future story," the relationship between the parties, or a win-win solution. Shuttle diplomacy is similar to adjudication in that it is about resolving a narrow set of issues but differs in that it does not surrender the outcome or resolution to a third-party panel or board. It is important to note, however, that despite its intentionally narrow focus with respect to outcome and its generally limited ability to uncover deeper issues, shuttle diplomacy has the potential to provide genuine relief to parties in dispute and enable them to move on. Thus, it can clear the way to healthier interactions between the parties in the future.

## Case Considerations

Shuttle diplomacy is most useful in cases where the following criteria are met: (a) future interaction between the parties is limited or unnecessary, (b) parties do not expect nor desire a future relationship, (c) objectives are practical and matter of fact, and (d) all other pathways have been considered carefully, and shuttle diplomacy is deemed the most likely to empower the parties involved or at least provide a reasonable chance of resolving the immediate dispute.

While shuttle diplomacy can be offered to assist some students who would otherwise walk away, it may involve significant risks and requires thoughtful application. Educators are justifiably hesitant to use this pathway as it counters many of the fundamental principles guiding student learning and student affairs practice. For instance, it can shield participants from the discomfort and dissonance (and therefore reduce the concomitant opportunity to mature and learn) that is experienced when individuals are required to directly communicate their needs and listen to the views of the other party(s) involved (Evans, Forney, & Guido-DiBrito, 1998). It also discourages parties from delving into the underlying issues and dynamics that are likely to have contributed to the conflict. As a result, of all the resolution pathways on the spectrum, shuttle diplomacy may offer the least by way of educational growth potential.

Shuttle diplomacy may also result in unintentional collusion with parties who perpetuate unhealthy or dysfunctional behavior. A student may present a seemingly pragmatic set of objectives when beneath those objectives lies a traumatic event or complex history that informs the conflict. An administrator who offers shuttle diplomacy may unwittingly be seen as consenting to or approving of the use of avoidance as a coping strategy by one or both parties. In other situations, facilitators may collude when they are unaware that one party is using shuttle diplomacy as an opportunity to target another party, either by distorting the issues or oversimplifying the conflict. Thus, the targeted party may sign off on an agreement that is not in his or her own best interest or that violates his or her rights. Awareness of these potential risks should make facilitators particularly vigilant in testing the reality and fairness of any agreement reached, especially one that looks too easy.

Despite its risks, shuttle diplomacy can offer a lifeline to a student when all other campus pathways and policies fail to address his or her needs. This can often be the case for students whose identity or conflict style is marginalized by the dominant culture on campus (Rifkin & Wing, 2001). For example, consider the dilemma of a female Muslim international student whose country of origin observes strict cultural guidelines around male/female relationships. If she has engaged in a romantic relationship that violates her own cultural traditions and it results in a breakup and a conflict occurs (e.g., a dispute over returning a gift), she may not seek more formal conflict resolution services offered on campus. The risks of pursuing a formal process that may result in unwelcome visibility by exposing the relationship to others or that may prolong uncomfortable interaction with her former partner may trump the benefit of resolving the conflict. However, the privacy, confidentiality, pragmatism, and indirect approach of shuttle diplomacy may meet her needs and therefore prevent her from experiencing the frustration that would flow from having no meaningful options.

## Facilitator Competency

The complex issues involved in offering and applying shuttle diplomacy require that administrators using this method demonstrate a core set of competencies. To ensure appropriate application, facilitators of shuttle diplomacy should be seasoned administrators who have completed formal mediation training. This ensures the following important skill sets: (a) ability to identify the issues at play and confirm with parties a proper understanding of desired outcomes, (b) active listening and communication, and (c) interpersonal skills that assist in picking up on subtle underlying messages. In addition, facilitators engaged in shuttle diplomacy should exhibit a solid understanding of cultural competence and social justice considerations. Understanding that dynamics beyond what is obvious or articulated are likely to be influencing the conflict and knowing how to appropriately account for such dynamics in a shuttle diplomacy case is critical (Wing & Marya, 2007). Failure to see a red flag and account for the issue can result in destructive rather than constructive conflict resolution (Rifkin & Wing, 2001).

## Technology as the Ultimate Shuttle Diplomacy Tool to Date

We recognize that this volume is not meant to define the end of a change process but rather to capture a fluid moment in time and mark a point in history where all indicators suggest a readiness for change in student conduct work. With this in mind, perhaps the shuttle diplomacy options found in Online Dispute Resolution (ODR) services provide the best examples of creative shuttle negotiation, at least to date.

The proliferation of ODR Web sites and services illustrates one arguably untapped potential for technology-assisted conflict resolution. This is a trend that warrants attention, particularly as our campus communities continue to embrace and respond to the rapid pace of technological change. One example of inquiry in this area is found at the University of Pennsylvania, where students attending the law school mediation clinic are asked to research and report back on online resolution options available to individuals and organizations in conflict. There are, in fact, quite a few. As in our previous discussion of shuttle diplomacy, the purpose of exploring the use and value of ODR is to highlight its advantages, disadvantages, potential pitfalls, and proper application. Therefore, the class also calls for an instructive review of the essential qualities of mediation and compares them to what might and might not be possible to replicate in cyberspace.

The ODR sites that are explored in these classes, as well as ODR sites in general, differ from one another in a variety of identifiable ways: the types of services offered, the level of automation involved, whether human facilitators are used, whether the sites invite blind bidding only or also offer some discussion-based resolution of disputes, and whether the sites employ e-mail shuttle diplomacy (asynchronous) or simultaneous (synchronous) chat room capability. Finally, because ODR is often on the cutting edge of grappling with knotty technological issues like security, privacy, and intellectual property, the class provides a lively format for discussing the intersection of these issues and the future of conflict resolution in an increasingly technological world.

Because students have grown so conversant with mediation skills in face-to-face disputes, they are acutely aware of the lost potential in cyberspace ODR. Key mediator techniques like reframing, active listening, encouraging candor, and probing for underlying interests may be lost online. Nevertheless, even in cyberspace mediators can still encourage parties to share their interests and even feelings, brainstorm options, and summarize what has already been shared.

Again, similar to the use of the spectrum approach for campus conflict, and the inclusion of shuttle diplomacy as a tool along that spectrum, educators and students alike must be encouraged to keep an open mind to new conflict resolution devices, even when some seem initially counterintuitive. Students (and others) are frequently amazed and excited by the many thus far untapped and creative ways (e.g., using Web cams, voice-activated technology, language translation capabilities, etc.) technology can contribute to the design and implementation of new forums for dispute resolution, and ultimately to additional ways of generating agreement and understanding among people.

## Conclusion

Shuttle diplomacy can seem counterintuitive to the traditionally trained student affairs practitioner, given the educational and experiential backgrounds common in this profession. Nonetheless, shuttle diplomacy is an important and legitimate form of conflict resolution. This spectrum pathway provides a creative option and offers flexibility, both of which are necessary and important characteristics of any conflict resolution program committed to serving a diverse campus population.

## References

Evans, N. J., Forney, D. S., & Guido-DiBrito, F. (1998). *The development of college students: Theory, research, and application.* San Francisco: Jossey-Bass.

Fisher, R., Ury, W., & Patton, B. (1991). *Getting to yes: Negotiating agreement without giving in* (2nd ed.). Boston: Houghton Mifflin.

Rifkin, J., & Wing, L. (2001) Racial identity development and the mediation of conflicts. In C. L. Wijeyesinghe & B. W. Jackson III (Eds.), *New perspectives on racial identity development: A theoretical and practical anthology* (pp. 182–208). New York: New York University Press.

Schrage, J. M., & Thompson, M. C. (2008, June). *Using a social justice model for conflict resolution to ensure access for all students.* Presentation at the Donald D. Gehring Academy for Student Conduct Administration, Salt Lake City, UT.

Warters, W. C. (2000). *Mediation in the campus community: Designing and managing effective programs.* San Francisco: Jossey-Bass.

Wing, L., Bowland, S. Y., Guinee, L., Abdul-Hadi Jadallah, A., & Roy, B. (2008, Summer) Framing the dialogue: Social justice and conflict intervention. *ACResolution, 3,* 3–4.

Wing, L., & Marya, D. (2007, May). *Social justice mediation.* Session presented at the Social Justice Mediation Training, University of Michigan, Ann Arbor.

# 12

# INCORPORATING PRINCIPLES OF CONFLICT RESOLUTION AND SOCIAL JUSTICE INTO FORMAL STUDENT CONDUCT CODE PATHWAYS

*Nancy Geist Giacomini*

If the only tool you have is a hammer, you tend
to see every problem as a nail.

*Abraham Maslow*

At the 2008 Donald D. Gehring Academy for Student Conduct Administration, several visionary colleagues brought themes of conflict resolution, restorative justice, and social justice together in one room for what may be the first intentional effort to join these practices and theories in a shared resolution model. The inclusive Spectrum Model produced by Jennifer Meyer Schrage and Monita C. Thompson (2008) visually expanded the existing Model Student Conduct Code (Stoner & Lowery, 2004) long embraced by the Association for Student Conduct Administration (ASCA), and student conduct administration as a whole, to allow students and administrators more process options for resolving conflict and campus "misconduct" than those detailed in the model code.

Ed Stoner, coauthor of the 1990 Model Student Disciplinary Code and the subsequent 2004 Model Student Conduct Code, joined 2008 Academy participants over lunch one day for the program "Is There Room in Student Judicial Affairs for Social Justice: Reframing the Model Student Conduct Code." Stoner entertained questions and talked about ways to build from the good work he produced with his publication partners Kathryn Cerminara and John Wesley Lowery and that of our fellow judicial colleagues to further transform the educational language and developmental emphasis of conduct codes (Stoner & Cerminara, 1990; Stoner & Lowery, 2004).

Taken together, what began as a four-day collaborative exchange within and between Academy program tracks has brought us to this national platform. Here we may consider together how to honor our best student development and social justice ideals while still supported by the solid and considered foundation provided by Stoner, Cerminara, and Lowery in crafting the 1990 and 2004 model student codes. This chapter reflects upon the most formal pathways for managing student conduct and conflict as found in Schrage and Thompson's (2008) Spectrum of Resolution Options visual model and begs the original question, "Is there room in student judicial affairs for social justice?"

In the context of this book, I favor exploring present language and legalese in our traditional campus code processes as a means to transform existing systems into better and best inclusive practices. My interest and expertise rests more on advancing this lens we call social justice as a means to inform change in student conduct administration, particularly when layered on top of what we might consider our existing lenses of student rights, student development ,and restorative principals. I do not revisit the historic and important reference points found in laws, policies, and mandates that have shaped student conduct practice today, as these can be found elsewhere in this volume. Rather, I hope to help colleagues reflect upon their present codes and "adjudication" practices in an effort to reclaim developmental, restorative, educational, and socially just values and principles in sound and meaningful ways.

This chapter respects the need for community standards and codes of conduct and honors them as an expression of the values, ideals, and expectations in unique communities of learners. It further values the nature, intent, and practical application of formal code pathways for managing the most egregious or pervasive student misconduct. But equally important, this chapter tests the ability of our most formal resolution processes to rise to the occasion of change in light of current campus trends, demographics, climate, diversity, and needs of the individual and the community.

## Building Up From the Model Code

Stoner shares my appreciation for the wisdom in Maslow's epigraph at the beginning of this chapter: "If the only tool you have is a hammer, you tend to see every problem as a nail." He would also be the first to admit that the pioneering Model Student Disciplinary Code (Stoner & Cerminara, 1990) was never meant to be the broad hammer it has become for nailing down every case of misconduct on campus. Many thorny campus issues do not fit neatly into the traditional adjudication models that campus administrators, informed by the courts over the past several decades, have carefully crafted. These thorny issues are treated as nails nevertheless.

This is not to say that the most formal code processes are not fully appropriate and sound as model pathways for handling certain campus cases of misconduct. Such cases may well include acts of violence, and/or threats to the health and safety of the institution's community. Cases also include those situations that may result in the most serious of sanctions because of the severity of a single incident or a pattern of inability or unwillingness on the part of a student to respect community standards. My assertion here, aligned with that of Stoner's and ASCA's, is that an *adjudication* model simply is not required to stand alone or be overly legalistic for each and every case of campus misconduct. Neither is it the best practice to develop codes that are detailed to the detriment of appropriately tailored responses that reflect a level of care for a student's individual circumstances, stage of development, educational needs, or the restoration of a community.

Just as we would not call a meeting of a behavioral review committee, mental health assessment team, or risk management group to consider every student, neither must we initiate our most formal conduct processes when each referral comes to our desk. While our codes are intended to offer a clearly outlined, formal pathway designed to protect the student and the institution, to overly formalize the management of every incident overtaxes the administrative system; moderates the significance and attention given the most serious reports; keeps students from alternative, viable resolution pathways; and inaccurately models adjudication as the best and only means of resolution.

Authors throughout this volume make the case that what we have come to call an adjudication model is asked to do too much, grounded in the wisdom that one clear and due institutionalized process ensures fairness and equity for every student. The resounding assertion is that one process cannot be made to fit every incident of conduct and conflict on campus. We get the job done, but at what and at whose expense?

## Agreement or Adjudication as Formal Pathways for Conduct Management

A great many things have been written about campus adjudication models and codes of conduct templates over the years. Stoner and Cerminara's

(1990) original Model Student Disciplinary Code established well-documented case law together with practical applications that support the inclusion of certain necessary steps in our campus processes for them to be deemed fair to individuals and balanced against administrative efficiency and community considerations. Historical reference points in the field are outlined in chapters 2 and 8 of this book as well.

Before considering the finer points of how creators of conduct codes today might further develop the two most formal resolution pathways as conceptualized in the Schrage and Thompson Spectrum Model (2008), let's look first at the common forums developed in higher education to administer reports of code violations. Most reports of alleged misconduct are received in writing (hard copy or electronic) by the staff charged with responding to such complaints. These complaints can typically be raised by any member of the institution's community.

Students are informed of the reported infraction in what is to be a timely fashion and are typically required to attend an individual meeting to share their side of the story, review their rights, and consider their resolution options. These meetings are also opportunities for a staff member to check in with the student about his or her fuller college experience, problems the student is experiencing, academic success, and so on. But, as with any administrative system, individual meetings can be as cursory, administratively rigorous, or developmental as time and the individual staff member allows (Zdziarski & Wood, 2008).

This one-on-one meeting is the responding student's entry point into the system as provided by the institution. More likely than not, the student is provided with two well-established pathways to resolve the complaint. As depicted in Schrage and Thompson's (2008) Spectrum Model, the student may generally agree with the report, accept the formal conduct charges, and waive the option for a more formal process through adjudication (informal resolution). Students choosing this pathway accept responsibility for the incident in question and leave the meeting either with sanction in hand or one that is forthcoming. Some systems allow the administrator at this level to apply sanctions only up to a certain point of severity, perhaps excluding suspension and expulsion. If this is the case, the system may require a more formal process or a supervisory review or application of the sanction. In cases of agreement, students largely waive their right to further challenges specific to conduct charges and perhaps sanctions. Many systems leave open the option of an appeal for procedural concerns to protect the student and the institution.

On the other hand, a student may opt to have the incident heard more fully in a meeting or hearing attended by other stakeholders, and facilitated by an individual or panel that in turn will determine responsibility and any subsequent institutional action. This is conceptualized in the Spectrum Model (Schrage & Thompson, 2008) visual as adjudication (formal resolution). Case law and legal precedent have helped shape these administrative systems to provide a student at this resolution level with a timely written notice of the hearing, an opportunity to hear and answer to conduct charges, to hear the statements of witnesses, and to receive a written outcome based on the information presented. Outcomes are based on whether a code violation "more likely than not" occurred or on the higher standard of whether the information shared was deemed "clear and convincing" by the individual or panel facilitating the procedure. Procedures at this level also provide the student with some manner of appeal. Among the most fundamental of guiding principles is that processes and sanctions must not be arbitrary or discriminatory (Stoner & Lowery, 2004).

Sanctions arising from these two formal code pathways range from a limited term warning such as a period of disciplinary probation or deferred suspension through permanent expulsion from the institution. Often lesser sanctions are paired with educational referrals to programs that include substance abuse education and assessment, anger and conflict management, and the like. Community service hours may be applied, and students may be asked to write reflection exercises. Subsequent meetings with the adjudication staff may be set up, and the students may also be provided at a handful of institutions with the institutionalized option of participating further in mediation or restorative circles. But given the nature of the more formal code processes, these developmental options are still frequently considered sanctions.

Variations or companion processes can be found on campuses that are administered by or for graduate programs, academic departments, off-campus crimes, violations by Greek organizations, and so forth. In addition, all campuses can and should provide an expedited process for the most serious of incidents that allows for the institution to take immediate action (i.e., removal from a residence hall or campus community and/or suspension of classes) pending a full process.

## What's In a Name?

The aim of this chapter beyond introducing the formal code processes is to consider how best to infuse these existing pathways with a fuller expression of core values including student development, individual rights, educational missions, social justice, and community restoration. A good starting point is in the language used within and about the processes themselves.

The Spectrum Model (Schrage & Thompson, 2008) aside, *adjudication* and *arbitration* as terms are imperfectly applied to student code processes. This language represents vestiges of familiar but dated codes that incorrectly model themselves after the legal profession. That said we could discuss to infinity the best words available to communicate policies and procedures in student communities. Ultimately what is important is not that we all choose the same language, but that our institutionalized language expresses our intent and values when addressing student misconduct and conflict. Taking adjudication and arbitration, for instance, we might weigh those legal concepts against more developmental expressions. In so doing, one campus might finally settle on *administrative hearing* as the expression of choice, while another prefers simply *conference* or *meeting*. In fact, Stoner says: "If it fits your campus culture and allows you to achieve your goals, I do not care if you call it a cantaloupe!" (E. Stoner, personal communication, January 21, 2009).

While considering the importance of language, I find myself returning to the concept of *structural determinism* as described by Delgado and Stefancic (2001). In their work on critical race theory, the authors define structural determinism as "the idea that our system, by reason of its structure and vocabulary, cannot redress certain types of wrong" (p. 26). Though this definition reaches far beyond the context it is used here, to me it begs the question of whether and why colleges and universities structurally limit their own ability to redress student misconduct most effectively and developmentally by virtue of our own chosen language.

If structure and vocabulary go hand in hand, as Delgado and Stefancic (2001) suggest, then the good news is that the way is already paved for change in how we administer student conduct codes in higher education. This movement is revealed in the language found in the new model code (Stoner & Lowery, 2004) that takes "judicial" out of "judicial affairs," expressed in related codes and office name changes across the country, and notable even in the name change of the premier association devoted to student conduct work—what was once the Association for Student Judicial Affairs (ASJA) is, after 20 years now, the Association for Student Conduct Administration (ASCA).

## Building Up From Common Ground

So how then do we best embody our history; student developmental, social, and restorative justice theories; student rights; community responsibility;

and conflict resolution practice all within our most formal conduct processes and language? In fact, that groundwork has been laid by Stoner and Lowery (2004).

Under the revised Model Code (Stoner & Lowery, 2004), consider that the language is consistently respectful of students as individuals while honoring rights, nondiscrimination, fairness, evenhandedness, and dignity, together with protecting and respecting the rights of the community and the rights of the college to promote high educational standards. This core value continues, "Whatever process it adopts, the institution will want to remember the basic student affairs precept that it is important to treat all students with equal care, concern, honor, fairness, and dignity" (p. 15).

In addition, there are several nods to conflict resolution including mediation and restorative justice practices. The code allows for the system to pursue or not pursue a referral upon investigation (Stoner & Lowery, 2004), and offers

> an arbitration or a mediation requirement prior to reaching a more formal Student Conduct Board Hearing stage. Such an option is acceptable because the concept of due process is flexible, requiring no more than is necessary to provide fair notice and an opportunity to be heard. In other words, in some cases a formal fact finding process is not required; an informal meeting between the students involved and college or university administrators suffices, as long as accused students are informed of the charges and given an opportunity to tell their side of the story. Other schools may not want to require such an initial meeting because such meetings could consume all of the administrator's time with little benefit. Local experience will dictate whether it is effective to attempt to resolve alleged Student Code violations through such a meeting, although the most common practice is to emphasize efforts at mediation or other informal resolution. (pp. 47–48)

The code endorses language that sets the expectation for students to be responsible to their campus communities and to demonstrate good citizenship (Stoner & Lowery, 2004, pp. 33–34). Further, the code recognizes the demands of small offices and small budgets in that the authors allow for one administrator to wear several hats, with the caution that an institution is wise to separate the "functions of informal investigating and/or mediating . . . from that of determining whether a violation has occurred and setting the sanction" (p. 21).

Still further, the model allows for total sanctioning flexibility, which again makes room for blending a formal process with educational and developmental sanctions, including those that address conflict resolution, social justice, and restoring community (Stoner & Lowery, 2004).

The irony of the original question posed at the 2008 Gehring Academy, "Is there room in student judicial affairs for social justice?" is that the better question might just be, "Is there room in student judicial for student *judicial*?!" The point is that there is much to draw from in the new model code (Stoner & Lowery, 2004) and companion script as templates for tailoring efforts to include conflict resolution processes grounded in social justice principles at individual institutions.

Building from the common ground provided in the model code (Stoner & Lowery, 2004), let's then consider how we might address omissions or shortcomings when crafting future institutional codes, practices, and language. For one, not much attention is paid to issues of victimization and community restoration as might be provided within a code. Neither is there a mention of how a community might be cared for and restored even while a criminal proceeding is pending and perhaps standing in the way of completing a campus process.

The language of the new code also reflects familiar ethnocentric trappings not uncommon in many of our country's formal adjudication systems. For instance, a hearing officer or board chair is empowered to set a calm rather than confrontational tone for the hearing, and all questions are directed by or through the hearing officer or student conduct board (Stoner & Lowery, 2004, p. 65). This is not to argue that it is outside the rights of an institution to create an appropriate setting for important dialogue only to challenge the definition of *appropriate* through different sets of lenses. Most of us might agree, for example, that participants in a formal process might not be allowed to swear, raise their voices, become physical, and so on, but how then do we also honor and account for the marked differences between people and between social groups when it comes to expressing oneself when faced with conflict or placed in a defensive position? If not accounted for in the language of an institution's code or set of expectations in preparation for a hearing/meeting, at least it might be accounted for in the training of the facilitators and chairs who help guide the dialogue. Better still, accounting for differences in conflict management styles between individuals and social groups in general can be accomplished by offering alternative pathways that provide a less adversarial process in favor of dialogue and restoration.

The code opts out of mentioning or defining the perhaps sticky concepts of neutrality or impartiality, instead favoring the importance of avoiding bias. Authors of institutional codes might research and consider the newer attention being given to terms like *multipartiality* and *multicultural competencies* as the ideal to work toward in a discovery process in which all parties are honored, fully heard, and respected through their stories.

Overall, the Model Code (Stoner & Lowery, 2004) provides a standard disclaimer that each college or university must collaborate with its own legal counsel to consider special needs or legal precedents relevant to that community while shaping its own codes and hearing scripts. With this sound legal advice, let's also add a requirement that codes be consistently reviewed in a collaborative forum of many diverse stakeholders including students, practitioners, and educators where new perspectives can be fully invited, heard, and reflected in our best practices.

Finally, with due respect to Thomas Jefferson as cited in Stoner and Lowery (2004), and to the authors themselves, the concept of framing the issue of discipline as "the most difficult in American education" (pp. 1, 3) establishes a troubling and dated lens to view the real issues found on college and university campuses today. Contextually perhaps, this was true in Jefferson's time, but is this true in today's campus climate? Stoner and I had some fun with this, a reminder of the importance of keeping a sense of humor and perspective mixed with equal parts of strategic planning and deep thought (E. Stoner, personal communication, January 21, 2009).

> Me: Is the issue of discipline more important than meeting the growing needs of our multicultural student body?
> Ed: Well, actually, Mr. Jefferson was teaching all white males.
> Me: More important than helping students afford college in the first place?
> Ed: I would venture to guess they were all sons of wealthy planters.

## Moving Away From the Lens of Insubordination

Ron Miller, a leading pioneer in holistic education, once observed that "to control and sort young people for the sake of institutional efficiency is to crush the human spirit" (http://www.lightafire.net/quotations/authors/ron-miller/). Student conduct administrators clearly do not set out to crush the spirit of students. But we have been raised professionally to view our efforts in the context of "harnessing the spirit of insubordination" (Stoner & Cerminara, 1990). Instead, the lens of social justice suggests that we continue to move beyond the framing of discipline as "difficult" and a means for "harnessing insubordination" and instead embrace language that is respectful and inclusive of all members of our changing student communities without bridling their spirit.

Similar to the comparison of language and scripts by David Karp in chapter 10, consider how this reframing plays out in the language of student conduct work in letters, conversations, policies, and formal procedures. The model code (Stoner & Lowery, 2004) today actively discourages much of the original legalistic language used in the original code (Stoner & Cerminara, 1990) to reflect changes in the field over time, yet words like *judicial, hearings, evidence, guilty,* and so on still remain a part of our vernacular as practitioners of this work. The point of reframing our shared language is to balance the administrative tone that may need to be set in a disciplinary context with language that also expresses a concern for individual welfare and community values as well. Table 12.1 provides but one example of how some of our traditional judicial language is beginning to change in favor of language that more directly communicates our shared values as educators in campus communities that aspire to be inclusive, just, and developmentally sound. It is up to each individual institution to evaluate and reframe its own code language to best express the mission, values, and procedures of its campus culture in a clear and concise manner.

If it sounds like so much semantics, think of a personal situation in which the way a message is delivered has made a difference in your own perception of system fairness and openness to your personal story. Examples might include being stopped and ticketed for a minor traffic violation, a stern truancy notice after taking your child out of school to visit Disneyland for a week, or a call from the hospital that places a recitation of Medicare rights over an expression of concern for the patient and family. The point is, there are many ways to communicate information, but the delivery governs

### TABLE 12.1
**Reframing Language Found in Traditional Campus Judicial Affairs Programs**

| *Existing Language* | *Reframed Language* |
| --- | --- |
| Judicial Affairs | Student Conduct Administration, Conduct and Conflict Resolution Process |
| Charge | Conflict, referral, conduct question |
| Prehearing | Administrative meeting, conference |
| Evidence | Sharing of information |
| Guilty/not guilty | Responsible/not responsible |
| Sanctions | Restorative or educational measures or community actions |
| Appeals | Individual and process safeguards |
| Hearing officer | Facilitator |
| Legal counsel | Adviser/advocate |
| Accused | Respondent |
| Victim | Complainant, harmed party |

how that information will be perceived and evaluated for system care, values, and fairness.

## From Language to Systemic Change

The value of including alternative pathways and inclusive language in managing student conduct and conflict is that it shows the community that even a large administrative system can be tailored in a personal and thoughtful way to best meet the needs of a diverse population. It does not do away with formal processes as a significant and fair option. Instead, once conflict resolution and social justice are understood and embraced by an institution, that shift becomes reflected in the language of the code by balancing fair play with the core values of student conduct administration. And, a change in language often heralds a change in vision. From vision comes action. Systems change takes time, but while germinating, it pays to give voice to the vision.

Finally, broadening the process menu under the spectrum and shaping balanced codes also makes fair and transparent what many educators already do when presented with student situations that do not quite fit the mold. In chapter 2, the authors cite Harwood (2008), who said that

> there are times when an assessment team finds that the subject is simply enraged about being charged administratively with a minor violation of a university rule. The situation then escalates because a campus bureaucrat holds strong and says he or she can't overlook the subject's infraction. "Sometimes," says Martin, "we have to say 'Break the rule. Make the exception. . . . if that's what it takes to defuse a volatile situation.'" (p. 76)

That resonates on an individual level, but let's take the example one step further. Cases in which we are most tempted to break our own rules prove to be the best indicators of weaknesses in our systems or in our interpretation of these systems. If we do a good job establishing and communicating fair community standards, then we are well within our rights to create alternative resolutions when a traditional response does not fit the situation or the student. As Stoner points out, this is not breaking the rules but rather an expression of "complying most fully with the rules" (E. Stoner, personal communication, January 21, 2009). These are the cases that we must consistently sit down with and dissect as lessons in refining systems and personal response plans in anticipation of the next case that may present itself in a similarly unique way. This elevates a good system to a great one by taking a willingness to do the right thing for one and lifting it to a systemic opportunity to do the thing right for all.

## Conclusion

The intent of this chapter is to respect and value traditional pathways of managing student conduct and conflict and further help the reader consider ways to support and work within campus-tailored models to nurture educational, developmental, and socially just opportunities in student conduct work. Formal conduct pathways including the less-formal agreement process and the more-formal hearing-type process are well established in managing campus misconduct. These pathways have clearly stood as the favored approaches to campus conduct issues even as other pathways, including mediation, have fallen away as well-intended but lesser or alternative options in the past.

Yet, we have also become accustomed to relying on a judicial hammer as a large and burdensome tool in student conduct work. When situations arise that don't fit the model just right, we force them to fit. We take roommate quarrels and label them *disruptive conduct* so that they can enter established systems. We charge student groups for hosting racially divisive parties that play out cultural stereotypes in Black face or immigrant garb. We counsel an assault survivor into a process that is not equipped to restore the harm that has been done. Very educational things may happen as a referral gets channeled through the process, but it is a formalized conduct process nonetheless. As such, it is structurally predetermined that someone other than the student will be empowered to make a decision about how to manage the incident, and the case may result in sanctions more punitive in nature than educational or restorative.

As Stoner was wise to remind me, Jefferson celebrated the spirit of insubordination without intending to subordinate a student's spirit. In honoring this, I invite the reader to remember that we are all empowered to fill our own administrative tool boxes with more than just a disciplinary "hammer." But even in the event that an institution is equipped with just that hammer, consider that we are still in control of how to use it as a meaningful tool in the educational and developmental process. Hammers can be hard headed or pliable, swung with grace or carelessness, kindness or malice, precision or reckless abandon. They can be leveled evenhandedly or used to exact advantage or subordination. When provided with only one tool, the holder of that tool still has a lot of decisions to make on what the impact will be.

# References

Delgado, R., & Stefancic, J. (2001). *Critical race theory: An introduction.* New York: New York University Press.

Harwood, M. (2008, April). Teaming up to reduce risk. *Security Management,* pp. 66–78.

Schrage, J. M., & Thompson, M. C. (2008, June). *Using a social justice model for conflict resolution to ensure access for all students.* Paper presented at the Donald D. Gehring Academy for Student Conduct Administration, Salt Lake City, UT.

Stoner, E. N., & Cerminara, K. L. (1990). Harnessing the spirit of insubordination: A model student disciplinary code. *Journal of College and University Law, 17,* 89–121.

Stoner, E. N., & Lowery, J. W. (2004). Navigating past the "spirit of insubordination": A twenty-first century model student conduct code with a model hearing script. *Journal of College and University Law, 31,* 1–77.

Zdziarski, E., & Wood, N. (2008). Forums for resolution in student conduct practice: The complete guide for student affairs professionals. In J. M. Lancaster & D. M. Waryold (Eds.), *Student conduct practice: The complete guide for student affairs professionals* (pp. 97–111). Sterling, VA: Stylus.

# PART THREE

## SUSTAINABLE INNOVATION

# 13

# USING NEEDS ASSESSMENT AND DELIBERATIVE PLANNING TO ENHANCE CONFLICT SYSTEMS DEVELOPMENT

*Richard T. Olshak*

Experience is a hard teacher because she gives
the test first, the lesson afterwards.

*Vernon Sanders Law*

In 1985 the National Institute for Dispute Resolution (NIDR) and the
University of Massachusetts Mediation Program published *Peaceful Persuasion: A Guide to Creating Mediation Dispute Resolution Programs for
College Campuses* (Girard, Rifkin, & Townley, 1985). This was the first publication specifically designed to aid colleges and universities in crafting mediation programs for the purpose of resolving disputes that arise on college and
university campuses. This was followed by Bill Warters' (2000) seminal book
*Mediation in the Campus Community: Designing and Managing Effective Pro-
grams*. The latter work was particularly influential since it was drawn from
experiences gained throughout the early evolution of campus-based mediation programs in the 1980s and 1990s. It was also exceptionally detailed in
examining the myriad of issues facing program designers.

This chapter builds from these previous works while expanding assessment questions to include the full spectrum of resolution options advanced
in this volume. Many campuses have focused solely on developing mediation
programs as a way to augment or complement disciplinary processes over the
past several decades, and thus fail to fully satisfy the goal of expanding conflict resolution services broadly enough to provide disputants with the best
fit when it comes to processes or pathways that meet unique needs and conflicts. To this end, the chapter (a) describes the importance of using needs
assessment when designing campus conflict resolution systems, (b) specifies

the questions and considerations that must be addressed in conducting a needs assessment, and (c) offers a template for planning and implementing effective conflict resolution systems.

For the purpose of this chapter, *conflict resolution systems* is an expansive term that includes all the various pathways that can be used for the constructive resolution of conflict as advanced in this book. Further, the focus of this chapter is on developing conflict resolution systems designed to meet the needs of students and communities. However, this same assessment approach can be used for professionals seeking to develop conflict resolution systems for other college and university constituencies, and can be modified for those developing systems outside higher education.

## The Need for Intentional Design

The development of conflict resolution systems in higher education is not a process that should be lightly entered into. Such a process is an investment of time, energy, personnel, and financial resources. Too often as a training consultant I have visited a college campus to provide mediation training only to recognize that the institution is ill prepared to implement or sustain a mediation program. This is not always the fault of the people responsible for the training or program design. My own experience in program development has been substantially affected by institutional politics, financial considerations, a lack of institutional support, and a lack of understanding of the complexity of conflict systems design.

As a result of these experiences, I became interested in developing a means for designing conflict systems in a deliberate way that would recognize and address the reality of administrative life in higher education. Coupled with my own experience in developing an administrative office, this chapter represents an idealized means for addressing program development and implementation. It is intended to first approach the process of systems design as an academic experience, conducting as much work as possible in an environment devoid of unrealistic and impractical expectations. Once a foundation can be developed, program implementation can proceed in a manner that makes program success and sustainability far more likely.

## Incorporating Needs Assessment

Before implementing a program, it is critical to first understand the needs of the specific community. My own experiences in this area have included (on multiple occasions) simply being directed or hired to develop a mediation program because someone in a position of authority determined that a mediation program was the best and only way to accomplish the goal of broadening conflict resolution processes on campus. But in reflection, I often have wondered how we knew that it was a mediation program that was needed for a particular community. What were the identified problems that such a program might address? And what about those conflicts that would not neatly fit into this method of resolution? By starting with the outcome in mind (e.g., "I want a mediation program."), we limit our possibilities and fail to serve the academic community to the best of our abilities. Thus, it is my assertion that we must begin with an open mind about what the outcomes will be, and design more comprehensive conflict systems that will maximize our service to the community.

Upcraft and Schuh (1996) define needs assessment as a "process of determining the presence or absence of the factors and conditions, resources, services, and learning opportunities that students need in order to meet their educational goals and objectives within the context of an institution's mission" (p. 128). Modified to meet our needs, we may look at needs assessment in conflict systems as the analysis of programs and services, formal and informal, designed to assist students in managing conflict situations during the course of their education.

This chapter argues for a deliberate but flexible approach to developing such conflict systems. The first assumption is that we will have a core group of people, or perhaps a single individual, who desire to see an improvement in how campus conflicts are handled at their college or university. The remainder of this chapter is intended to serve as a step-by-step process for such trailblazers to follow.

## The Key Questions

Four key questions must be addressed at the outset by the people initially invested in enhancing conflict systems as well as the people who subsequently become involved in the process. A shared vision among the initial stakeholders is critical.

### *The Question "Why?"*

The most basic question to address is *why* such an examination of conflict systems is necessary. Diamond (2006) offered a number of reasons college and university environments are resistant to the idea of change. Among these ideas are some key thoughts that have an impact on campus conflict systems. They include the following:

- College and university officials (faculty and administration) find it easier and much less risky to maintain the status quo than to initiate *risky* change.
- Unit loyalty leads to a sense of turf. Any efforts that result in a shift of resources tend to be looked at negatively.
- Assessment and accountability can threaten the status quo and are often avoided.
- Decreasing availability of funds in higher education has reduced the opportunities for colleges and universities to reward risk taking and innovation, particularly in nonacademic areas.
- Many leaders in higher education are unprepared to serve as catalysts for change and are often not knowledgeable about the change needed.

If we accept these points, it is imperative to invest first in the education of key people who can drive institutional change as well as those who have access to resources that will support the process of change. This will be possible if those responsible for prompting a discussion of campus conflict systems can assist those whom we deem to be change agents to better understand the strengths and weaknesses of current campus conflict systems, as well as the needs currently not being met by existing systems.

Note that the approach taken in this process is similar to the popular strengths, weaknesses, opportunities, threats (SWOT) analysis process used in many different fields but is tailored to more effectively turn into an immediate plan of action.

To address why, we must address the following:

- How would we ideally assist students in resolving conflict?
- How do we currently assist students in resolving conflict?
- What are the strengths of each approach?
- What are the weaknesses of each approach?
- What needs are not being met?
- How can we achieve our ideal?
- How can we meet those needs through change?

## The Question "What?"

An extension of the *why* question is the *what* question. Specifically, what are we proposing to change about our conflict systems, and how will this meet the needs we have identified? It is critical not to enter into the process with the outcome already established but rather to be open to whatever results a needs assessment process offers.

On two different occasions in my career, I have been directed to establish campus mediation programs because the people calling for the program had identified a shortcoming in the campus disciplinary process. While the disciplinary process was diligent and consistent in resolving violations of the schools' code of conduct, these processes did not satisfy the conditions of many cases. In some instances, code violations occurred because interventions that might have prevented behavioral issues had not been carried out, while in other cases the mere resolution of the code violation did little to address the underlying issues involved in the dispute. In both cases, seasoned educational leaders "guessed" that a mediation program would serve to better address these situations. Starting with the outcome in mind rather than addressing more compelling questions allows us to miss key opportunities to improve how we manage conflicts on campus.

It has been my experience that student affairs professionals tend to look at conflict systems in terms of formal programs. Thus, it is common to see a campus that has a formal disciplinary program and a formal mediation program oftentimes connected and even housed in the same administrative unit. In these cases in general, clear guidelines help professionals determine which cases head toward the disciplinary process and which ones are directed to the alternative mediation program.

But conflicts themselves do not always break out so evenly. Conditions surrounding campus conflict are complex and fluid, as is evident today in the growing impact of technology on the classroom experience and how this technology affects student interactions with others in a collegial environment (think distance learning and/or the advent of global campuses spanning multiple continents). Disciplinary administrators and boards often determine that violations have occurred but that traditional sanctions are not adequate to address underlying issues or issues never even anticipated just a few years ago. A mediation program staff often finds that disputes suitable for resolution outside disciplinary systems do not always lend themselves to resolution in mediation either, given the formal nature of the mediation process or the time required to participate in the process. Many students opt not to use voluntary mediation programs for these reasons, leaving students to find other (often less-constructive) means for resolving or avoiding the conflict.

Rather than see conflict systems in terms of formal structures, it is my assertion that we need to step back and consider a broader array of conflict resolution pathways and be less focused on investing solely in singular methods of resolution. The more important issue is that these conflicts must be resolved in constructive ways that meet the needs of the people involved.

Thus, direct face-to-face mediation may work well in some cases, but other disputants may not wish to communicate directly with one another. In other cases, the disputants may desire to leave decisions to a third party. Our conflict systems need to maintain a degree of flexibility that prepares us for successful resolution in those instances when our current conflict systems fall short of student needs.

By maintaining an open perspective on how to best resolve campus conflicts rather than predetermining what specific conflict pathways will be used, we are more inclined to offer students a broader range of options for resolving conflict. In this way, we avoid the mistake of forcing a conflict into a pathway of resolution that does not serve the interests or needs of the disputants.

To address the what, we must address the following:

- What gaps in conflict systems have we identified?
- What are the best ways of addressing these gaps? What changes must be made?
- Will these changes truly close the gaps that we see?
- What obstacles must we overcome to close the gaps?
- Could new problems arise from our efforts?
- How will our community respond to these changes?

### The Question "Who?"

Yet another consideration in moving forward with needs assessment is to establish *who* will be involved in the effort. While administrators are often tempted to develop new programs and services in an insulated planning environment free of potential distractions and interference, it is my belief that this is one of the reasons many programs die on the vine in their first few years of inception. While it may seem easier to develop a program in a controlled environment surrounded by kindred spirits, the disadvantage is that the community is not allowed to give significant input and develop ownership of the program. Thus, a program may be developed and implemented, but finding steady sources of referral can prove difficult.

A group assembled to conduct a needs assessment of conflict systems is not intended to remain a static one. Membership and inclusion may vary based on the stage of the assessment as well as on changing considerations. At the outset it is most efficient to establish a smaller group of committed individuals, not to conduct the needs assessment but to establish the process for conducting the assessment. Then a larger group can be established to engage in the needs assessment, providing the broadest and most diverse perspectives available. The next stage of the process might include engaging implementation groups to create new, or modify existing, programs or services. At the end stage, oversight or advisory groups can be charged with ensuring that the program is assessed in an ongoing and meaningful way, and that it is meeting the needs of the community.

When considering whom to invite to the table, make certain to extend invitations to a diverse and balanced group of people, including

- **Allies**—Who are the kindred spirits, the champions of the cause? These people can bring energy and excitement to the effort, and often have expertise that will be valuable as the effort moves forward.
  Critics—Who has been critical of existing programs and services, or who is inclined to be critical of any new programs or changes to existing ones? These people may be critical for good reason, based on previous experiences. These people may also bring a devil's advocate perspective that can be helpful in challenging allies to think outside their own comfort zones.
- **Stakeholders**—Who has a vested interest in existing programs and services, or who would have an interest in new programs or changes to existing ones? These people may serve as referral sources to conflict systems or may have parallel systems. Stakeholders might also include those who oversee the affected programs or services as well as those managing other such campus systems. People who currently or might in the future fund campus conflict resolution systems can also be considered as stakeholders. As an example, in one campus needs assessment I conducted, the assessment group included the vice president of student affairs, the dean of students, residence life staff, campus judicial officers, and counseling services staff. Another campus might consider shaping a group that includes members from general counsel, campus ministry, campus ombuds, campus police, academic departments, student employment, affirmative action, and others.
- **Students**—Although inherently stakeholders, students merit special mention here. It is important that student representation be as diverse as possible, reflecting not just cultural diversity but the diversity of conflicts that exist on campus. Rather than appointing a few favored students to this effort, consider diverse groups of students such as student government, student organizations composed mostly of underrepresented populations, Greek organizations, athletes, general interest students, and others.

Finally, who will lead the needs assessment process? Who will moderate the conversations that are to take place? One perspective suggests that an internal person, someone central to conflict resolution processes on campus, should be the person to take the lead. Advantages to this approach are that this person generally has a solid background in the campus community and the programs and services that already exist. In addition, relationships are often in place that will assist in bringing people together in the community. Conversely, perceptions of this person (or people) also already exist, and may serve to either further or frustrate the process. If an internal person, for example, is perceived as having a personal vested interest in the outcome of the assessment process, this can negatively affect the level of trust needed to engage in honest dialogue about campus conflict. Campus politics may also have an impact on the internal facilitator, as this person may not be able to make observations or share opinions that an external person could make without upsetting the internal culture. Finally, in many cases cost may be a determining factor on how an institution will proceed. Internal people can typically facilitate a process without the additional costs incurred by the use of an external facilitator.

External people also carry advantages and disadvantages. In many cases, external consultants carry additional credibility based on their professional experiences, such as having served as a consultant in similar situations for other institutions. With proper experience, external facilitators can ask questions that shed new light or get people to think differently about existing situations. External facilitators also have the advantage of being able to bring a different tone to the conversation, even using the needs assessment as an opportunity to educate those involved in the needs assessment process in the interest of ensuring that everyone has a shared understanding of key assessment concepts. The key disadvantage to an external facilitator can be cost, as well as working around his or her schedule. Additionally, some campus climates may simply not respond well to an outsider coming in to assist in the discussion of internal processes and politics.

To address the who question, we must address the following:

- Who will be involved?
- Why are we choosing each of these people?
- Is anyone excluded?
- Do the people we have chosen to include reflect a commitment to diversity and social justice, or does the group simply reflect the privilege of the majority?
- Who will lead the needs assessment? Is this an internal or an external person?

## *The Question "How?": A Road Map to Program Development*

The fourth question, *how*, serves as a transition into the road map for conflict systems program development (see Table 13.1). It is important to note

## TABLE 13.1
### A Road Map to Program Development

**Step 1: Preparation**

- Establish initial core group of people (First Team) to design needs assessment process.
- Establish a realistic timeline that provides for extensive dialogue, community assessment, program planning, and implementation and advertising.
- Identify and address barriers/obstacles to the needs assessment process, including institutional values, campus politics, potential legal issues, financial considerations, and so on.
- Approach potential participants for the formal needs assessment.
- Create the process to conduct a needs assessment.
- Establish who will lead a needs assessment process (internal vs. external).
- Incorporate any existing data that relates to conflict resolution processes on campus, including previous assessment of existing programs and services.

**Step 2: Formal Needs Assessment**

- Establish the facilitator(s) and participant list (Second Team) for the needs assessment process.
- Conduct an initial needs assessment workshop (full day to two days recommended).
  A sample outline of such a workshop includes
  —defining and understanding conflict;
  —exploring styles for managing conflict;
  —identifying sources of conflict for students;
  —identifying means for resolving student conflicts;
  —identifying gaps that exist for students in conflict;
  —identifying student populations that are traditionally underserved by existing conflict systems;
  —brainstorming on how to change existing programs and services, or how to implement new programs and services that will close the gaps identified;
  —developing a plan of future action, as well as working groups to carry out the plan.

- Create a report solidifying the work of the needs assessment group.
  In the report, note
  —background that led to the needs assessment,
  —process used to execute the needs assessment,
  —summary of recommendations resulting from the needs assessment,
  —recommendations on how to operationalize these recommendations.
  This report should be submitted (for approval/endorsement) to key decision makers who will have the final say on recommended changes, as well as the funding needed to carry out such changes

**Step 3: Planning and Implementation**

- Establish a small group (Third Team) responsible for the overall implementation of recommendations made; smaller groups can be established to facilitate any specific change or set of changes—subgroups can be developed based on the specific conflict resolution pathway.

### TABLE 13.1 (Continued)

- For each conflict resolution pathway, engage in the following activities.
  - —benchmarking: Examine other programs for best practices; in determining which programs to benchmark, consider peer institutions, national leaders (regardless of peer comparison group), and local institutions.
  - —networking: This term is applied to using professional contacts in conflict resolution and higher education to engage in informal brainstorming as well as to discuss experiences that other professionals have had in managing conflict systems.
  - —student assessment: Conducting focus groups to discuss how students resolve conflict and how students react to current conflict resolution practices on campus can be useful in designing changes; it also serves as an opportunity to gauge student reaction to possible changes. (Note: This should be done once for all the conflict resolution pathways to avoid student burnout on assessment efforts.)
  - —brainstorming: Once benchmarking, networking, and assessment processes have been completed, the team has sufficient information to develop a proposal for altering current conflict resolution practices or adding new ones.
  - —Items to address in a proposal include
    - ○ program to be added/altered—What is being proposed?
    - ○ rationale—Why is it being proposed?
    - ○ mission and scope—What constraints will the program work within?
    - ○ referral systems—How will cases be referred? By whom? Is specialized training needed to serve as a referral agent? What exchange of information is needed to ensure proper case management and record keeping?
    - ○ resources needed—What human resources will be needed? Financial resources? Technology resources? Facility resources?
    - ○ Assessment—How will the program be assessed? When will it be assessed? For what will it be assessed? Who will conduct the assessment? (Note: Program assessment is the subject of chapter 14 in this book.)
    - ○ Education—How will the community be educated about the program?
    - ○ Advertising—How will students be made aware of the program? How will faculty and staff members know to refer students to the program?
    - ○ Staff—Who will provide the service? How will these people be recruited and selected? What type of training will staff need, and who will provide this training? How will supplemental training be provided? How will staff be assessed in their performance?

that this is not a prescription for the only way to conduct a needs assessment. It is impossible to design one process that works for 2- and 4-year schools, liberal arts and trade schools, public and private schools, and so on. Rather, this outline should serve as a guide to conducting a needs assessment process. The very first task of the initial planning group should be rewriting this outline to meet your institution's own needs.

## Conclusion

Developing and improving campus conflict systems is a highly detailed process. By having a clear strategy and road map, coupled with motivated stakeholders, the process can also be enriching and enlightening. A full assessment process will ultimately lead to improvements in campus conflict resolution systems that will benefit students in conflict, adapt to changing students and changing environments, and will have a positive impact on student development.

Many things need to be considered in improving existing and developing new conflict resolution programs and services. No single outline can account for the complexity each professional will face in her or his institutional environment. Edit and augment the approach offered in this chapter to meet your own individual needs. Finally, remember that professionals at other institutions have been down the road you are preparing to travel. Draw on their experiences. Learn from their lessons. Despite marked differences across colleges and universities, as a student affairs profession we share notable similarities in terms of the successes and frustrations we experience in our work with students and campus conflicts. The human experience transcends our institutions. We can assist one another in improving the quality of life on our campuses by developing and sustaining thoughtful creative processes that best meet the assessed needs of our diverse and changing student communities.

## References

Diamond, R. (2006). *Why colleges are so hard to change*. Retrieved October 15, 2008, from http://www.insidehighered.com/views/2006/09/08/diamond

Girard, K., Rifkin, J., & Townley, A. (1985). *Peaceful persuasion: A guide to creating mediation dispute resolution programs for college campuses*. Amherst, MA: Mediation Project.

Upcraft, M., & Schuh, J. (1996). *Assessment in student affairs: A guide for practitioners*. San Francisco: Jossey-Bass.

Warters, W. (2000). *Mediation in the campus community: Designing and managing effective programs*. San Francisco: Jossey-Bass.

# 14

# SUSTAINING A WORTHY INVESTMENT

## Assessing Conflict Resolution Programs

*Richard T. Olshak*

All assessment is a perpetual work in progress.
*Linda Suske*

In 2005, as a part of a larger survey on conflict resolution, I examined 69 campus-based mediation programs. Of these, 29% of program administrators acknowledged that no assessment was being conducted to ensure that the program was achieving desired goals. Of those who did report using assessment practices to evaluate effectiveness, 45% employed user (disputant) satisfaction surveys as the sole means for program assessment. Another 25% of the programs complemented user surveys with surveys of mediators. Of the programs studied, administrators of only six programs (9%) reported using comprehensive assessment practices to evaluate program effectiveness and community satisfaction/impact.

In environments of often negligible financial resources, it seems more critical than ever that conflict resolution professionals make reasoned and documented arguments for the continued use of financial and human resources, as well as to make successful arguments for securing new resources. The purpose of this chapter is not to explore the topic of program assessment in higher education, as there are multiple outstanding resources (Palomba, Banta, & Associates, 1999; Upcraft & Schuh, 1996) currently available to practitioners. Rather, the purpose is to offer a practical strategy for assessing campus-based conflict resolution programs specifically.

## Why Don't We Assess?

How is it that in only 9% of the mediation programs surveyed, administrators reported conducting assessment practices that go beyond user satisfaction surveys? The anecdotal information I have collected suggests several reasons for lack of assessment.

- Busy, busy, busy—Practitioners are often wearing multiple hats, and many of the people responsible for coordinating conflict resolution programs feel they don't have the time or support to conduct a thorough assessment.
- Fear—Practitioners have also expressed a concern for what assessment efforts may show, not so much for individual cases but in terms of the lack of program use and/or lack of the overall impact of the program. By staying away from formal and intentional assessment, some practitioners avoid calling attention to a program that might not be deemed of significant value by the program's operational division or by the broader campus community.
- Lack of knowledge—Some practitioners have been up front with me about their unfamiliarity with assessment and their concern about doing something wrong. Because of the many tasks they have, they feel unable to conduct a worthwhile program assessment.

As a practitioner myself, I understand each of these concerns. But to allow these concerns to carry the day does a disservice to the programs we manage and to the populations we profess to serve. How can we truly know, beyond a feeling that we get, that a program is accomplishing the goals we have established (assuming we have established goals) and is meeting the needs of the populations we serve? How can we justify avoiding assessment while allocating and being accountable for resources? And how can we expect our campus communities to see conflict resolution programs as anything more than a pet project if we avoid being accountable for the impact (or lack of impact) of the program?

## Why Should We Assess?

It is my view that assessment is a critical part of program sustainability, and when done correctly should serve as the greatest argument for the existence of comprehensive conflict resolution programs. As Warters (2000) noted

> A good evaluation, if planned from the program's beginning, can be a valuable management tool. Planning the evaluation as the program is being developed will sharpen everyone's thinking about the entire program: its

mission, its goals, its objectives, and activities designed to meet those objectives. By organizing the evaluation, program coordinators can give their program greater structure and increase their chances of success. Ideally, program planning and evaluation should work hand in hand. (p. 151)

Expanding further on Warters' perspective, it is my argument that program assessment is a critical piece of the life cycle of any conflict resolution plan. Rather than seeing assessment as something outside the program, we should see it as inseparable. One such model has been used historically in student affairs programs across the board at Illinois State University. The model is best summarized in Figure 14.1. In this model, the life cycle of a program actually begins with the type of needs assessment I outlined in chapter 13.

**FIGURE 14.1**
**Resource Allocation**

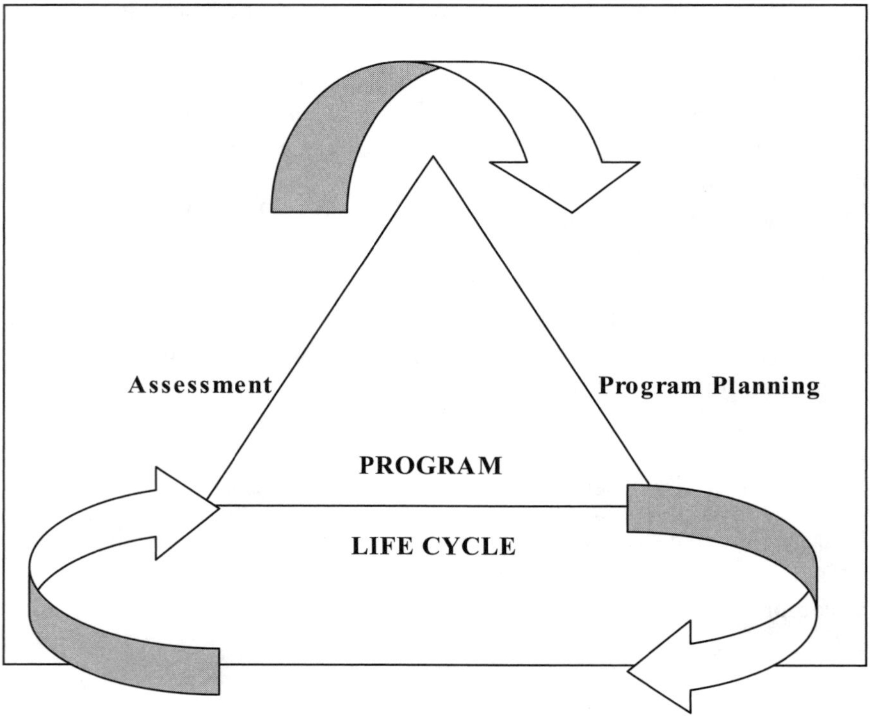

*Note.* Adapted from unpublished materials by Brent Paterson.

Based on that assessment, a program plan is put into place for the alloca-tion of resources (human, financial, space, technology). We then use the assessment process to ensure that the allocation of resources is having the effect that was desired during the program planning phase. This requires a comprehensive ongoing analysis of the entire program.

Moreover, Warters (2001) states that an effective assessment effort can serve multiple purposes, including

- Justifying and explaining the program,
- Program planning and decision-making,
- Improving services,
- Addressing a specific problem area, and
- Assessing volunteer needs and impact. (pp. 152–153)

Given the potential purposes that assessment can serve, coupled with an environment that demands accountability for every dollar spent, it is time to overcome obstacles to program assessment for the benefit of our programs and the students we serve.

## How Do We Assess? A Three-Stage Assessment Process

There are many different thoughts on how to most effectively assess a stu-dent affairs program. The approach offered in this chapter is a recommended best practice for conducting an overall assessment of a conflict resolution program in a college or university setting. It should be altered as appropriate to meet the specific needs of a particular environment. In general, I recom-mend the three stages be completed on a continuous basis every 5 years to ensure continual program review while also acknowledging the complexities involved and resources required to engage in such efforts.

### Preassessment

To be successful, an effective assessment process should be understood, inclu-sive, meaningful, manageable, and flexible (Bresciani, 2006). Prior to embarking on a comprehensive assessment process, some key questions must be addressed.

#### What Are We Seeking to Assess?

An effective assessment effort must be meaningful to those who will be using the information collected. Determining what will be measured is key to addressing the issue of meaning and manageability. How will success or effectiveness be measured for a particular program? Will it be a straight cost-benefit analysis? Will it be concerned with the satisfaction of those using the services being provided? Or will the assessment seek to measure the overall impact of the program on the quality of institutional life? An ambitious and comprehensive assessment may attempt to address all these questions in some form.

### Who Will Conduct the Assessment?

Similar to developing a conflict resolution program, the assessment process will likely require the involvement of different people at different stages in the process. Consider who will need to be involved at the various stages, including program members, users of services, referral agents, funding sources, and other people who may be directly or indirectly affected by the program. An inclusive process will seek out all those with relevant perspectives and feedback.

### How Will the Assessment Be Conducted?

Many factors can be used to engage in program assessment. Interviews, statistics, focus groups, document analysis, observations, and other methods can be employed to address the questions being asked. Drawing from the Council for the Advancement of Standards (CAS) self-assessment elaborated on later in this chapter, many different methods may be used to gather information from various stakeholders. It is not uncommon at the first stage of the process to conduct interviews and convene focus groups while simultaneously examining program documents and statistics. In the second stage of the process (benchmarking), the focus is on examining external programs, again using interviews and documentation review, sometimes supplemented by site visits. In the final stage (external review), many of the methods used in the CAS self-assessment process are revisited but conducted by different evaluators.

### What Will Be Done With the Results?

Program assessment processes require a great deal of time, energy, and in some cases money. Therefore, it is important that all involved understand at the outset of the process what is going to come of the results. Will the information be used to justify the continued existence of the program? Will results be used to justify the argument for new resources? Or will the assessment be used to make incremental changes in the program? Those getting involved in such an effort should understand in advance how their efforts will be used. Conducting a comprehensive assessment process simply so the results can sit on a shelf will ultimately do more harm than good to the morale of those involved.

## Stage One: The CAS Self-Assessment Process

A good beginning place for a comprehensive program review is to conduct a CAS self-assessment. CAS (2008) is a consortium of more than 30 professional organizations committed to the establishment of consistent professional standards for all student affairs programs. Until 2006, there were no formal standards in place for conflict resolution programs, and those programs using CAS modified student conduct standards to include conflict resolution programs. Today, CAS has incorporated conflict resolution standards in response to increased program interest and availability, making it far more convenient for those evaluating conflict resolution programs.

The CAS self-assessment process is described in detail on the CAS Web site and in the publications available for purchase. In short, the process is designed to examine whether programs are in compliance with professional standards as well as to measure how well programs meet various learning and developmental outcomes (CAS, 2008). In effect, the process first assists professionals in identifying areas of strength and weakness in each program evaluated. The next recommended step is to attempt to address areas of weakness through benchmarking.

It is worth noting here that in addition to the standards established by CAS, other professional standards of practice can be incorporated in a CAS review process either to supplement the process or to replace the process entirely. This may be useful depending on the type of conflict resolution services offered, as well as who is providing such services. Various standards have been established by the Association for Conflict Resolution (http://www.acrnet.org), the International Ombudsman Association (http://www.ombudsassociation.org), the American Bar Association (http://www.abanet.org), and the American Arbitration Association (http://www.adr.org). Additional information related to standards of practice and assessment can be found at http://www.campus-adr.org.

## Stage Two: Benchmarking Process

The goal of the benchmarking process is to seek to improve areas of program weakness by considering what other institutions and programs have done in those areas. By examining best practices, we can get an understanding of how other institutions have met similar challenges. This is predicated on the idea that few challenges are truly unique, and that we benefit from the experiences of others rather than seeking to reinvent the wheel.

The benchmarking process is relatively straightforward. A group of people are charged with examining other programs that have been identified as being worthy of study. This may include comparison schools, schools of similar size, schools in the same general geographic area, or schools that have been identified as having model conflict resolution programs. For example, when assessing mediation programs at Illinois State University, we considered schools that are considered comparison schools, such as Ball State, Bowling Green, and Miami University. We also considered other public universities in Illinois, as well as programs that we considered to be excellent in areas where we needed to improve including the University of Central Florida, Rochester Institute of Technology, University of Michigan, and the University of Illinois.

Depending on the information sought, members of the benchmarking team may collect documents, examine Web sites, conduct interviews, or visit other campuses to gain a better understanding of why things work the way they do at those campuses and thus gain a better understanding of how to improve their own program.

To better understand benchmarking, Upcraft and Schuh (1996) provide an outline for conducting a successful benchmarking process, which includes the following steps:

*Define the problem*—In this case the results of a CAS assessment will help identify what the specific problems are.

*Determine if benchmarking is appropriate*—While we will seek to gather information from other institutions, some problems may be completely unique to a particular environment. In such cases it may be difficult to find relevant benchmarking questions to address.

*Determine what to benchmark*—Remember that we are not benchmarking entire programs but specific components of these programs. Go into a benchmarking effort with a clear goal in mind and with predefined questions.

*Determine who should be involved*—An inclusive assessment process is desirable but challenging when it comes to benchmarking. In general, benchmarking is best conducted by those who have a solid grasp of the system being benchmarked and the context within which the assessment information is being sought. In other words, specific expertise and context is highly desirable. To remain inclusive, consider the varying levels of knowledge and awareness that key stakeholders have, and attempt to include these people in the process.

*Determine which comparable organizations will be benchmarked*—I have already noted that different types of institutions may be selected based on likeness of schools, geographic location, and best practices. It may also be that particular types of programs are more desirable to benchmark than others. For example, a mediation program based in a counseling center faces specific issues unique to counseling centers. As such, schools to benchmark would be those that have programs housed in counseling centers.

*Determine what information will be gathered*—It is best to have preestablished questions for interviews and to seek specific types of printed and electronic information. Working from a script will ensure consistency in the benchmarking process, particularly when multiple teams will be conducting the benchmarking practices.

*Determine how the information will be collected*—In most cases, significant information can be gathered by reviewing Web sites and published material available from the institution being benchmarked. In many cases this is supplemented with telephone interviews consisting of specific questions about the program and about the material already reviewed. In some instances, it may be determined that a campus visit is necessary to see the program and the people involved; in other cases such a visit is a luxury made affordable because of close proximity.

*Analyze the data*—Compare the data to the questions asked and the challenges identified by the CAS assessment process. How does this data shed light on how challenges facing a program can be addressed? With this in mind the group conducting the benchmarking review will issue a report detailing its findings and offering recommendations based on its review.

*Take action*—With a report in hand, program directors and higher administrators must review the findings and examine recommendations made. Do the recommendations make sense for the program? If not, how can the recommendations be tailored to better meet the program's needs? What changes can be made? What conditions must be met for these changes to be made? Taking big action is generally preceded by taking smaller actions that help create an atmosphere that is supportive of change.

*Assess the action taken*—Once changes have been made and appropriate time has been allowed to provide reviewable results, we must determine if the changes we made had their intended effect. Did the action solve the problem? Did it create new problems? Have other problems emerged since the time of action that may now necessitate additional review? Only by examining these questions intentionally will we know if our goals have truly been met.

### Stage Three: External Review

In the final stage of the program assessment process, the institution will bring in at least one external (outside the institution) consultant who is considered to be an expert in the programs being assessed. In cases where a specific program is examined (such as mediation), one external expert in mediation would likely suffice. In cases where multiple programs are being assessed simultaneously, it may be preferable (though costlier) to bring in people whose expertise matches the programs being assessed. In general, most external reviews will include one or two external reviewers.

External reviewers do not conduct the entire process on their own. One difficulty with bringing in external experts is that their own programmatic biases may not meet the needs or realities of the institution being reviewed. It is preferable to assemble a team of people from within the institution to work with the external reviewer(s) to fully examine the program and to ensure that an internal perspective is considered in the discussions.

Prior to outlining the process, I would like to share my own experience as an internal consultant to an external review of a student health service. Three external experts in health care were invited to facilitate the review. One brought a community medical perspective, another brought the perspective of an accomplished director of a campus health service, and the other held the perspective of someone working in student health insurance. The three were complemented by a group of internal representatives who worked as part of the team to review all aspects of the health service. One faculty member and one student were appointed to the team, as was the dean of the College of Nursing. I was appointed as a representative of the student affairs division, despite having no knowledge of health services.

As a group, we read through documentation of the program and conducted interviews with all personnel in the student health service over a 3-day period. We then met as a group and continued to meet electronically until a final report was issued. The entire process, from the time of my appointment to the time of the final report, was 6 months in length. The final document was a 34-page report that validated some of what previous internal assessments had found, while challenging others. The resulting recommendations were far more expansive than I believe an internal team would have accomplished on its own.

So how is an external review conducted? It begins with an internal documentation of the entire program. This includes mission, initiatives, summary of resources, and a description of each program or service offered, as well as summaries of personnel and staff development, outreach, and diversity. An internal SWOT analysis weighing the strengths, weaknesses, opportunities, and threats experienced within a program or unit is often included as a means for alerting an external review team to issues that are the most critical to address. All previous data from the CAS self-assessment and benchmarking processes are included, as well as an update of any developments since the conclusion of the benchmarking process. This is provided to the external consulting group whose composition we will address shortly. This team is then charged with drafting questions based on the internal documentation and developing a course of action for addressing those questions. The external review team determines who in the community it wishes to interview and determines the questions that need to be addressed in each interview.

Consistent with my own experience as a program reviewer, I see the external review process as being the domain of the external consultants and internal stakeholders, rather than including internal program personnel. As such, a conflict resolution review would likely include students, faculty, referral sources, and other constituencies in addition to the external consultants. It would not include staff that provide the programs and services. This eliminates defensiveness and turf battles that might lead to muting information critical of the program yet necessary for productive change to be made.

This group concludes with the creation of a final report. From my perspective, it is critical for this report to be made public and posted on a Web site for transparency to the process, and so that accountability can be maintained for the institution, the division where the program is housed, and for the program itself. The conflict resolution staff is then charged with enacting those recommendations supported by the institution.

## Conclusion

The conclusion of the external review is far from the conclusion of the assessment process. Once recommendations are made, reviewed, and acted upon, we should see shifts in the programs and services provided. Following the model (Figure 14.1) on page 210, the conclusion of the external review will lead to changes in program planning and thus changes in resource allocation, and the entire cycle starts anew.

While the assessment process described in this chapter is ambitious and intense, it ultimately has the best chance to result in positive and sustainable improvements in the programs and services we offer. By seeing such a process as an opportunity rather than a burden, we can ensure that we will get the most out of the process, resulting in getting the most out of our conflict resolution programs and services.

## References

Bresciani, M. J. (2006). *Good practices in outcomes-based assessment program review.* Sterling, VA: Stylus.

Council for the Advancement of Standards. (2008). Retrieved December 12, 2008, from https://www.cas.edu/Presentations%20&%20Tutorials/NASPA_CAS_20 08.ppt

Palomba, C., Banta, T., & Associates. (1999). *Assessment essentials: Planning, implementing, and improving assessment in higher education.* San Francisco: Jossey-Bass.

Upcraft, M., & Schuh, J. (1996). *Assessment in student affairs: A guide for practitioners.* San Francisco: Jossey-Bass.

Warters, W. (2000). *Mediation in the campus community: Designing and managing effective programs.* San Francisco: Jossey-Bass.

# 15

# TEACHING SOCIAL JUSTICE ON CAMPUS FOR SELF-AWARENESS, COMMUNITY SUSTAINABILITY, AND SYSTEMS CHANGE

*Judy Rashid*

The unwillingness to approach teaching from a standpoint that includes awareness of race, sex, and class is often rooted in the fear that classrooms will be uncontrollable and that emotions and passions will not be contained. To some extent we all know whenever we address in the classroom subjects that students are passionate about there is always a possibility of confrontation, forceful expression of ideas or even conflict.

*bell hooks, 1994, p. 39*

In a collection of works that focused on teaching for social justice, Linda Christensen (2000) wrote that although conflict does occur when students "rise up" (p. vii), transformative acts such as engagement and empowerment also occur. In essence, engagement in diverse ideas causes conflict, which causes change, which causes learning to occur. Fried (2006) refers to learning as a comprehensive, holistic, transformative activity that integrates academic learning and student development and the campus as a learning system. This learning system is in the classroom, the residence halls, the cafeteria, the athletic field, study abroad programs, and student organizations. To promote the study and examination of social justice issues for students, most colleges and universities either have curricular requirements for social justice course work or a campus culture that promotes such engagement outside the classroom (Tritton, 2008).

This chapter addresses the relevance of teaching social justice on campus—in the classroom and in student affairs—and the challenge of maintaining a balanced and reasoned approach.

## Teaching Social Justice: The Impact on Teaching, Research, and Civic Engagement Inside the Classroom

After Thomas Tritton served as president of Haverford College for 12 years, he returned to the classroom in 2007 as president in residence at Harvard University Graduate School of Education where he designed a course titled Social Justice in the Undergraduate Experience. In his article "Teaching Social Justice in Higher Education," Tritton (2008) reported that before teaching the course he explored how colleges promote social justice issues with students. He pointed out that while in this pursuit, he quickly realized there was little coordination or consensus among colleges pursuing social justice goals. It was also apparent that no well-developed base of scholarship on the definitions, objectives, and outcomes of course instruction in social justice existed.

Students who took the course with Tritton examined Brian Barry's (2005) theoretical approach to distributive justice where fairness and equality are achieved in all aspects of society; bell hook's (2003) view of higher education as a combination of autobiography, history, and literary analysis; and Martha Nussbaum's (2006) unconventional approach to three unsolved aspects of justice, namely, the disabled, nonhuman animals, and global justice. In addition, through small group discussions, students examined the most effective ways that colleges could have the most impact in teaching social justice. Furthermore, the students examined whether the focus in the study of social justice should be on research or teaching, curricular or extracurricular, through specific courses or across the curriculum, how to form partnerships with those outside the academy, how to encourage more than one viewpoint on controversial issues, and to what extent can or should academic critique influence the public agenda. Each group was also responsible for leading a class session on the social justice topic of its choice. The class settled on four main topics: health care and social justice, justice for nonhuman species, diversity and social justice, and housing and social justice. These topics demonstrate, as pointed out by Tritton (2008), that one can make any course better by engaging social justice concepts from nearly any disciplinary perspective.

Just as Tritton's approach engaged the students in the critical exploration of teaching and applying social justice theory, Pettit (2006) similarly concurred that we in the academy can "cultivate the highest capacities of human beings when we assist them in critically evaluating questions about how we can better flourish together in our communities, rather than isolating communities and reacting to each other without ever really knowing why we do so" (pp. 475–476). As a result, to help "advance the cause of searching for better ways to think about and to teach social justice" (p. 477), Pettit offers the following five rules:

- Differentiate between unjust and unfortunate states of affairs. Situations are often discounted as unfortunate when one does not critically examine the causes of the misfortune. This means that teachers of social justice must use history, sociology, and public policy to pursue any structural changes that might make a real case for the possible existence of injustice rather than mere misfortune.
- Avoid misanthropy. This is defined by Pettit as "distrust or negative evaluation of human beings as such" (p. 478). Regardless of the nature of the indictment (e.g., corporate corruption, racism, sexism), those who teach social justice must believe in the inherent ability of the human being to do something about social justice. A negative outlook on human capacity to be part of the solution is counterproductive and creates a sense of hopelessness.
- Observe the pedagogical priority of injustice to justice. This rule implies that we must learn about justice by beginning with injustice. Theories of justice are better taught by first examining injustices, which are often common areas of agreement among diverse groups. This approach allows participants to converge on particular outcomes without feeling the stress of not being able to solve large-scale issues.
- Put actual political discourse back into theories of political discourse. This rule means paying some attention to the mechanisms of discourse and communication. It means getting actively involved in the community to make things happen (e.g., making phone calls, writing letters to legislators and newspapers, listening to constituents) rather than merely studying the theory of the process. Involvement builds in the student a tolerance for uncertainty, conflicting opinions, long debate, competing interests, confusion, bargaining, compromise, and imperfect solutions. This in turn helps to shape a citizen that will remain steadfast in the process instead of becoming aggravated and possibly walking away.

- Link discussions of social justice and injustice to actual opportunities to pursue justice or to confront injustice. This linking of social and political ethics to opportunities for action, according to Pettit, brings the first four rules together, which enables one to possibly claim the presence of injustice rather than merely an unfortunate state of affairs.

By adhering to these five rules in teaching social justice, students are enabled to become educated rather than trained and would be expected to engage in intellectual discourse. On the contrary, as noted by Fried (2006), teaching in the academy has "usually been understood as the transfer of information" and learning is the "ability to acquire, recall, and repeat information" (p. 3) . This "positivist epistemology" (p. 3), as explained by Fried, views learning as a body of knowledge that exists objectively, separate from the person who is learning. On the opposite side, Fried cites that "constructivism" (p. 4), a challenge to positivism, addresses questions of personal meaning wherein "individual perspective and life experience shape each person's interpretation of information" (p. 4).

The teaching of social justice is a means of provocation of thought, thus supporting the notion that the educational goal should be to help students address personal questions of meaning, experience, or involvement. This approach further allows the individual to explore endless possibilities and respond collectively to societal needs as determined by each generation.

## Outside the Classroom

In 2003 the Council for the Advancement of Standards in Higher Education (CAS) identified 16 individual learning and development outcome domains (Komives & Schoper, 2006). As I see it, the following eight of these domains are areas of impact in teaching and applying social justice:

- intellectual growth
- effective communication
- realistic self-appraisal
- leadership development
- meaningful interpersonal relationship
- collaboration
- social responsibility
- appreciating diversity

These domains served as the basis for establishing learning outcomes in a collegiate course in negotiation and conflict resolution taught by a student affairs administrator during fall 2007 and spring 2008. In a research study of the assessment of learning outcomes, Rashid (2008) concluded that the use of these domains prove helpful in establishing and assessing learning outcomes, which enable students to acquire new skills, knowledge, and/or attitudes in the practice of negotiation and mediation. Teaching students conflict management and resolution enabled this researcher, as a student affairs administrator, to demonstrate that academic learning and student development processes exist simultaneously and should be highlighted more in the academy.

To demonstrate this inherent existence, Street (1997) found that most of the research that examined the affects of the college environment on college students outside the classroom dealt with the role student organizations play in student involvement and student development. Historically, college student organizations "play a significant role in student life on most American college and university campuses" (Street, 1997, p. 6) and particularly in student leadership development (Komives, 1994). More specifically, Street (1997) describes student organizations as "learning laboratories" (p. 4) that offer many opportunities for students, including the chance to develop meaningful relationships, pursue special interests, clarify a sense of purpose and identity, and develop interpersonal, leadership, organization, and social skills.

There are many variables at play within student organizations that influence individual and group behavior. Schmitz (1997) explored the adaptation of organizational behavior theory to college student organizations depicting the student as the core of the group being surrounded and influenced by task, technology, structure, leadership, and culture all in the university environment. It is the job of educators to equip students of all ages with the relevant skills needed to navigate the constant interplay of these variables.

The challenge is for student affairs professionals to assume their appropriate role as equal partners in the educational training and development of not only student leaders (McIntire, 1989) but also all students. For example, on the college campus there seems to be a general assumption that student leaders of campus organizations are automatically effective leaders who are "flexible, prepared, knowledgeable about self, and are able to create therapeutic climates, intervene critically and to successfully apply 'problem-solving processes'" (Conyne, Harvill, Morran, & Killacky, 1990, p. 34). This may very well be an expectation of group leaders but cannot be left to chance by student affairs professionals. Without proper training, many students who are chosen to lead organizations, for example, are unable to effectively assume leadership responsibilities (Lamoureaux, 1994). These "idealistic, energized students are quickly 'burned out' by unrealistic demands they place upon themselves and by the frustrations that develop as a result of the absence of a systematic approach to solving their organizational problems" (Duvall & Ender, 1980, p. 145), in addition to coming to terms with their personal self-identity.

As a result, there is constant conflict in student organizations caused primarily by role conflict, interdependence, and scarcity of resources (Franck, 1983). These findings further indicate the potential to teach the principles of social justice as a means to increase self-awareness and to manage interpersonal conflict. Critical reflection of thoughts and ideas along with self-introspection enable students to gain invaluable life skills.

## Conclusion

Racial, ethnic, cultural, and language diversity deepens the quest by different groups for cultural recognition and rights (Banks, 2004). In essence, when men and women simultaneously reflect on themselves (self-awareness, as in the title of the chapter) and on the world, they increase the scope of their perception and "begin to single out elements from their 'background awareness' and to reflect upon them" (Freire, 1970/1993, p. 64). This "problem-posing education" according to Freire, causes people to "develop their power to perceive critically the way they exist in the world with which and in which they find themselves; they come to see the world not as a static reality, but as a reality in process, in transformation" (p. 64). Thus, this quest by different groups for cultural recognition and rights challenges the "assimilationist notions of citizenship," as noted by Banks (2004, p. 290), in which all groups are expected to forsake their own culture to fully participate in the dominant mainstream culture. On the other hand, the twenty-first century and beyond calls for "a delicate balance of unity and diversity . . . as an essential goal of citizenship education in multicultural nation states" (Banks, p. 289).

As a result, it is vital for campuses to be engaged in building community through social justice research, teaching, and civic engagement. Curricular and co-curricular experiences in social justice provide a forum for the student to acquire new skills, knowledge, attitudes, and enhance students' ability to work with people whose personality, background, expectations, and values differ from their own.

Many world problems that affect us all need our collective attention. Today, citizenship education is just as vital a part of literacy as basic skills in reading, writing, and mathematics (Banks, 2004). We must teach our students how to communicate with each other—not to fear one another because of differences but to learn from one another as we seek to address the pertinent challenges of our time. We are cautioned by the late Martin Luther King Jr. that "we must learn to live together as brothers or die together as fools." Let us take heed within the academy to provoke thought among our students through teaching social justice for all and for all things.

# References

Banks, J. A. (2004). Teaching for social justice, diversity, and citizenship in a global world. *National Forum, 68*, 289–298.

Barry, B. (2005). *Why social justice matters.* Cambridge, UK: Polity Press.

Christensen, L. (2000). *Reading, writing, and rising up: Teaching about social justice and the power of the written word.* Milwaukee, WI: Rethinking School.

Conyne, R. K., Harvill, R. L., Morran, D. K., & Killacky, D. H. (1990). Effective group leadership: Continuing the search for greater clarity and understanding. *Journal for Specialists in Group Work, 15*(1), 30–36.

Duvall, W. H., & Ender, K. (1980). A training model for developing leadership awareness. In E. B. Newton & K. L. Ender (Eds.), *Student development practices: Strategies for making a difference* (pp. 145–168). Springfield, IL: Charles C. Thomas.

Franck, B. (1983). Conflict: Is it tearing your organization apart? *Campus Activities Programming, 16*(5), 26–29.

Freire, P. (1993). *Pedagogy of the oppressed* (Rev. ed., Myra Bergman Ramos, Trans.). New York: Continuum. (Original work published 1970)

Fried, J. (2006). Rethinking learning. In R. P. Keeling (Ed.), *Learning reconsidered 2: A practical guide to implementing a campus wide focus on the student experience* (pp. 3–9). Washington, DC: National Association of Student Personnel Administrators.

hooks, b. (2003). *Teaching community: A pedagogy of hope.* New York: Routledge.

Komives, S. R. (1994). Women student leaders: Self-perceptions of empowering leadership and achieving style. *NASPA Journal, 31*, 102–112.

Komives, S. R., & Schoper, S. S. (2006). Developing learning outcomes. In R. P. Keeling (Ed.), *Learning reconsidered 2: A practical guide to implementing a campus-wide focus on the student experience* (pp. 17–41). Washington, DC: National Association of Student Personnel Administrators.

Lamoureaux, G. P. (1994). *Leadership training: A special focus on Berkshire Community College student leaders.* Unpublished doctoral dissertation, University of Massachusetts, Amherst.

McIntire, D. D. (1989). Student leadership development: A student affairs mandate. *NASPA Journal, 27*(1), 75–79.

Nussbaum, M. C. (2006). *Frontiers of justice: Disability, nationality, species member-ship.* Cambridge, MA: Belknap Press, Harvard University Press.

Pettit, J. (2006). Five rules for teaching social justice. *Political Theology, 7*(4), 475–489.

Rashid J. (2008, September). *Conflict resolution education: Assessing student learning outcomes.* Paper presented at the annual conference of the Association for Conflict Resolution, Austin, TX.

Schmitz, C. A. (1997). *The translation of organizational behavior theory of college stu-dent organizations.* Unpublished doctoral dissertation, University of Southern California at Los Angeles.

Street, J. L., Jr. (1997). *Leadership development: A comparison of strategies for college student organizations.* Unpublished doctoral dissertation, University of Southern California, Los Angeles.

Tritton, T. R. (2008). *Teaching social justice in higher ed.* Retrieved September 19, 2008, http://www.insidehighereducation.com/views/2008/03/03/tritton

# 16

# AN IMPLEMENTATION MODEL

## Campus Conduct and Conflict Management at the University of Michigan

*U-M Division of Student Affairs Office of Student Conflict Resolution and Housing Student Conflict Resolution Staff*

The University of Michigan must continually change to meet—and to anticipate—the needs of an evolving society. To do so, we must be prepared to rethink what we do and how we do it, and to explore new paths that will lead us in entirely new directions. . . . Michigan's academic excellence presents itself in a student experience that draws on a diversity of ideas, beliefs, ethnicities and personal backgrounds. Ours is an environment that shapes our students and is shaped by them. Let's build upon that as we prepare students for life—and an interdisciplinary life at that.

*Mary Sue Coleman, president*
*of the University of Michigan*

Over 40,000 undergraduate and graduate students are enrolled at the University of Michigan (U-M) in Ann Arbor. Students from all 50 states and nearly 6,000 international students—the sixth highest total in the nation—help create a rich and diverse learning environment. About 25% of the university's students self-identify as students of color.

The U-M Division of Student Affairs Office of Student Conflict Resolution (OSCR) is responsible for administrating campus conduct policy and resolving conflict. During the 2007–08 academic year, OSCR staff assisted with nearly 399 requests for services. Over 700 additional cases involving alleged violations of the *Statement of Student Rights and Responsibilities* (the campus behavior policy) were referred by OSCR to the Housing Student Conflict Resolution (HSCR) process.

## The Office of Student Conflict Resolution's Mission and Guiding Principles *by Jennifer Meyer Schrage, OSCR Director*

The same commitment to student learning and development that typifies best practices in student affairs informs U-M's approach to campus conflict resolution. OSCR seeks to provide services to students, faculty, and staff that align with the values of the institution and are in accordance with OSCR's mission to "build trust, promote justice and teach peace" in a diverse campus community. A crucial step toward realizing this mission has been the development of meaningful alternatives to the formal conflict resolution services outlined in campus policy. The significant system changes associated with this development are rooted in the awareness that providing student-driven, educationally focused, and socially just conflict resolution services is not possible with a one-size-fits-all process for every incident that happens on campus. In this chapter we review how we strive to live up to this commitment of providing more meaningful and effective alternatives to traditional campus conduct processes.

In 2006 the OSCR began to develop a broader menu of conflict resolution pathways for U-M community members to use in addressing and resolving conflict. We use the term *conflict* broadly to encompass interpersonal, intragroup, and intergroup conflict as well as behaviors that are in conflict with U-M values articulated in the *Statement*. While our formal resolution process remains an important and educational venue for many incidents, the OSCR team experience demonstrates that many conflicts call for a less-formalized approach. When appropriate, this less-formal approach can be offered to provide a more educational, effective, satisfying, and timelier experience for all parties in a conflict. To this end, the OSCR experience has reaped some interesting results. In the 2006–07 academic year, only 4% of cases referred to OSCR were resolved in alternative conflict resolution (ACR) pathways. As we have continued to refine our systems and expand ACR offerings, the number of cases using these processes has greatly increased. In the 2007–08 academic year, more than 70% of cases were resolved in ACR.

With the support of the U-M Division of Student Affairs leadership, the OSCR team continues to explore innovation and refine its program. We do not assert that OSCR's program provides the one right answer. Rather, we hope that our experiences and successes raise questions and provide support and insight that is of value to other campuses.

**FIGURE 10.1**
**The Spectrum of Resolution Options**

Informal                                                                 Formal

No Conflict Management | Dialogue/Debate/Discussion | Conflict Coaching | Facilitated Dialogue | Social Justice Mediation | Restorative Practices | Shuttle Negotiation | Adjudication (Agreement) | Adjudication (Arbitration)

Social and Restorative Justice Foundation

*Note.* Schrage & Thompson; 2008.

## The Conflict Resolution Process *by Robert Coffey and Akilah Jones, OSCR Assistant Directors*

### Overview

The university's *Statement of Student Rights and Responsibilities* outlines the core community values that are foundational to maintaining U-M's scholarly community and describes student rights and responsibilities as members of this community. The *Statement* also outlines behaviors that contradict the values of the university and are thus considered violations subject to action under the *Statement*. Finally, the *Statement* describes the process for resolving campus conflict. This process and the OSCR's associated services are intended to be educational and restorative and in alignment with eight core campus values: civility, dignity, diversity, education, equality, freedom, honesty, and safety. The residence hall community has a separate but collaborative process that is discussed on pp. 236–239.

Incidents covered under the *Statement* may be resolved through OSCR's Formal Conflict Resolution (FCR) pathway, ACR pathways, or when appropriate, the HSCR process. OSCR's FCR pathway is used for alleged violations of the *Statement* when parties desire a more structured approach to resolution and/or formal documentation. Accordingly, when students are found responsible for a *Statement* violation in cases using the FCR process, the violation is formally documented as a discipline record with the university.

OSCR may administer ACR to address issues under the *Statement* when parties' desired outcomes call for a more flexible approach, *and* if all parties agree that ACR is the most appropriate way to address the conflict. In the event that ACR is successful, no disciplinary record is incurred. In the event that an incident involving a potential *Statement* violation does not reach successful resolution through ACR, the complaining party has the right to pursue resolution through the FCR process.

ACR pathways are also used by parties seeking resolution for conflicts that do not involve potential *Statement* violations. In the event that the *Statement* does not apply and attempts at ACR are not successful, OSCR attempts to assist the parties in finding additional resources to aid them in their pursuit of conflict resolution.

The OSCR unit is equipped with individual staff teams, which include student staff members devoted to offering the pathways for resolution. These teams include an FCR team, an ACR team, and a team that provides administrative support for the FCR and ACR processes.

## Intake Process

Parties access OSCR's services through referral from faculty and staff, students, campus and community police, through self-referral via OSCR's Web-based service request form, or by simply walking into the office and requesting assistance. At least one party in the conflict must be a student for OSCR to provide services. All parties who express an interest in learning more about OSCR's conflict resolution services are scheduled for an initial appointment with an intake facilitator. Faculty and staff seeking services consult with an OSCR professional staff member serving as an intake facilitator, and students are paired with a peer intake facilitator. OSCR's peer intake facilitators are undergraduate and graduate interns knowledgeable about OSCR's services. The majority have completed additional facilitation training, such as mediation and/or motivational interviewing.

This intake meeting is critical for several reasons, and therefore all parties must participate in this part of the process. Parties in the conflict often have a limited or incomplete understanding of how disputes may be resolved and assume that only a quasi-legal and adversarial process is desirable or available. These assumptions can drive a party's decision to prematurely ignore or dismiss a range of possibilities as he or she navigates the process. While some parties' social identities may lead them to feel more comfortable investing in a traditional judicial process, others may come from cultural communities where they have experienced maltreatment at the hands of a formal authority and are less trusting. The primary focus of the intake is to orient parties to the conflict resolution pathways available to them, help them identify desired outcomes, and then match those needs and interests with one or more pathways.

During the initial appointment, OSCR intake facilitators provide parties with information about each conflict resolution pathway, including the role each person would play, what parties could expect from the process, and typical outcomes achieved through resolution. While parties often wish to describe and explore the presenting conflict during their initial appointment, intake facilitators are trained to help parties first identify the most appropriate conflict resolution pathway by focusing on what they hope to accomplish through the conflict resolution process. Intake facilitators are also prepared to candidly broach the subject of social identity and to help parties consider whether identities such as race, gender, socioeconomic class, ability, or sexuality inform the conflicts they face. Left unaddressed, elements of the conflict related to social identity can limit or undermine the process and the outcome.

## Formal Conflict Resolution (FCR) *by Jordan England, OSCR Student Conflict Resolution Coordinator and Akilah Jones, OSCR Assistant Director*

OSCR's FCR process is initiated by any U-M community member filing a formal complaint. The FCR process is facilitated by a resolution coordinator (RC) from the FCR staff team. This coordinator is responsible for working with the complainant and respondent to achieve resolution of the conflict, while ensuring that the process adheres to *Statement* procedures and is in alignment with community values.

Resolution Coordinators (RCs) review newly submitted complaints, confirm that the complaining party has met with an intake facilitator, and may contact the complainant with questions regarding the complaint. If the RC determines that the alleged behavior describes a potential *Statement* violation and that the complaint is supported, the responding student is provided with a written notice of allegations and goes through the intake process. Complaints that do not meet these criteria may be referred to the ACR process.

During the FCR process the complainant and respondent meet separately with the RC to review the conflict and are provided with an opportunity to discuss their perspective on the incident, explore resolution options, and talk about desired outcomes. If both parties agree about what occurred and can reach a consensus about an outcome in alignment with the community's values, the case may be resolved. The responding party exits the resolution process with a set of educational and restorative measures that he or she has helped to design. Most parties using the FCR process resolve their case by coming to an agreement. As previously noted, a case resolved in the formal pathway is formally documented as a discipline record with the university.

If parties disagree about what happened and/or how best to resolve the conflict, the case will proceed to arbitration. Readers may recognize this as similar to a traditional campus administrative hearing process, but there are noticeable and important differences in language and implied philosophies. These are not semantic accidents but intentional system changes that influence the language and values of conflict resolution and social justice in a meaningful way. In arbitration, a third-party arbiter, consisting of a staff/faculty member or a panel of students, *facilitates a dialogue* with involved parties. The arbitration involves a structured conversation, with a *respectful exchange of questions and statements* about the incident and alleged violation. The complainant and respondent may present information and invite witnesses to participate to provide insight for the arbiter in determining an appropriate outcome for the conflict. At the conclusion of the arbitration, the arbiter, based on the facts revealed during the hearing, makes a recommendation of *responsible* or *not responsible*. If the student is found responsible, the arbiter also recommends a *package of educational and restorative measures*. The recommendation is sent to the dean of students, who may affirm or modify the outcome of responsibility and/or the package of educational measures. Either party may appeal the outcome of the arbitration.

*Program Strengths*

One of the strengths of OSCR's FCR process is having the RC serve as a facilitator, rather than an arbiter, of the resolution process. In the facilitation role, RCs work to ensure that the process is fair and just for all involved parties, that due process rights are protected, and that all participants are treated with dignity, civility, respect, and compassion. RCs practice multicultural competence, remaining conscientious of their own identities and cognizant of the various issues of culture, identity, privilege, and oppression that may be involved in a conflict. Neither advocates nor advisers, RCs are keepers of the process, ensuring access to meaningful and relevant conflict resolution for all participants.

In addition to being fair and just, OSCR strives to ensure that the FCR process is educational and restorative. Dialogue is a valued part of the process. When possible, parties have the explicit opportunity to hear and understand each other's viewpoints. In cases where parties are in agreement about the issues involved in the cases, the complainant and respondent are actively involved in deciding how to repair the harm done to the community. OSCR believes that educational measures should not be punitive; rather, the measures are designed to benefit the community and to prompt growth and development for all the parties involved.

## Special Issues

A number of potential issues should be considered in shifting to an educational and restorative model. One challenge is the paradigm shift this approach may present to process participants and campus administration. Many students enter OSCR's FCR process expecting or even seeking a punitive or legalistic system. OSCR's FCR process introduces students to the educational and restorative paradigm at the intake meeting, then reinforces it throughout the process.

Administrators may also be accustomed to a more legalistic and punitive approach. Ensuring that a conduct policy authentically represents the voices of students, faculty, and staff and is therefore community owned is critical. The U-M *Statement of Student Rights and Responsibilities* was initially authored by students. It is reviewed periodically by a student committee that works with faculty, staff, and students to propose any necessary amendments to the policy. OSCR's role in this amendment process is entirely informational. By remaining in a facilitator role, OSCR ensures that the process reflects the culture and values of the community rather than risk appearing as the campus prosecutor charged with defining and enforcing the values of campus.

OSCR also works to ensure that language used in the process or as part of practice and procedure aligns with the campus culture. Terms such as *guilty*, *not guilty*, *judicial*, *accused*, and *sanctions* reinforce perceptions of campus conflict resolution as punitive or legalistic and may undermine attempts to move toward educational and restorative practices.

The process of crafting educational measures also requires attention. A package that is tailored to the details of the incident at hand; that offers opportunity for learning, reflection, and restoration; and feels relevant to the responding student will likely net more educational and restorative value than a predetermined, one-size-fits-all or zero-tolerance package. Student involvement in the development of educational measures is critical. We have found it necessary to coach students through this process, helping them to move away from preconceived ideas of punishment, and craft a package that is appropriate to their circumstances.

Campuses also may want to consider the impact that a restorative and educational process may have on the timeliness of case resolution. OSCR strives to resolve all cases in a timely fashion, however, many factors can cause cases using this approach to take longer to resolve than is ideal. These include the complex and sensitive nature of some cases, the requirement that complainants and respondents take an active role in the process, the multiple meetings that may be involved in the resolution process, the fact that some cases may first attempt to use an ACR process, and occasional deferral of our process for students facing concurrent civil or criminal proceedings.

## Alternative Conflict Resolution *(ACR) by Robert Coffey,*
## *OSCR Assistant Director and David Votruba, OSCR Student*
## *Conflict Resolution Coordinator*

What further sets OSCR's conflict resolution model apart from traditional resolution models are the multiple options for resolving disputes offered through ACR services. Assisted by an intake facilitator, parties can consider and choose from a menu of ACR pathways, including conflict coaching, mediation, shuttle negotiation, a restorative justice circle, and facilitated dialogue. Each of these pathways may be considered for the purpose of resolving interpersonal, intragroup, or intergroup disputes that do or do not arise under the *Statement.* As with the FCR process, a student must be a party in the conflict for OSCR to assist.

In addition to these ACR pathways, OSCR offers ACR for Alcohol and Other Drugs (AOD) for students who acknowledge their involvement in minor alcohol and drug-related incidents and are interested in resolving these matters without incurring a disciplinary record. The ACR for AOD program is a brief, peer-facilitated educational and motivation enhancement intervention that provides students with the opportunity to explore and consider AOD-related issues, behaviors, and choices. All students who choose to complete the ACR for AOD program are provided with customized referrals to additional campus-based educational, diagnostic, and treatment resources. The ACR for AOD program is a restorative diversion program, similar to models discussed in chapter 9.

Once a student has selected an ACR pathway, the case is transferred to an RC in the ACR staff team. The RC then contacts the other party(s) involved with news of the initiating party's interest in ACR. Once all parties have consented to participate, the RC manages the logistics associated with providing the service, including identifying volunteer mediators, restorative justice circle facilitators, or dialogue facilitators; reserving a suitable space; and confirming the day and time with participating parties.

*Program Strengths*

The ACR program ensures that OSCR's services are relevant and accessible to parties, regardless of whether their dispute represents a viable complaint under the *Statement*. The OSCR ACR pathways have been used to address and resolve disputes between housemates, student leaders, students exiting intimate partner relationships, and between student organizations. While ACR can be used to resolve a wide range of conflicts, disputes in which (threatened or actual) violence is a factor or that otherwise require an immediate response may not be appropriate for ACR. In such cases, the RC will consult with colleagues before making the decision on whether to offer ACR as an option.

*Special Issues*

Staff from student conduct and conflict resolution offices who are considering implementing or expanding ACR programs should ask several important questions. First, how might campus climate and culture influence the development of ACR programming? What roles might students play in the development, implementation, training, or facilitation of ACR pathways? What other time, staffing, and financial resources will be required to develop and sustain these programs? In what ways might the development of new ACR programming affect existing conduct services both on and off campus? Who is likely to benefit from the development of these services? Who, if anyone, is likely to object to their development? What campus groups and populations are more or less likely to use these services? What conflicts or misconduct fall out of bounds for ACR pathways and require a formal agreement or arbitration pathway regardless or in addition to the preferred choices of the parties? And what can be done to ensure that the ACR processes are implemented in an efficient, educational, and socially just manner? Answers to these and other questions will likely depend upon many campus-specific factors, including the type of campus, the extent and types of student involvement on campus, and the campus climate as a whole. By considering these questions during the earliest phases of program development and remaining cognizant of them during the implementation, practice, and assessment phases, student conduct and conflict resolution offices can help to ensure the long-term success of their ACR programming.

## Program Assessment and Evaluation *by Jordan England and David Votruba, OSCR Student Conflict Resolution Coordinators*

OSCR is committed to providing quality programs and services. OSCR strives to meet this commitment by first selecting and designing programs and services grounded in existing theory and research; second, implementing these programs and services reflectively and with an eye toward continuous improvement; and third, subjecting its programs and services to rigorous, ongoing evaluation and assessment.

OSCR employs a two-pronged approach in its evaluation and assessment efforts: (a) an ongoing assessment completed by participants in all OSCR programs and services, which allows for quick and consistent access to general evaluative and educational outcomes feedback; and (b) a more focused and methodologically rigorous assessment designed to test predetermined hypotheses pertaining to a specific program or service.

OSCR's ACR and FCR General Assessment is a 44-item survey-based assessment measure that includes quantitative and qualitative items and is completed anonymously via a secure, third-party Web site. Survey responses are analyzed in aggregate at predetermined intervals to protect the confidentiality of OSCR's process participants. All participants in OSCR's ACR and FCR programs are informed at the conclusion of their involvement with OSCR that they will be sent an e-mail invitation to participate in the ACR and FCR General Assessment.

OSCR's ACR for AOD Evaluation is designed to examine the effectiveness of one specific OSCR program: that is, a brief educational motivation enhancement and conflict resolution intervention for students involved in minor alcohol and other drug-related incidents. This more focused and methodologically rigorous project consists of pre- and post-intervention questionnaires and is intended to test specific hypotheses concerning the ACR for AOD program. While OSCR intends to use this project internally to inform the development of its programs, it also hopes that research results will prove generalizable and useful to colleagues engaged in similar work at other institutions. Because of the comparatively complex nature of this project's design, the sensitivity of the information, and OSCR's intention to disseminate its results, the project was reviewed and approved by U-M's Behavioral Sciences Institutional Review Board.

To ensure the highest-quality assessments, OSCR develops these projects, including associated measures, in consultation with colleagues, internal and external research consultants, and existing relevant literature. OSCR has also used existing educational outcome and assessment measures, such as the *College Outcomes Survey* (American College Testing, 2000), and the standards developed by the Council for the Advancement of Standards in Higher Education (2006) to inform its assessment questions. Additionally, OSCR uses Internet-based assessment methods whenever possible to allow for maximum flexibility, efficiency, and economy.

## Conflict Resolution in the Living-Learning Community
*by Stacy Vander Velde, HSCR Assistant Director*

It is often the case that the best grassroots efforts of changing conflict resolution and mediation practices begin in the residence life community. For years residence life programs have trained and empowered their student and professional staffs to help identify and resolve conflict between residents at the earliest stages possible. OSCR builds on these successes through a collaborative relationship with the university housing system.

The U-M housing system consists of 13 residence halls, houses over 9,000 students, and employs close to 400 live-in student staff members, and 65 professional staff members who live in or on campus. Residence Education, a sub unit of University Housing, provides for local conflict resolution in the living and learning community. Residence Education is responsible for adjudication of any violations of the Community Living Standards (CLS), which are part of each resident's housing contract and applies only to residents. University Housing residents are also responsible for living up to the university values articulated in the *Statement.* Thus, conflicts that occur within housing may be managed locally within Residence Education or centrally by OSCR.

To assist Residence Education and OSCR in determining how and when to manage conflict locally in the residence halls or centrally through the OSCR's conflict resolution processes, the units' staff jointly wrote "A Commitment to Collaborate." This internal document provides a road map of guiding principles to inform case management. The implementation of this document has aided both units in discussions on how to proceed in situations that may involve violations of the CLS and the *Statement,* and provides a concrete reminder of our shared values around positive and productive student-centered conflict resolution.

The specific criteria in the "Commitment to Collaborate" that inform the decision to resolve a conflict through the OSCR as opposed to HSCR include whether the alleged behavior (a) presents a potential threat of danger to people or property; (b) presents potential imminent danger to people or property; (c) is of a repetitive nature and the accused student is not responding to local process and/or restorative measures; (d) involves harassment (racial, sexual, or other) and indicates a potential impact on the campuswide climate; (e) indicates that the responding student may need to be put on notice that repetition could result in suspension or expulsion; and (f) occurs outside the residence halls, or the responding student is not a member of the residence hall community. These criteria have been incorporated in the CLS housing contract for residents so that students understand the available venues for conflict resolution and what will result in referrals to those venues.

These criteria have been helpful in determining the most appropriate student-centered venue for resolving conflicts and have paved the way for better communication and stronger relationships between departments. Further, these criteria have invited robust dialogue and ultimately increased confidence in case management.

In addition to the "Commitment to Collaborate," the work with residents during the HSCR process is informed by social justice, the Residence Education Community Development Model (CDM), and restorative justice. As with OSCR, social and restorative justice is at the core of all work with residents. Residence Education's CDM guides staff interactions with residents.

## *Process*

When a conflict arises in Residence Education, multiple pathways for resolution exist. For those situations that are determined to be based on the "Commitment to Collaborate" criteria that OSCR is the appropriate administrative venue for management, Residence Education will consider the following actions: (a) participate as disputant under OSCR's ACR process or (b) file a complaint under the *Statement* for resolution in the FCR process. All incidents are reviewed in this way. For example, an incident involving alcohol might result in the affected Residence Education staff member's initiating ACR services such as a restorative justice circle and/or referral to the ACR for AOD diversion program.

In determining the preferred method of resolution, Residence Education administrators will evaluate what specific outcome they are seeking and whether this can be achieved through an ACR process. In past years, this has resulted in increased referrals to the ACR process, thus providing better understanding and rebuilding relationships between Residence Education and the responding student(s). On occasion, because of the severity of an incident, the impact on the community, and/or the need for formal documentation, it will be necessary for Residence Education to pursue resolution through an FCR process. Both of these options for resolution align with the Residence Education's mission to foster the academic, cultural, intellectual, personal, and social development of students living in the residence halls, while encouraging and supporting each others' development.

In Residence Education, two resolution pathways exist when the CLS are alleged to have been violated and the cases do not call for central management under the "Commitment to Collaborate." The first option is housing arbitration, which is distinct from an OSCR arbitration. Housing arbitrations are used to resolve any situation where the CLS is alleged to have been violated. These arbitrations are initiated through an informal meeting with the hall director or area coordinator in which the resident has the opportunity to discuss the case, accept or deny responsibility for the alleged violation(s), and participate in reaching a solution. The outcomes of housing arbitrations are designed to address harm done to the community as well as harm to the individual resident who engaged in the behavior. While the hall director or area coordinator acts at the arbiter in the housing arbitration, it is our practice to actively engage and work with the resident on how to repair the harm done.

The second pathway for resolution, a community circle, is appropriate for cases involving first offenses where there has been a clear impact on the community and where the responding resident is accepting responsibility. This resolution pathway brings together the responding resident with other affected parties to discuss the incident. Together the resident and affected parties develop an agreement that reflects how the resident can repair the harm done, thus repairing relationships and restoring his or her status within the community.

Since developing the community circle pathway, we have noted a decrease in the number of cases resolved through arbitration. Our internal assessment efforts have indicated that residents have positive perceptions of their experience participating in a community circle, that their sense of community increased, and that they would participate in a community circle again.

## Conclusion

It is our conviction that the diversity and dynamism of today's campus climates necessitate that student conduct and conflict resolution departments provide a fuller spectrum of resolution pathways and empower process participants to make informed and meaningful choices in these pathways if these departments are to remain relevant and functional in their campus communities. In this way, we are living up to our mission to build trust, promote justice, and teach peace by offering a full range of innovative, substantial, and culturally competent conflict resolution options. Readers are invited to visit our Web site, http://www.oscr.umich.edu, and contact the U-M campus conflict management teams in OSCR and Housing's Residence Education with inquiries as we continue to assess, evaluate, and refine our programs.

## References

American College Testing. (2000). *College outcomes survey.* Iowa City, IA: Author.
Council for the Advancement of Standards in Higher Education. (2006). *CAS Professional Standards for Higher Education* (6th ed.). Washington, DC: Author.

# 17

# SHARING STORIES
## Program Innovations of Our Colleagues

*Edited by Nancy Geist Giacomini*

S tudent affairs colleagues are among the best collaborators in higher education today. In the course of our daily work, we engage in meaningful and often difficult dialogue and decision making with stakeholders ranging from students and their parents, attorneys and community members, the press, faculty, supervisors, and staff and colleagues from across departments and institutions. It is through these dialogues that we shape the context and meaning of our conduct work as educators and practitioners to best meet the needs of our unique campus cultures.

Chapter 17 concludes our journey with a sampling of models and practices shared by colleagues from across the country who volunteered their individual stories to help fellow colleagues move from the *what* and *why* of a fuller spectrum approach for resolving conflict and conduct to several notable and creative versions of *how*. By sharing these theory-to-practice innovations, I join chapter contributors in the hope that we have equipped readers with the theories, questions, tools, and reference points needed to write their own versions of an inclusive resolution model. No two campus models will evolve in the same way, but if we start with a common end to build and develop systems that exemplify and support our core values with the ideals of justice, then no matter our individual paths, we will find common ground along the way.

## Community Training and Education at American University

Be patient. Mediation and alternative dispute resolution are not at the constant forefront of society so getting the word out needs to be a constant and diverse effort.

*Christy Anthony*

American University (AU) is a 4-year private undergraduate and graduate institution affiliated with the United Methodist Church, with 5,800 undergraduates and 3,300 graduate students. About 3,300 students live in residence halls. AU is urban, located in the nation's capital, and boasts a large international population.

American University Conflict Resolution Services is used by about 100 students per year and is part of Student Conduct and Conflict Resolution Services. The full-time staff devotes 30% of their time to the conflict resolution effort. Others assist at times of high volume. Three student staff members, about 80 volunteer mediators, and one support staff member split their time between conflict resolution and student conduct. In addition to assistance from local community mediation programs, the university launched a graduate internship position in partnership with the graduate program in International Peace and Conflict Resolution.

Conflict Resolution Services' role on campus is threefold: to provide direct conflict resolution services to students, faculty, and staff (including mediation and conflict coaching); to provide community education regarding mediation and other means of dispute resolution; and to provide initial and ongoing training for volunteer mediators.

### Direct Services

Conflict Resolution Services provides confidential, voluntary, and free mediation and conflict coaching to any member of the AU community. Referrals come from sources that include faculty, counseling center practitioners, residence life staff, and student leaders. Some student conduct cases are referred to this process as an optional first path to resolution when relationships are at stake. In general, we will offer a formal mediation for a dispute if one party is an AU student, faculty, or staff member. If all parties do not agree to mediation, we offer conflict coaching to those interested.

### Community Education

A community whose members are aware of the benefits of conflict resolution is more likely to use the service. Additionally, an awareness of alternative means of dispute resolution encourages community members to seek resolution that ameliorates rather than divides relationships. To those ends, our office provides class presentations, coaching roles in mediation courses, presentations to staff, and extended presentations to student groups. Finally, we conduct passive outreach for students, faculty, and staff in the form of electronic and hard-copy postings in a variety of campus media outlets.

## *Mediator Training*

Each semester, our office hosts a free 20-hour mediation training session available for up to 30 students, faculty, and staff. Participants submit applications and are selected based on their interest, general understanding of the goals of mediation, and ability to contribute a unique and diverse perspective to training and to our mediator pool. At the conclusion of training, mediators are eligible to volunteer in our services. We work with academic departments and local agencies to offer a broad perspective on mediation styles and cultural issues. Additionally, Conflict Resolution Services offers ongoing training to mediators including practice sessions, speakers, readings, and other learning opportunities.

Author: Christy Anthony is assistant director of Student Conduct and Conflict Resolution Services. She can be reached at anthony@american.edu, telephone: 202-885-3328. Information: conflictresolution@american.edu, telephone 202-885-1313, or http://www.american.edu/ocl/sccrs

## Using Restorative Principles to Reinforce Ethical Behavior at Michigan Technological University

The more opportunities you create for students
to be involved, invested and influenced, the
stronger your community will be.

*Robert Bishop*

Michigan Technological University is a 4-year public institution of some 7,000 students, 2,100 of whom live in residence halls. Michigan Tech is an isolated, rural campus with a 3:1 male-to-female ratio of scholars. The Office of Student Judicial Affairs, Housing and Residential Life, and Student Activities collaboratively administer the restorative program under the direction of three professional staff and one administrative support staff.

During the 2006 fall semester, the Division of Student Affairs began researching and implementing restorative practices as a partner or alternative to traditional student judicial processes. Growing concerns existed with regard to a progressive decline of direct, interpersonal communication between students. Based on this, Michigan Tech looked for new ways to engage students using restorative practices as a gateway for those interested in developing a stronger community. Educating students about civility, integrity, character development, ethical and moral leadership, civic engagement, spirituality, and interpersonal relationships permeates each facet of the program.

From this, the Student Judicial Affairs Office unveiled a unique approach to sanctioning residence hall students for minor policy violations in the 2008 fall semester. The staff adapted an experiential Challenge Course developed by faculty in the university's School of Business into an Ethics Module for hearing officers to include as a sanction for resident students found responsible for minor violations. The Ethics Module is a 2-hour program geared to help students improve communication and learn how their actions affect the residence hall community. Students engage in a series of hands-on activities. A trained facilitator then debriefs each exercise to connect exercise to infraction as a means to reinforce the concept of individual responsibility in a learning community.

The program goal is to enhance the residence hall community by facilitating shared ownership for the ethical development of all residents. When there is a violation of community standards, those found responsible have a hands-on opportunity to enhance self-esteem and develop respect for a cooperative learning environment. Students typically view traditional sanctioning methods as a punishment or an inconvenience. Allowing opportunities for students to participate and learn in their sanctions reinforces the academic mission of the university.

Author: Robert Bishop is associate director of Student Judicial Affairs and Student Development. He can be reached at rmbishop@mtu.edu. Information: studentaffairs@mtu.edu, telephone 906-487-2212, or http://www.mtu .edu/dean/judicial

## A Residential Conflict Management Program at New York University

Given the sensitive nature of many conflicts, it is important to provide residence life staff with the language to work with students in conflict so that staff members can frame conflict management and mediation in a way that allows students to understand that working through a conflict can be part of the learning process.

*Melissa Tihinen*

New York University (NYU) is a 4-year private, urban institution of about 50,000 students, 12,500 of whom live in residence halls. The residence hall system spans about 30 blocks in lower Manhattan and Brooklyn. Most halls were not built as residences at all but rather as apartment buildings and hotels. Therefore, each building has a unique layout and set of challenges. International students make up 9.7% of NYU's student population.

The NYU Department of Residential Education and the NYU School of Law Mediation Clinic share administration of the residential conflict management program that serves about 60 students per year. The program is guided by one law professor who teaches the Law School Mediation Clinic and one professional staff member in the Department of Residential Education. In addition, 12 to 16 law students serve the program as mediators, together with 33 hall directors and assistant hall directors and about 350 resident assistants (RAs). The service is free. Budget costs are minimal and are generally related to training residence life staff and providing them with first-responder conflict intervention skills. The law school helped develop the program and conflict management training materials as part of a course in dispute system design.

Roommate and other student conflicts are stressful for the students and are often challenging for staff members. While conflicts present challenges, they are also opportunities for student development. To address this, the NYU Department of Residential Education and School of Law began collaborating during the 2006–07 academic year. The resulting Residential Conflict Management Program offers a multiphase conflict management process and allows residential students in conflict to meet with law school mediators to discuss their conflict in a confidential, safe environment. The program began as a pilot in selected residence halls with mixed results. It became obvious that mediation is difficult to promote among students who are frustrated with their living situation. During the spring 2008 semester, coordinators conducted a needs assessment to enhance the program and make it more accessible for students and staff.

## Needs Assessment

*Survey and Interviews*: To better understand the needs of professional residence hall directors, the coordinators developed an anonymous survey asking staff for feedback on how the program can best address the needs of students and RAs. Following the survey, hall directors were interviewed to provide more detailed information.

*Focus Groups*: RAs were invited to participate in focus groups to discuss perceptions of and possible improvements in the program. Focus group participants discussed conflicts they experienced in the residence halls and brainstormed how the program might help them function better as RAs.

## *Outcome of Needs Assessment*

*Staff Training:* Based on the assessment, program coordinators developed materials and held two comprehensive conflict management training sessions for RAs. Improvements concentrated on ways to translate conflict into an opportunity for learning valuable life skills. Training allowed RAs to role-play talking with students about the program, and mediation in particular, in more student-friendly language.

*Student Outreach/Program Promotion:* The Resident Living Agreement Form was revised to include information about the program and framed conflict as an opportunity for learning and a healthy part of living with others. Materials, such as sample cleaning schedules, were created and placed online to assist students in improving living space interactions.

*Process Enhancements:* The mediation process was revised to better account for previous conflict management intervention by the hall staff and to assist student learning. A follow-up mechanism was also added so that students who participated in mediation could continue to receive support.

Authors: Melissa Tihinen is the judicial educator in the NYU Department of Residential Education. She can be reached at melissa.tihinen@nyu.edu, telephone 212-994-4635.

Sarah Burns is professor of clinical law, NYU School of Law. She can be reached at sarah.burns@nyu.edu, telephone 212.998.6464. Information: conflictmanagement@nyu.edu, telephone 212-998-4311, or http://www.nyu.edu/residential.education/students/howto_roommate.html

## Conflict Resolution at Northeastern University

Listen to the needs of your community. We had originally planned on starting a peer mediation program until we challenged ourselves to get feedback from our community. Our community was asking for training and education on conflict resolution more than they were asking for mediation services. Once we listened to their needs, we found the positive response was greater than we could have anticipated.

*Colleen Ryan*

Northeastern University, located in inner-city Boston, has about 15,000 undergraduate students, with 7,600 of them living in residence halls. The university is a 4-year private institution with a unique cooperative learning component that encourages students to attend for 5 years with two or three 6-month co-op assignments interspersed throughout their academic career. Co-op assignments are full-time paid positions with companies and organizations in partnership with Northeastern. Assignments can be in the local area or abroad.

The Conflict Resolution Program is cosponsored by the Spiritual Life Center and the Office of Student Conduct and Conflict Resolution. Initial training workshops included some 200 student participants. In the program's first semester, 10 students used the conflict coaching and mediation resources. An additional 30 residence life staff members have also been trained.

The program is led by a staff member in the Office of Student Conduct and Conflict Resolution who works with a committee of four other staff members. Two of the committee members have received at least forty hours of mediation training. As it evolves, the program staff hopes to form a partnership with the program chair of the graduate program for College Student Development and Counseling to assess opportunities to pursue a graduate practicum in the office. The staff also hopes to provide mediation and conflict coaching training to staff members in the future to best handle incoming requests.

Northeastern University announced the launch of the Conflict Resolution at NU program in the fall of 2008. In an effort to meet the need for conflict resolution on campus, the Spiritual Life Center and Office of Student Conduct and Conflict Resolution joined forces to develop a program designed to educate and train students in conflict resolution techniques, as well as provide resources for those who are currently experiencing conflict. The program strives to change the negative perception of conflict to an understanding that conflict, when handled well, can be an experience that deepens and strengthens relationships. The program provides proactive and active resources for all Northeastern University students.

*Proactive resources* include training workshops designed for student organizations and residence hall floors. The following training workshops can be customized according to the needs of the community:

- What Conflict Style Are You? is based on the Thomas-Kilmann Conflict Mode Instrument (TKI, 1974) and designed to help students assess their *default approach* to conflict drawing from the five conflict styles outlined by the TKI.

- "How to Talk and When to Listen" is designed to instill basic skills needed to appropriately address conflict. The workshop's focus is on interest-based negotiation, a method outlined in *Getting to Yes: Negotiating Agreement Without Giving In* (Fisher, Patton, & Ury, 2001).

*Active resources* for students currently experiencing conflict are also offered. These resources include conflict coaching and mediation. The goal of conflict coaching is to ask questions of the student that will encourage him or her to think about the cause(s) of the conflict and brainstorm potential options for resolution. Additionally, the coach shares resources that include tips for managing conflict. Conflict coaching is a good option for students interested in resolving conflict on their own rather than involving a third party. What a student learns from conflict coaching will empower him or her to approach the conflict in a productive way.

Mediation services are available for all student-to-student disputes. It is a voluntary and confidential process in which a neutral third party facilitates a conversation between conflicting parties. The parties determine their own resolution.

The program staff has been receiving many requests for workshops as well as requests for conflict coaching and mediation. Early efforts in working with the Department of Residential Life, the Student Government Association, the Resident Student Association, and other student organizations have created a successful word-of-mouth network most referrals are coming from. The program's philosophy focuses on educating the community to enable a grassroots approach to constructive conflict engagement.

Author: Colleen M. Ryan is an assistant director of the Office of Student Conduct and Conflict Resolution at Northeastern. She can be reached at co.ryan@neu.edu, telephone 617-373-4390. Information: conflictresolution@neu.edu, telephone 617-373-4390 or http://www.northeastern.edu/conflictresolution

## Conflict Coaching and Mediation at Nova Southeastern University

Start small with a pilot program in the beginning. Bring as many key people throughout the campus into your decision making as possible to get

full buy-in and support. From the very beginning
develop and maintain documentation and data
to report your results and outcomes.

*Bob Hosea*

Located in Fort Lauderdale, Nova Southeastern University (NSU) is Florida's largest independent higher education institution with more than 26,000
undergraduate, graduate, and professional students. The university currently
houses up to 1,492 students. Student Mediation Services (SMS) is a conflict
management and resolution assistance service for students administered by
the Division of Student Affairs and housed in the Office of the Dean. The
program is available to all students enrolled at NSU.

Currently the SMS assists about 130 students annually including mediations and conflict coaching. It is coordinated by a part-time graduate assistant, assisted annually by 15 to 20 trained volunteers who work an average of
5 hours per week. These volunteers are students from the university's graduate degree programs in conflict analysis and resolution and in college student
affairs. Using trained volunteers from a graduate program provides a win-
win situation for everyone. For the service, these students are interested in
assisting without cost and they are readily available. For the students, this
opportunity builds confidence and adds good experience to a résumé. Many
also gain academic credits through internships and practicum. Other institutions may find great student volunteers not only from conflict resolution
programs but from psychology, social work, and marriage and family therapy
programs.

SMS was developed and implemented in 2005 by the Division of Student Affairs to support NSU students by providing a variety of dispute resolution services including conflict coaching, mediation, restorative justice,
facilitation, presentations, and trainings. As opportunities present themselves
SMS staff works collaboratively with the administrators of the university
judicial process and the residential judicial program to address conflict issues
that have surfaced as part of a student's behavioral incident. Students may
be referred to an SMS service to learn constructive and productive conflict
management skills and strategies as part of their judicial sanction.

In the fall of 2006 SMS developed and implemented the conflict coaching service that offers one-on-one individualized and confidential assistance
to all NSU students interested in developing or enhancing their understanding of conflict and the styles, skills, and strategies for dispute management
and resolution. SMS conflict research regarding residential freshmen has

indicated that many residential students (88%) had not gained classroom or hands-on conflict management or resolution experience during their secondary education years. The finding points to the significance of conflict management/resolution educational assistance and services such as conflict coaching as a mechanism to support the development of higher education students.

Geared toward de-escalation, management, and resolution, one-on-one coaching is intended to minimize uncontrolled conflicts that become positional and limit opportunities for resolution. Coaching provides students with the knowledge to address and resolve their conflict without further third-party involvement. Whether as an educational experience or to address a current conflict, the session is designed to fit the needs of the person seeking assistance. Over one or two sessions, lasting from 30 minutes to 2 hours, a participant develops new understandings and skills to approach or reengage in a current conflict, seeking cooperative and realistic outcomes. Participants are aware that if their resolution attempts do not develop satisfying outcomes they can request assistance through mediation. Most, however, prove able to manage their conflict following coaching without mediation.

The service provides clients with drop-in and appointment-based sessions with a trained and neutral coach. Our program uses a hybrid conflict coaching model based on the Problem Solving for One model developed by Alan Tidwell (1998) and the Skills Development Coaching model developed by Ross Brinkert (2002). Our model incorporates conflict approach assessments, communication skills enhancement exercises, conflict resolution strategy development, and role playing exercises to enhance the individual's ability and confidence.

Conflict coaching has been very beneficial. Sessions have been used by students for a variety of conflicts including roommate, work setting, and club/organizational disputes. The service also provides assistance to employees of the Division of Student Affairs. During academic years 2006 through 2008 the service provided about 50 sessions annually to residential students (45%), students in clubs and organizations (24%), other students (3%), and Student Affairs Division student employees and its full-time employees (28%). The service has begun to train Residential Life staff members in the basics of conflict coaching to support and enhance their work with residential student conflict issues.

Author: Bob Hosea coordinates Student Mediation Services (SMS) for NSU's Division of Student Affairs. He is currently in the dissertation stage for completion of a PhD at NSU in conflict analysis and resolution with a concentration centering on the application of conflict analysis and resolution theory and

practice in the higher education setting. He can be reached at hosea@
nova.edu. Information: http://www.nova,.edu/studentmediation/

## A Comprehensive Approach to Social Justice at Oberlin College

The success of our program is due to the buy-
in of the OC community from the start and the
institutional support from the college president.
Have your program independent from the formal
grievance procedures and try to get your CEO's
support and collaboration with you!

*Yeworkwha Belachew*

Oberlin College is a 4-year private liberal arts institution located in Oberlin,
Ohio, with a student population of about 2,822, 2,400 of whom live in residence halls. Oberlin College attracts students interested in service and activ-
ism in high numbers. Many students with a strong interest in music are also
drawn to Oberlin College to develop their skills in the conservatory. The
conservatory also attracts a high percentage of international students.

The Office of the Ombudsperson was created in fall 2000 and is dedicated to improving the quality of intracampus discourse by providing conflict resolution tools and improving communications skills across campus.
Because of the high volume of requests in the first semester, the ombudsperson expanded resources for the mediation program and convened a design
team consisting of students, faculty, and staff in December 2000. In 5
months this team developed a mediation program tailored to the needs of
the college community. The program was designed to reach beyond conflict
resolution to facilitate communication between people of diverse backgrounds, providing *socially* and *culturally* relevant mediation. The Oberlin
College Dialogue Center (OCDC) was created in 2001 and is based on the
social justice model of mediation. OCDC promotes change through conflict
transformation, mediation, community building, and dialogue. Since its creation, the center has served more than 2,000 individuals including students,
faculty, and staff. The ombudsperson acts as a coordinator of OCDC. Her
administrative assistant provides secretarial support for the program.

Proactive resources include voluntary mediation, facilitated group dialogues, an annual social justice institute, and training for students, faculty,
and staff to serve as volunteer mediators on campus.

*Mediation training*: Training takes place over 5 days and involves a total 50 hours of intensive activities. The first 2 days focus on providing theoretical and practical understanding of social justice concepts that help mediators-in-training develop or sharpen multipartial competencies. The final 3 days focus on developing mediation skills through a social justice lens. Participants are certified by Oberlin College in accordance with the state of Ohio's mediation mandates.

*Annual Social Justice Institute*: On Labor Day weekend, September 6–7, 2009, the Office of the Ombudsperson will sponsor the fifth 2-day Social Justice Institute. The goal of the institute is to create a cohesive bond among participants and to integrate them into the Oberlin College community by exploring multicultural issues at Oberlin and in the larger society. This is accomplished through discussion, role playing, and highly interactive exercises focusing on the debilitating issues of privilege and oppression, classism, heterosexism, racism, and sexism.

The following are active resources for students, faculty, and staff experiencing conflict:

*Facilitated dialogues*: The goal of facilitated dialogue is to create a less-hostile group atmosphere by helping participants set ground rules to achieve thoughtful and creative ways of addressing difficult issues. A housing cooperative or residence hall, a student organization or athletic team, or even a local institution such as the police department or high school may request this service. As with mediation, the techniques of facilitation are rooted in social justice concepts, hence there is an effort to help all participants feel that their voices are heard. Facilitators work to make sure that group-authored ground rules are observed. To counter the reluctance that may arise for individuals to speak in large-group settings the facilitators provide opportunities for people to contribute anonymously. Public notes are taken so that participants can see that their contributions are acknowledged. Meetings are documented and provided to the group that initiates the request to allow participants to continue the dialogue.

*Mediation*: Because some conflicts between two or more individuals may be better resolved through mediation, college community members are encouraged to consider mediation as a means of resolving disputes as often as possible. The ombudsperson assigns mediators in pairs to support the program's goal of multipartiality. Mediators help parties in conflict to identify needs and interests as well as possible solutions. OCDC mediators recognize the differences in power and privilege and address these dynamics so that *all parties can be supported and have their voices heard*. Oberlin currently has 37 trained student, faculty, and staff volunteer mediators and facilitators on campus who assist with a wide range of issues. All OCDC mediators practice multipartiality, independence, and confidentiality. The Office of the Ombudsperson and OCDC foster an environment that helps prevent, diminish, and resolve conflicts that under other circumstances might result in a formal judicial response.

When staff at the Office of the Dean of Students believes that mediation is a fitting alternative to a formal judicial process, a judicial coordinator may refer students to the OCDC through the Office of the Ombudsperson. Mediation is made available by the OCDC when the ombudsperson is able to verify that both parties in conflict are seeking mediation voluntarily and that it has been recommended as an acceptable alternative by a judicial coordinator. OCDC mediators work with both parties to develop a written document that includes a statement of agreement on each issue. The statement of agreement becomes part of the contract drawn up and signed by the parties at the completion of the mediation process. In cases referred by a judicial coordinator, the parties must give permission to inform the referring judicial coordinator whether mediation has resulted in a mutually satisfactory resolution. Cases that do not have resolution, may be remanded to the judicial system. Because participation in the mediation process is voluntary, and the final result is a product of mutual agreement, the individuals participating in the mediation own the outcome. A copy of the contract is not kept by the ombudsperson and cannot be used for any formal judicial process.

Authors: Kimberly Jackson Davidson is associate dean of students at Oberlin. She can be reached at Kimberly.Jackson.Davidson@oberlin.edu

Yeworkwha Belachew is the ombudsperson at Oberlin. She may be reached at Yeworkwha.Belachew@oberlin.edu, telephone 440-775-6728 or ombuds @oberlin.edu. Information: http://www.oberlin.edu/ombuds/

## Mediation and Advocacy at Saint Louis University

Make sure to collaborate with different areas within your university. Our use of the law student mediators provides them with the experience they need, and provides us with another outlet for conflict resolution.

*Meggie Biesenthal*

Saint Louis University (SLU) is a 4-year private Jesuit institution of some 12,733 students. Located in midtown St. Louis, 89% of first-time freshmen and 53% of all undergraduate students live in residence halls. The mission of the Mediation and Advocacy Program (MAP) is to provide an alternative method of conflict resolution in which students can feel empowered to effect change in their relationships, acquire life skills in communication and empathy, and express themselves in healthy and productive ways leading to a more developed sense of self and a reflective attitude that will assist them in their life beyond SLU. The two complementary components of this program are a mediation program to resolve student disputes and an advocacy program to assist students in preparing for conduct hearings and to better inform the community about student rights.

Disputes between students such as roommate conflicts, floormate disagreements, or other relational matters brought to the attention of the Student Conduct Office are referred to MAP. These students are offered the opportunity to meet and participate in mediation before initiating conduct charges. Mediations result in agreements created by the students that detail guidelines on how they will resolve the present conflict, communicate with each other, and deal with conflict in the future. Mediators are members of SLU's School of Law's Mediation Clinic, and have received thorough mediation training from a practicing mediator. The mediation program also uses mediators to conduct group mediation sessions (or team-building exercises) for campus groups that express an interest in resolving conflicts among their members. Mediation is offered to student groups, teams, and classes whose members express interest in the program. The first group mediation session took place in January 2009 to develop behavioral guidelines for a competitive mock-trial team.

The second component of MAP involves advocating for students who are charged with violations of the code of conduct. The Student Conduct Office has trained a group of undergraduate volunteers to serve as advocates. Any student going through a hearing before one of the conduct boards is offered the assistance of a student advocate. Since the commencement of the program at the beginning of the 2008–2009 school year, 71% of students facing a formal hearing enlisted the assistance of an advocate. Advocates guide charged students through hearing preparations including the creation of impact statements, deciding whom to call for witnesses, building questions, and proposing mutually agreeable outcomes. Advocates are also used when making changes to conduct processes and policies, and they are involved in creating and implementing programs and resources to educate the student community about rights and responsibilities.

Students greatly benefit from the assistance of advocates, as indicated through assessments conducted with each student. Having the help of a peer who is intimately familiar with the hearing process and trained thoroughly on expectations and procedure helps students to fully understand how the process works and to be better prepared for their hearing and the results. Advocates work to help students understand the policies they allegedly violated. By helping students better understand university policy, advocates are in the unique position of being able to empower students to take responsibility for their actions. When evaluating their work throughout the semester, advocates indicated that the students they worked with were truly grateful for their assistance. Advocates were confident that these students would have received less-desirable outcomes from their hearings had they not enlisted the assistance of advocates.

The program has also improved efficiency in the conduct office. Students and parents who previously needed almost daily meetings with staff in the office to discuss the impending hearing now depend on advocates with even better results. The duration of an average hearing has been reduced from a procedure that took numerous hours to complete to an hour-long process. The preparation time of staff members for a hearing has also been significantly reduced.

This new programmatic efficiency is further enhanced in that students are receiving more satisfying individual attention. Assessment results indicate that students reported higher levels of satisfaction and the feeling that they received a fair outcome than was reported in the semesters prior to the program's implementation. Student advocates have been a tremendous asset to our office and the perception of the university conduct process, not just for students but for their families as well.

The MAP is premised on the notion that an active engagement in resolving conflict will allow students to test their own skills of communication, formulate ideas and strategies for negotiation, respond to conflict in productive and healthy ways, and allow students to give, process, and receive immediate feedback from their peers rather than solely from administrators. By providing training, guidance, and other basic resources, the program teaches students how to develop life skills that will ultimately improve their relationships and their perspective on empathy, community responsibility, diversity, and ultimately *cura personalis.*

Authors: Meggie Biesenthal is a graduate assistant in SLU's MAP. She can be reached at foxmc@slu.edu, telephone 314-977-7326.

Sarah Klucker is program director of SLU's Office of Student Conduct. She can be reached at sklucker@slu.edu, telephone 314-977-7326. Information: http://www.conduct.slu.edu

## Partnerships and Code Revisions at the University of Florida

Look for partnerships with a law school if you have one, although there are often mediation programs in education, business, etc., so if you don't have a law school all isn't lost. You can also look to your local city for a partnership as well. Finally, conflict resolution is very consistent with our core values of educating our students on how to live and thrive in our global community. If you need to sell your program, I think that is the angle to take.

*Chris Loschiavo*

The University of Florida (UF) is a 4-year public institution with 52,000 students. The university houses 7,000 students in residence halls and another 3,000 in family housing. UF recently revised its student conduct code to include conflict resolution using the Model Student Conduct Code by Ed Stoner and John Lowery (2004). We wanted to be sure the code was educationally focused and removed as much legal language as possible. To that end, we also knew we needed to change the name of our office from Student Judicial Affairs. After a lot of discussion, we decided on Student Conduct and Conflict Resolution as the best option.

The Student Conduct and Conflict Resolution Office staff administers the new initiatives described here and anticipates enlarging the program to serve 300–400 students in its first full year. The director and assistant director administer the new conflict resolution efforts along with their traditional administrative roles. They are assisted by student legal services and law school faculty and are increasing their trained ranks across campus to support conflict resolution processes.

As with many institutions, the Student Conduct Code at UF must be approved by the board of trustees. We felt it was important to add language addressing alternative dispute resolution to our code at the same time other changes were being made. I spoke with the associate dean of students and the dean of students and they agreed. They spoke with our legal counsel and our vice president of student affairs, and we got permission to explore adding conflict resolution to the Student Conduct Code. Through collaboration with our student legal services office, our students, and dean of students staff members, we identified the kinds of issues in which alternative dispute resolution, particularly mediation and restorative justice, could be a helpful resource. The issues we identified include property damage, theft, problem houses (party houses), neighborhood concerns, residence hall noise, and roommate conflicts.

Once we identified the need and support for such a program, we began the process of drafting the general language for our Student Conduct Code to include alternative dispute resolution. After several drafts and discussions, we arrived at a language that was acceptable to all, and in September 2008, the Student Conduct Code was approved by the board of trustees.

The next step involved finding development resources. Fortune struck when I learned that the Gainesville Police Department had hired an individual to develop a restorative justice program for the city. We met to discuss the goals for each program and how we could assist each other. We agreed that this was an important partnership. Subsequently, the city leader agreed to volunteer as a university mediator, and I agreed to assist in training facilitators and sharing materials that I helped develop at my previous institution. Additionally, we have spoken about how to encourage students and community members to use the restorative justice and mediation programs.

We also contacted staff at the law school dispute resolution center to gauge their interest in providing mediators/facilitators for restorative justice conferences and circles. They agreed this was an excellent opportunity but were concerned that volunteers would be underused. We addressed this by using students in the dispute resolution center not only to facilitate and mediate but also to offer conflict resolution trainings and workshops for students and organizations.

We will continue our steady progress with stakeholder meetings and an ongoing evaluation of our new code and programs. Ultimately, we hope to continue offering advice and consultation services for faculty, staff, and students in conflict as well as formal mediation, victim/offender mediation, and restorative justice on campus and through the city. Finally, we are investigating the creation of a bias response team to address incidents of bias on campus.

Author: Chris Loschiavo is assistant dean of students and director of student conduct and conflict resolution. He can be reached at chrisl@dso.ufl.edu, telephone 352-392-1261, ext 203. Information: http://www.dso.ufl.edu/sccr/

# References

Brinkert, R. (2002). *Conflict coaching: CERT's use of conflict coaching, 2*(2). Retrieved from http://www.campus-adr.org/CMHER/ReportArticles/Edition2_2/Brinkert 2_2.html

Fisher, R., Patton, B., & Ury, W. L. (2001). *Getting to yes: Negotiating agreement without giving in.* New York: Penguin Books.

Stoner, E. N., & Lowery, J. W. (2004). Navigating past the "spirit of insubordination": A twenty-first century model student conduct code with a model hearing script. *Journal of College and University Law, 31,* 1–77.

Thomas, K. W., & Kilmann, R. H. 1974. *Thomas-Kilmann Conflict MODE Instrument.* Mountain View, CA: Xicom and CPP.

Tidwell, Alan. (1998). Problem solving for one. *Management Development Forum, 1*(1). Retrieved from http://www.esc.edu/ESConline/Across_ESC/forumjournal.nsf/3cc42a422514347a8525671d0049f395/e8b8f6dd2b8fe87c852567ba006cd936?OpenDocument

# ABOUT THE EDITORS

**Nancy Geist Giacomini** is a private educator, mediator, facilitator, and author based in Chester County, Pennsylvania. She completed her educational leadership degree at the University of Delaware while she was a Conflict Resolution Program (CRP) associate in the Institute for Public Administration. While in CRP, she taught in the master's program, mediated special education disputes for the Delaware Department of Education, and facilitated statewide dialogue. Her doctoral research, *Enhancing the Collaborative Capacity of Individualized Education Programs (IEPs) in Delaware Schools,* helped shape statewide IEP facilitation training and coaching. Prior to her move to CRP Giacomini was University of Delaware's assistant dean of students for judicial affairs for over a decade. She was awarded the prestigious annual Institutional Award for Women's Equity in 1997 for overall campus leadership and as chair of Sexual Assault Awareness Week.

Giacomini is an annual Association for Student Conduct Administration (ASCA) faculty member and the 2008–2010 coordinator for conflict resolution faculty. She piloted the first conflict resolution specialist program at the 2008 Donald D. Gehring Academy where the Spectrum Model (Schrage & Thompson, 2004) was introduced. She and Jennifer Schrage shared a featured session presentation related to the spectrum and conflict resolution in ASCA at the 2009 ASCA Annual Conference. Her previous ASCA leadership includes summer institute cochair/chair (1995 and 1996), annual conference program cochair/chair (1996 and 1997) and president (1998). Giacomini was honored with the Gehring Award in 2004 for her ongoing service to ASCA.

She was a contributing editor for *Mastering Mediation: A Guide for Training Mediators in a College and University Setting* and coauthor of the chapter "Managing Student Conduct & Conflict Through Mediation and Other Alternative Dispute Resolution Processes" *in Exercising Power with Wisdom: Bridging Legal and Ethical Practice with Intention.* Giacomini's national conflict resolution work has included training for Centre Consulting, Inc., where her team helped implement the new U.S. Air Force National Security Personnel System. She is on the educational staff at Longwood Gardens in Kennett, Pennsylvania, teaching a curriculum-based K–12 outdoor program.

**Jennifer Meyer Schrage** provides leadership to the University of Michigan (U-M) Division of Student Affairs Office of Student Conflict Resolution (OSCR). During her tenure as a director at U-M, she led the OSCR team in departmental realignment and championed, with colleague Monita C. Thompson, the nationally recognized Spectrum Model, which includes mediation, restorative justice, and related innovative methods. In addition to her credentials as an educator and administrator, Schrage is a talented mediator, having completed training with the Office of Civil Rights at the Arizona Office of the Attorney General and through the Social Justice Mediation Institute. Schrage earned her Juris Doctor degree from the University of Arizona College of Law and graduated cum laude from Northern Arizona University. Schrage is a member of the State Bar of Michigan (SBM) and the SBM's Alternative Dispute Resolution Section.

She approaches conflict resolution from a social justice perspective and has devoted her career to building more peaceful and just communities. Schrage has written, consulted on, and presided over training sessions, and made presentations on such topics as mediation, cultural competence in conduct work, restorative justice, preventing disabilities discrimination, promoting diversity, and building community. Her work has been published in the Council on Law in Higher Education's *Student Affairs Law and Policy Quarterly*. In 2009 she was interviewed and quoted in the *Chronicle of Higher Education* as part of a special series on innovative practices and restorative justice in student conduct work. She served as faculty for the Donald D. Gehring Academy for Student Conduct Administration in 2007, 2008, and 2009 and was a featured presenter on the Spectrum Model and social justice at the 2009 Association for Student Conduct Administration annual conference.

Schrage has experience in student conduct work and teaching and as an attorney and professional consultant. She previously served as director of Student Judicial Services and adjunct faculty in business law at Eastern Michigan University. Prior to her career in higher education, she practiced as an attorney at the national headquarters for the United Auto Workers Legal Services Plan.

# ABOUT THE CONTRIBUTORS

**Michael M. DeBowes** is director of Student Judicial Affairs at Old Dominion University where he oversees the student conduct system for academic and nonacademic violations of university policy. Prior to working at Old Dominion, DeBowes served as assistant director of the Center for Student Ethics and Standards at the University of Vermont. He received his MEd in higher education and student affairs administration from the University of Vermont. DeBowes was the 2007 recipient of the Association for Student Conduct Administration's New Professional of the Year award.

**Keith Edwards** is director of Campus Life at Macalester College in St. Paul, Minnesota, where he oversees residence life, student activities, orientation, and the campus conduct process. He received his PhD from the University of Maryland in college student personnel with a concentration in social justice education. Edwards founded and served as the first chair of the American College Personnel Association's Commission for Social Justice Educators and has made presentations at more than 40 colleges and universities across the country.

**Andrea Goldblum** is director of Judicial Affairs at Ohio State University. Prior to her tenure at Ohio State, she served as director of Judicial Affairs at the University of Colorado at Boulder where she helped create the first restorative justice program in higher education. She also has experience in residence life and housing, Greek life, advising student organizations, ombuds, and academic integrity. Goldblum completed an MA in higher education administration from the University of Michigan and is currently enrolled in the master's in the Study of Law Program at Ohio State University School of Law.

**Michele Goldfarb** is associate ombudsperson at the University of Pennsylvania where she previously served as director of the Office of Student Conduct for eleven years. She has expertise in and led workshops on academic integrity, ethics, conflict resolution, and she has significant experience in mediation. She received her JD from the Washington College of Law at American

University and currently serves as an adjunct professor with the University of Pennsylvania Law School's clinical programs.

**Ryan C. Holmes** served as the director of Off-Campus Communities at La Salle University in Philadelphia. He was responsible for building relationships between La Salle and the surrounding community as well as serving as a university hearing officer and mediator. Holmes holds an MA in bilingual/bicultural studies from La Salle, as well as a MA in counseling and personnel services from the University of Maryland. He currently serves at the vice-chair for outreach for the American College Personnel Association's Commission for Social Justice Educators. Holmes has accepted a new position as assistant dean of students at University of Texas El Paso.

**David R. Karp** is interim associate dean of Student Affairs and director of Campus Life at Skidmore College in Saratoga Springs, New York. He is also associate professor of sociology. Previously he was chair of Skidmore's Department of Sociology, Anthropology, and Social Work and director of the Program in Law and Society. Karp's scholarship focuses on restorative justice in community and campus settings and on prison programs preparing inmates for return to the community. He has published five books and more than 75 academic papers. His most recent books are *Restorative Justice on the College Campus* and *Wounds That Do Not Bind: Victim-Based Perspectives on the Death Penalty*. He holds a PhD in sociology from the University of Washington.

**Tamara L. King** is judicial administrator and director of Judicial Programs at Washington University in St. Louis where she works with students, faculty, and staff to uphold community expectations. King also serves as an adjunct faculty member at Washington University School of Law. She received her JD from the New York University School of Law. King also currently serves as the president of the Association for Student Conduct Administration (formerly the Association for Student Judicial Affairs)—the first African American to do so.

**Richard T. "Rick" Olshak** is associate dean of students at Illinois State University where he previously served as director of Student Dispute Resolution Services. He is the author of *Mastering Mediation: A Guide for Training Mediators in a College and University Setting*, past president of the Association for Student Judicial Affairs (now the Association for Student Conduct Administration), and is a founding partner of the Campus Mediation Project. Olshak received an MS degree in college student personnel administration and is a doctoral student in the Higher Education Administration Program at Illinois State.

**Judy Rashid** is dean of students at North Carolina A&T State University, where she also serves as an adjunct faculty member in the university studies department. She has been involved professionally in campus conflict management, education, and training for 20 years, and is a certified mediator. Rashid is a senior student affairs administrator with Student Affairs Administrators in Higher Education, where she also serves as a founding legacy member of its foundation. Rashid received her PhD in higher education from North Carolina State University.

**Tosheka Robinson** served as coordinator for Student Development and Campus Community Outreach at Arizona State University. While at Arizona State, she coordinated Student Advocacy Services, chaired the Campus Environment Team, and facilitated workshops for the campus LGBTQA Safe ZONE program. She holds an MEd in higher and postsecondary education from Arizona State.

**Edward N. Stoner II** performs confidential investigations for management in private-sector companies and in higher education institutions. He also provides advice on a variety of campus issues, trains judicial boards, and develops effective student affairs policies. He is the author of the nation's most widely used model code for college student conduct. Stoner graduated from the University of Virginia.

**Simone Himbeault Taylor** serves as associate vice president for Student Affairs at the University of Michigan. Himbeault Taylor has guided strategic planning and change management efforts at the unit and divisional level and has led campuswide student learning initiatives. She writes about, presents, and consults on issues related to student learning and development and organizational effectiveness. She received her PhD from the University of Michigan's Center for the Study of Higher and Postsecondary Education, and currently serves as an adjunct assistant professor, teaching courses related to student learning and development and college impact.

**Monita C. Thompson** is assistant dean of students and codirector of the Program on Intergroup Relations at the University of Michigan. Her work of more than 15 years in intergroup relations and social justice education focuses on the training, development, and support of peer educators in skills and techniques of intergroup dialogue facilitation, conflict management, and on becoming a social change agent. She is the author of several publications related to intergroup education and is the coeditor of the forthcoming book *Building Bridges, Creating Change: The Power of Facilitation in Intergroup Dialogue.*

**Donica Thomas Varner** is assistant general counsel at the University of Michigan. Her practice areas include employment defense litigation, student affairs, immigration, and document retention and production issues. A significant portion of her time is spent advising academic units and the Division of Student Affairs on legal issues arising from student behavior. Varner graduated from the University of Michigan Law School. She is a member of the State Bar of Michigan, the American Immigration Lawyers Association, the National Association of College and University Attorneys, and the Wolverine Bar Association.

**William Warters** is a faculty member in the Master of Arts in Dispute Resolution Program at Wayne State University. He is director of the grant Fund for the Improvement of Postsecondary Education (FIPSE) that funds the Conflict Management in Higher Education Resource Center (http://www.campus-adr.org), developer of the new Conflict Resolution Education Connection clearinghouse (http://www.creducation.org), and author of *Mediation in the Campus Community: Designing and Managing Effective Programs.* He holds a PhD from Syracuse University's Maxwell School of Citizenship and Public Affairs.

**Jay Wilgus** is assistant dean of students at the University of Utah, where he has direct responsibility for Greek Life and shares responsibility for a caseload of student conduct and student advocacy issues. Wilgus earned his JD at the University of Utah in 2005 and an MA in dispute resolution from Pepperdine University. He is a certified rape crisis counselor and gives frequent presentations on topics surrounding crimes of sexual violence and the role of men as allies in ending sexual violence.

## Research Contributor

**Jordan England** served as Student Conflict Resolution Coordinator for the University of Michigan Division of Student Affairs Office of Student Conflict Resolution. She received her M.Ed. in Counseling and Personnel Services from the University of Maryland. England provided significant research and related support for this book.

## Special Campus Program Overview Contributors

Christy Anthony, assistant director, Judicial Affairs and Mediation Services, American University

Yeworkwha Belachew, ombudsperson, Oberlin College

Meggie Biesenthal, graduate assistant, Mediation and Advocacy Program, Saint Louis University

Robert Bishop, associate director of Student Judicial Affairs and Student Development, JD, Michigan Technological University

Sarah Burns, JD, professor of clinical law, New York University School of Law

Robert Coffey, doctoral student in higher education at Michigan State University and former assistant director of the University of Michigan Division of Student Affairs Office of Student Conflict Resolution

Kimberly Jackson Davidson, associate dean of students, Oberlin College

Jordan England (see Research Contributor, p. 264).

Bob Hosea, doctoral student and coordinator for Student Mediation Services, Division of Student Affairs, Nova Southeastern University

Akilah Jones, assistant director, University of Michigan Division of Student Affairs Office of Student Conflict Resolution

Sarah Klucker, JD, program director, Saint Louis University's Office of Student Conduct

Chris Loschiavo, JD, assistant dean of students and director of student conduct and conflict resolution, University of Florida

Colleen M. Ryan, assistant director, Office of Student Conduct and Conflict Resolution, Northeastern University

Melissa Tihinen, judicial educator, Department of Residential Education, New York University

Stacy Vander Velde, assistant director, Student Conduct and Conflict Resolution, University of Michigan Division of Student Affairs Housing

David Votruba, PhD, Student Conflict Resolution Coordinator, University of Michigan Division of Student Affairs Office of Student Conflict Resolution

# Also available from Stylus

**Student Conduct Practice**
*The Complete Guide for Student Affairs Professionals*
Edited by James M. Lancaster and Diane M. Waryold
Foreword by Linda Timm

"*Student Conduct Practice* includes the thinking of notable experts in the profession and offers a smorgasbord of practical, insightful, up-to-date information for the student conduct and larger student affairs community. The editors [have] compiled an astute guide that can be read from cover to cover or referenced as a particular issue arises. Whether you are an experienced professional or just commencing your professional journey, I highly recommend this guide as a source for practical guidance, relevant information and food for thought."—*Journal of College Student Development*

**Creating and Maintaining Safe College Campuses**
*A Sourcebook for Enhancing and Evaluating Safety Programs*
Edited by Jerlando F. L. Jackson and Melvin Cleveland Terrell
Foreword by Constance B. Clery / Preface by Gregory Roberts

"[The] editors tackle the complex issues of safety at America's multiple and diverse college campuses. They note the significance of institutional type, location, and student composition in shaping the campus environment and the influence these factors have on developing a safe campus environment. This is an extraordinary undertaking (to address standards of safety while acknowledging and accounting for institutional difference), but the editors and respective authors of the 14 chapters of this work do justice to the task.

College administrators, especially those in student affairs, should rely on this work to stimulate their thinking about routine safety practices."—*Journal of College Student Development*

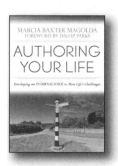

MARCIA B. BAXTER MAGOLDA
**Authoring Your Life**
*Developing an Internal Voice to Navigate Life's Challenges*
Foreword by Sharon Daloz Parks

"Given today's complex and ever-changing life demands, *Authoring Your Life* offers a timely, crucial map of possibilities for helping ourselves and others to grow and to meet the implicit and explicit demands of post-modern life. In a highly accessible manner, Baxter Magolda consciously, thoughtfully, and gently teaches us about her robust 'cyclical model' for how to authentically grow from life's challenges and experiences through what she calls 'learning partnerships.' By sharing real life experiences from courageous adults, and how they made sense of and navigated their way through them, she illuminates the internal landscape of personal growth as a developmental process. This book, informed by constructive-developmental theory, will enable us to nurture adult development." –*Ellie Drago-Severson,* Associate Professor of Education Leadership, Teachers College, Columbia University, and author of "Helping Teachers Learn" and "Leading Adult Learning"

22883 Quicksilver Drive
Sterling, VA 20166-2102

Subscribe to our e-mail alerts: www.StylusPub.com